PLAYBOY PRESS EXECUTIVE LIBRARY

PLAYBOY'S Investment Guide

MICHAEL LAURENCE

PLAYBOY PRESS

Copyright © 1971 by Michael Laurence. All rights reserved.

Published simultaneously in the United States and Canada by Playboy Press, Chicago, Illinois. Printed in the United States of America.

This book is a revised, expanded and updated version of material that previously appeared in PLAYBOY and VIP magazines. Copyright © 1967, 1968, 1969, 1970, 1971 by Playboy.

PLAYBOY and Rabbit Head design are trademarks of Playboy, 919 North Michigan Avenue, Chicago, Illinois 60611 (U.S.A.). Reg. U.S. Pat. Off., marca registrada, marque déposée.

Playboy Plays the Commodities Market originally appeared in PLAYBOY magazine, August 1967. Copyright © 1967 by Playboy. Reprinted by permission of publisher.

Beating Inflation: A Playboy Primer originally appeared in PLAYBOY magazine, March 1968. Copyright © 1968 by Playboy. Reprinted by permission of publisher.

Playboy's Guide to Mutual Funds originally appeared in PLAYBOY magazine, June 1969. Copyright © 1969 by Playboy. Reprinted by permission of publisher.

Playboy Plays the Stock Market originally appeared in PLAYBOY magazine, March 1970. Copyright © 1970 by Playboy. Reprinted by permission of publisher.

Playboy Plays the Bond Market originally appeared in PLAYBOY magazine, August 1970. Copyright © 1970 by Playboy. Reprinted by permission of publisher.

Collecting for Fun and (Maybe) for Profit originally appeared in PLAYBOY magazine, September 1971. Copyright © 1971 by Playboy. Reprinted by permission of publisher.

Puts and Calls originally appeared in VIP magazine, Summer 1969. Copyright © 1969 by Playboy. Reprinted by permission of publisher.

for A. C. Spectorsky

CONTENTS

Preface   6

I. THE STOCK MARKET

1. How to Make a Billion Dollars   12
2. Picking Winners   21
3. Finding and Using a Broker   38
4. Investment Costs: Commissions and Taxes   49
5. Investment Gadgets: Preferred Stock, Warrants, Rights, Puts and Calls   60
6. The Psychology of Successful Stock Speculation   78

II. MUTUAL FUNDS

7. Who Needs Mutual Funds?   88
8. The Dilemma of Success   107
9. What to Look for and What It Will Cost   110
10. Load Versus No-Load   120
11. Discount Merchandise: Closed-End Funds   129

III. THE BOND MARKET

12. How Bonds Work   143
13. Governments and Municipals   149

14. Corporates and Convertibles	162
15. Speculating in Bonds	173

IV. THE COLLECTOR INVESTMENTS

16. The Collector Mentality	179
17. What to Collect for Profit	187
18. How to Collect for Profit	210

V. THE COMMODITIES MARKET

19. Pork Bellies Versus AT&T	229
20. Trading Techniques	239
21. Controlling Your Broker	249
22. Tax Magic: Spreads and Straddles	256
23. The Psychology of Successful Commodity Speculation	263

VI. CONCLUSION: SUCCESS IS A STATE OF MIND

24. Conclusion	269
Bibliography	273
Index	279

PREFACE

Most investment books are not written for an audience that is both youthful and well heeled. Investment books, in fact, are usually aimed at married folks in their 50s who are trying to puzzle out how to generate a retirement income. The information served up to them is conservative, sometimes reactionary. And understandably so, because these people are concerned with investing their life savings, and they won't have another life to repair mistakes.

But such information has little meaning for a man in his 20s or early 30s just beginning to knock down a substantial salary—one that promises to grow, rather than diminish, in decades to come. Unlike his senior counterparts, he can afford to take risks. Indeed, he welcomes risk, because he senses, quite correctly, that only large risk brings large reward. Even if he runs up losses here and there, as surely he will, he can afford them. His best earning years are still ahead of him. His salary is more than sufficient to cover day-to-day needs; so he doesn't need a second income. Instead, he wants to increase his stake: to try to run a few thousand into $10,000, $10,000 into $100,000, or $100,000 into a million.

These seem ambitious goals. They would be impossibly ambitious for the retirement-minded couple. But for a man with 30 or even 40 productive years ahead of him, such a goal isn't so unreasonable. In fact, it might even be called prudent. He has the money and, more important, he has the *time*. In the investment world, as we will see, money is just part of the equation. Even a multimillionaire can't invest well if the markets are bad. But a man with only modest investment capital, so long as he has years ahead of him and can afford to take a risk here and there, need not chase opportunity. He can wait for it to come to him.

As a rule, investment books are either too simple or too complex. A novice who's interested in commodity speculation, for instance, won't learn much from the conventional introductory sources, because they will invariably tell him little more than he already knows—even if he knows virtually nothing. However, if he happens across one of the more sophisticated works, written by a commodity speculator for the enlightenment of fellow speculators, he will likely find that it is gibberish. Successful speculators don't write very well. Why should they if they can speculate successfully? And good writers tend to avoid the investment area—which they see as complicated, venal, boring and too much work. Few writers have the time, or the interest, to delve deeply into the world of personal investment. Fewer still have the resources or the temperament to put their money where their words are. As a result, investment books tend to be sophisticated but unintelligible, or readable but uninformative.

This book tries to be sophisticated and readable. A happy arrangement with PLAYBOY allowed the author not only to devote a substantial amount of time to researching and writing the book but to dabble, sometimes extensively, in each of the major markets discussed. Most of the advice contained in these pages was gleaned not from interviews or newspaper clippings but from hard personal experience—sometimes painful, sometimes exhilarating, but always instructive. There is no substitute for having been there, believe me.

This book discusses all the major investment media where an amateur—with cash, patience and knowledge—can reasonably expect profit. Basically, this includes stocks, mutual funds, bonds, art objects and commodities, each of which is discussed in turn. In all of these broad categories, simple ownership is all that's required. Areas where *work* would be needed as well—buying and renovating town houses, for instance, raising thoroughbred horses or setting up a chain of car-wash franchises—have been ruled out, on the assumption that the would-be investor already *has* a rewarding job and does not want to take on another. The author had originally intended to include a section on real-estate investment, until diligent research proved that real-estate profits invariably accrue not from land ownership but from land *development*.

This is work in the extreme, and all too often the results are either ugly or ecologically unsound. None of the five broad investment categories discussed herein yield socially undesirable results. In fact, to the extent that these broad investment areas promise to enrich those who get involved in them, their social usefulness is boundless.

This book grew out of a series of articles published in PLAYBOY between 1967 and 1971. If the clarity of its prose is to be commended, thanks should go not to the writer but to PLAYBOY's exacting and rigorous editorial standards. The original material has been updated, reshaped and greatly expanded upon. Much new material reflects today's fast-changing investment climate (especially regarding inflation and interest rates) and incorporates criticism and suggestions from readers of the early articles. Even readers who are familiar with the original pieces—many of which number among the most popular nonfiction ever published in PLAYBOY—should find new and useful information.

While the book was written to be read from cover to cover, each of the five major sections can stand by itself. The man who is specifically interested in dabbling in mutual funds, for example, can turn directly to part 2 and there find sufficient information to set him on his way. He will not have to grope through earlier pages in search of definitions or unexplained concepts. Each section begins from the premise that the reader knows little or nothing about the subject at hand and then builds up, page by page, to a reasonably sophisticated level. Although the book is frankly and unabashedly written for relatively youthful investors who are willing to assume some element of risk (often a large element), conservative approaches are also discussed, but not extensively. Wherever possible, techniques are outlined whereby a novice can begin an investment campaign with only a few hundred dollars. After all, one must begin somewhere. But in all cases the book will be just as useful for the man with thousands or tens of thousands. In the investment world, as in life itself, the more you have, the more you get.

Preface

It is customary for authors to applaud the help of others. In the case of this book, their number is legion, so that names alone would fill pages. These people should know who they are, and I thank them collectively and sincerely. I do owe a special debt to Mrs. Kathy Fast, of the PLAYBOY Editorial Research Department, who, in many months of poring over the manuscript of this work, ferreted out scores of factual errors. Mrs. Fast is so meticulous and so competent that I am tempted to say that any mistakes remaining are her fault, not mine. But I won't.

I
The Stock Market

Stock Prices: 1925-1971

Performance of two major stock-market indices since 1925. The Dow-Jones Industrial Average reflects the price movement of the common stock of 30 large and long-established blue-chip firms. The Standard & Poor's index reflects the action of 500 different stocks, and thus provides a better picture of "average" market performance. Technical data: Standard & Poor's figures have been multiplied by 10 to give a more-or-less common base (100 in 1925) with the Dow-Jones Industrial Average. The S & P average reflects 500 stocks only from 1957. Prior performance is based on 90 stocks, converted to a compatible base. Sources: Dow-Jones figures from Securities Research Company, Standard & Poor's figures from Board of Governors, Federal Reserve System.

1. HOW TO MAKE A BILLION DOLLARS

The names H. Ross Perot and Edwin C. Whitehead are hardly household words. Yet for current or would-be investors in stocks, they should be, for the stock market has been exceedingly kind to both men. In fact, it made them both billionaires—at least for a while. Neither man went about it in the way an ordinary investor might, but, then, your ordinary stock dabbler doesn't usually roll up ten-figure gains. Whitehead had the good fortune to inherit Technicon Corporation, a medical-equipment manufacturer, headquartered in Tarrytown, New York, that produces a machine called an AutoAnalyzer—much in demand by hospitals seeking to analyze blood samples. In 1969 Whitehead decided to test the public market for his company's shares. He sold half a million of them and was presumably gratified to see the price run up to $55 apiece. Not only did this provide a nice profit on what he had sold, but it meant that the 19.5 million additional shares that he had prudently retained enjoyed a value—on paper, anyway—of $1,072,500,000. The falling market of 1969–70 wrested Whitehead out of the billionaire class almost as abruptly as he had been thrust into it, but he's hardly hurting. As these words are written, in August 1971, Technicon is selling around $40, which means that Whitehead's holdings are now worth $780 million. As J. Paul Getty supposedly observed, the first billion is always the hardest.

Perot's case is even more interesting. Failing to inherit a company, he started his own. Moreover, he seems to have made *his* billion in a single year, a feat without precedent in the annals of speculation. In 1959 Perot quit working as an IBM salesman and, with a stake of $1000, founded Electronic Data Systems Corporation, a firm offering computer skills and systems to those who need them. Needless to say, the company prospered. In 1968 Perot took it public by selling 650,000 shares at $16.50

each. Like Whitehead, he had the good sense to keep some for himself—in this case, an additional nine million shares. A year later, when eager buyers were bidding $162 a share for EDS, Perot—had he cared to add up his holdings—would have found them worth $1,458,000,000.

Perot, too, has since been knocked out of the billionaire ranks (his holdings are currently worth just $666 million) —but not out of the news. He served as chairman of United We Stand, a lobby that supported President Nixon's early policies in Vietnam. In this capacity he tried unsuccessfully to fly a planeload of Christmas gifts to U.S. war prisoners. More recently he turned up with ten million dollars cash to bail out a failing brokerage house that happened to be one of his firm's clients. And at the depths of the 1969–70 stock-market collapse, he smilingly sustained paper losses—in two mind-blowing days—of $573 million. Easy come, easy go, one assumes.

Given his political persuasions, it seems fittingly ironic that Perot should have passed the elusive billion-dollar mark during the "moratorium" month of October 1969. October, Mark Twain once observed, is "one of the peculiarly dangerous months to speculate in stocks in." The other dangerous months, Twain continued, "are July, January, September, April, November, May, March, June, December, August and February." Since Twain lost more in stocks than he could earn even as a fantastically successful writer, the cynicism that colored his judgment is forgivable. Like most writers, he knew little or nothing about the stock market. In fact, a variation of the typesetting machine in which he invested—and which bankrupted him in the 1890s—subsequently made millions for investors with a marginally better sense of timing. Twain also singled out the wrong month. As Perot's experience might attest, October happens to be a very *good* month to speculate in stocks in. Most of the declining markets of the past generation (1946, 1957, 1960, 1962, 1966 and 1970) turned around then, a curious coincidence that prompted a veteran Wall Street observer to proclaim that "October outranks all other months as a buying time" for short-term stock profits. Perot's and Whitehead's good fortune can also be cited to confirm the observation—if it needs confirmation—that no single route to riches is swifter or more rewarding than the stock market.

The stock-market debacle of 1969–70 proved that prices can drop as quickly as they increase. In fact, like the stone of Sisyphus, they generally retreat more quickly than they advance. But fallen stocks mean bargain-basement price levels, where shrewd investors, both amateur and professional, can gobble up discounted merchandise. Almost to a man, the investment community ridiculed President Nixon in April 1970, when he declared that if he had any money, he would be buying common stocks. In retrospect the president proved as shrewd an investor as he is a politician. Within weeks after his pronouncement, the stock market began moving higher. Many observers now feel it will never re-touch its 1970 lows.

The message is that while stocks move both ways, they seem to increase more consistently than they retreat. In other words, in the long run they will generally prove profitable. And, at last count, almost 30 million Americans were betting on stock profitability. These are the investors who (as the saying goes) own a share in American industry. Some of them may have purchased stocks to conserve their capital, others to avoid taxes, to hedge against inflation or to nail down a decent income to see them through retirement. A very few, like Perot, created their stockholdings as an almost unanticipated by-product of their own foresight and hard work in forging a corporate empire. But the vast majority of stock players these days, silent or vociferous, are in the market with just one goal—to make money—and, whether the market is going up or down, a surprising number succeed.

Stated in its simplest terms, transactions in the stock market involve sheets of paper called *shares*, or *stock*, representing fractional ownership of a corporation. Some companies, of course, are privately held; while they have shares and shareholders, it's impossible for the public to invest in them. But the preponderance of the nation's largest companies are publicly held, with ownership spread among hundreds, thousands or even—in the case of the telephone company—millions of shareholders. Companies issue stock for one reason—to raise money—and long experience shows that money is most easily raised when potential investors know they can subsequently sell their shares, presumably for a profit. Thus the stock market developed, to provide a convenient gathering place for would-be buyers and sellers.

Marxist critics of capitalism enjoy pointing out that money changing hands in the stock market rarely reaches the corporations involved, giving the game a surrealistic irrelevance. This is true but no more useful than observing that poker winnings don't usually go to the manufacturer of the playing cards. Without a ready market for corporate shares (economists call it a *liquid* market), companies could never raise the money with which to begin or expand their operations. People wouldn't buy stock unless they knew they could ultimately sell it. The liquidity of the marketplace is one of the basic underpinnings of capitalism as we know it, and today it is seriously threatened for the first time in history. Mutual funds and other huge institutional investors have grown so fat that they are finding it increasingly difficult (sometimes impossible) to sell the large blocks of shares they have accumulated. As a consequence, stock prices are bouncing around with a vehemence that would have been unimaginable just a few years ago. But this is good news for the small investor. The market is still liquid enough to accommodate any transaction he is likely to make, and the problems that plague the institutions only create more action—and profit —for the individual.

Before the investor begins playing, he's got to learn the rules. To start, he needs just two things: money and a stockbroker. Both are relatively easy to come by these days, but he's not likely to keep either without a third, more elusive prerequisite: knowledge. Scraping up money and locating a stockbroker will be considered farther on in this section, but since stock-market knowledge is surely the most important and difficult of the three, it will be considered first.

Actually, the stock market is not one market but many. In the United States, four predominate: the New York Stock Exchange (often called the Big Board); the American Stock Exchange, which tradition-minded Wall Streeters like to call the Curb, because years ago its operations were conducted on the curb of a sidewalk; the vast and important over-the-counter market, which is not really a single market at all but a collection of stock dealers scattered across the country; and a sort of demimarket, comprising another set of individual dealers, most of whom buy and sell large blocks of stock for institutional clients, but who also traffic in smaller transactions. Shares in most major U.S. corporations are bought and sold (*traded,* in Wall Street jargon) on the New York Stock Exchange; their younger and more speculative competitors show up on the Curb; and most of the rest, comprising tens of thousands of companies, large and small, are found over the counter. Besides the major exchanges, there are at least 15 others, the most important being the handful of markets serving Detroit, Boston, Pittsburgh, Baltimore, Chicago, San Francisco and their respective environs. These smaller exchanges feature stocks whose appeal is regional rather than national, but they also deal in shares that are sold on the larger exchanges. In addition, a feisty and relatively recent outfit called the National Stock Exchange, also located in New York, is trying to establish a market in shares even more speculative than those sold on the Curb.

Just as there are several types of stock markets, so are there several types of stock. By far the most common is called just that—*common stock*. When investors talk about the vicissitudes of their stocks, 99 times out of 100 they mean common stocks. The holders of a company's common stock, *in toto,* are the owners of the company. They get to vote in the firm's affairs (one share, one vote), and they participate in the company's profits in a similarly undemocratic fashion. From its profits the company might pay cash dividends—which means that the stockholder gets a check, usually quarterly—or it might retain its profits to finance new factories and otherwise expand its operations. In either case, if the company prospers, the shareowner should, too. His dividends, of course, are immediately spendable, and the company's retained profits should increase the value of his shares, which means he should receive that much more when he sells.

The "shoulds" are necessary because the shareowner doesn't usually gain or lose in direct proportion to the fortunes of the company in which he owns shares. This is because the value of a share is set not by the issuing corporation but by the buyers and sellers who make up the marketplace. A share of stock, like everything else, is worth only what another person will pay for it. This is the challenge and the excitement of the stock market, and all the techniques of stock playing (there are as many techniques as players) ultimately rest on this premise: that when the time comes to sell, the investor will find someone who, for one reason or another, is willing to purchase his shares at a price higher than the investor originally paid for them. In other words, when all is said and done, stock-market success is largely a matter of mass psychology, with the investor trying to guess just what sort of stocks future buyers will be willing to pay more for.

He might guess successfully for any number of reasons. Perhaps he buys shares at a point in history when potential stock buyers are gloomy about the future of the economy. Such an attitude prevailed most strikingly in the spring of 1932, though it was repeated as recently as 1966 and again in 1970, when President Nixon was telling investors to buy stocks and investors weren't listening. If public fears prove unfounded, then the value of many shares will rise. More typically, the successful investment will involve an assessment not of the entire economy but of the fortunes of a particular firm. Such stocks might involve companies whose profits an investor correctly divines are about to rise markedly; they might also involve firms that he was right to feel stand to benefit from unexpected outbreaks of war or peace, those that he accurately guesses will profit from new discoveries or those that, for any other reason, he senses will seem more attractive to stock buyers at some point in the foreseeable future.

Knowledge of the future is all that's required. But since the future is unknowable, knowledge of what's currently happening in business, in the economy and in the world around us is a workable substitute, as long as the investor never forgets that all the statistics in the Department of Labor or the *Wall Street Journal* can still prove ruinous unless he has an equally good knowledge of people, because it is people, not statistics, to whom he must ultimately sell his shares.

No matter to whom the investor sells, his chances of making a profit are good, even excellent. This would sound like a half-baked generalization if it weren't supported by hard fact. In a landmark study conducted at the University of Chicago a few years ago, Professors Lawrence Fisher and James Lorie, aided by a huge computer, evaluated the performance of every common stock traded on the New York Stock Exchange between 1926 and 1965. The study embraced 1856 stocks and 57 million possible transactions, representing every different Big Board investment that could have been made, held or liquidated at the end of each month during the 39 years programmed. The results must have surprised even Merrill Lynch, Pierce, Fenner & Smith, the nation's largest brokerage firm, which financed the venture. Assuming reinvestment of dividends and subtracting brokerage fees at both ends of every transaction (an expense that most studies conveniently ignore), the median return on a random common-stock investment turned out to be 9.3 percent a year. It didn't matter what stock was bought, when it was purchased or how long it was held. All that mattered was that one invest often enough and at random. One was bound to end up making money at a rate of over 9 percent a year. The study also revealed that 78 percent of all 57 million transactions showed a profit, which theoretically means that an investor's chances of picking a winning stock, blindfolded, from an outspread *Wall Street Journal* are something close to eight in ten.

The methodology is open to criticism, but the results stand on their own. (One major criticism is that the study stopped in 1965, just as the stock market was entering a five-year period of decline or, at best, stagnation. However, the cutoff reflects not design so much as programming time. The study will eventually be updated, and early indications are that even updated into the 1970s, the results will be impressive.) Not surprisingly, the Fisher and Lorie studies caused great jubilation in the stockbroker community, though the mutual-fund industry, which by and large had been achieving lower than random results, was less pleased. (Despite recent setbacks, the funds are now doing better, and readers inclined toward this less demanding form of investment are referred to part 2.) Even subtracting incomes taxes, the Fisher and Lorie figures are still remarkable. The after-tax return for an individual with a taxable income of $10,000 (based on 1960 dollars and tax rates) was 8.4 percent; for an individual in the $50,000 bracket, 7.4 percent.

Relying on this information alone, tyro investors in every tax bracket might do well to confine their initial transactions to common stocks listed on the Big Board, where the deck seems provably stacked in their favor. This would lessen the preparatory study involved, eliminating the need to brush up on preferred stocks, bonds, convertible bonds, rights, warrants, puts, calls, straddles and all the other investment arcana, discussed elsewhere in this book, in which investors can also make or lose money. But even if the investor concentrates his early efforts on common stocks alone, his choice is far from limited. To the 1200-plus common stocks listed on the Big Board should be added a like number on the Amex and perhaps another 1000 of the better-known over-the-counter offerings. Clearly, the investor faces more choices than he can possibly grapple with, and some way has to be found to reduce them to manageable proportions.

The easiest way is to begin by exploring not the vast universe of possible common-stock investments but the smaller and more negotiable universe of the investor's own experience. Almost all of us, if we thought about it long enough, could unearth an attractive stock from the personal world with which we're familiar. Perhaps it's the firm we work for, if we can confirm from personal knowledge that it's well managed and making fatter profits year after year. Or perhaps it's the competitor that always gives us so much trouble, that supplier who always exceeds quality standards, that hotshot firm a fast-rising friend works for or a corporation that regularly produces new products we can't do without. Was anyone unimpressed with the first Polaroid camera he saw? A purchase of Polaroid stock at any time up to 1965 would now have increased at least fourfold. That's better than 50 percent a year.

Unfortunately, the more a novice learns about the stock market, the less he'll be willing to rely on his own judgment. Once he begins reading the *Wall Street Journal* every morning, once he starts poring through the business and investment magazines, subscribing to an advisory service or two, hanging out in the brokerage boardroom watching stock figures shoot across the wall and listening to what the traders are whispering about, shuffling through the volumes of financial data that supposedly enable him to make better investment decisions—once he has immersed himself in all this, how can he bring himself to buy a stock like Polaroid just because he owns and enjoys one of the company's cameras? The message should be clear: Never assume that anyone knows more about the market than you do. The stock market, like the future, cannot be predicted. People who make correct forecasts are not oracular—just lucky. Your guess *has* to be as good as the next man's. For you, it's probably better, because it's personally suited to your own needs—psychological as well as financial. As we will see, this is crucially important.

2. PICKING WINNERS

Still, certain facts can help the would-be investor act intelligently. For instance, he ought to be able to interpret the stock-price figures in the daily newspapers. This is an especially useful point of departure. Not only is the information cheap and readily available, but since newspaper stock quotations consist solely of names and numbers, no one will be ruined by just reading them (as can result from a serious flirtation with a bad "How I Made a Million in Stocks" book).

Whatever paper he reads, the investor will find that the daily quotations of the listed stocks look something like this:

119 65¼ StdOilOh 2.70 679 119 119⅞ 117¼ 119⅞ +4⅜

Imaginative reading should reveal that the stock in question is Standard Oil Company of Ohio. The first two figures—119 and 65¼—are the highest and lowest prices at which the stock has sold during the year. (U.S. stock prices are invariably quoted in dollars and fractions of dollars, rather than in dollars and cents, and over the years investors have come to think that way themselves, because it makes calculations easier. Typically, dollar signs are dropped for brevity; so $65.25 becomes 65¼. Then, to save breath and provide the proper aura of detachment, dollars become *points,* so that an increase of $2.50 is "up two and a half points.") The year's high and low figures are quite instructive, but for some reason, only the better financial pages see fit to include them.

The figure following the company name represents the dividend the stock paid the previous year—in this case, $2.70 a share. Companies that regularly pay dividends other than cash, usually in the form of stock, are indicated by a lowercase letter after the dividend figure. An alphabet soup of other symbols carries additional significance, but since each wire service has its own symbology and since many newspapers deviate even from these, the investor would do well to consult the explanatory table that usually accompanies the quotations. The number following the dividend figure represents the day's trading volume, in hundreds of shares; in other words, 67,900 shares of Sohio were traded that day. If the investor had been watching the stock closely, he might recognize that this figure indicates quite a bit of trading action. Typically, fewer than 50,000 Sohio shares change hands daily.

The next figures describe the day's price movement—opening price, high price, low price and closing price—and the final figure reveals that in the last transaction before the market closed, the stock was selling at a price of $4.38 higher than that of the closing trade the previous day. (Many investors mistakenly think that the last figure—+4⅜ in this example—tells how much the stock went up that day. Actually, the change *during* the day is the difference between the opening price and the closing price—which, in this instance, was 119 and 119⅞, giving a daily change of ⅞ of a dollar, or 88 cents.)

The point of all this is to show that one small row of figures conceals a gold mine of useful information. It not only enables the investor to make a stab at charting the day's action in Sohio, but it also hides clues to the direction in which the stock is heading. Needless to say, the clues are ambiguous. In this case, since the closing price of $119.88 represents an advance of $4.38 beyond the previous day's close, the stock must have closed the previous day at $115.50. Then it opened the next day at $119, for an overnight jump of $3.50. Such a large opening gap is unusual. Either the market for Sohio is unstable or some new development has taken place overnight. (In this instance, both explanations applied.) The amateur investor might regard such action as ominous. Since the stock jumped sharply overnight and closed at its highest level of the year (actually, its highest level ever), he could well conclude that the stock is overpriced and should be sold.

A more seasoned investor might reach the opposite conclusion. Stocks that reach new highs tend to keep reaching new highs. So, on the basis of the same information, while the amateur is selling, the seasoned investor might be buying. Meanwhile, the professional investor could reach yet a third conclusion. The stock opened strong on a new high, but after the large initial leap it didn't forge much higher. Whatever pushed it up an opening $3.50 wasn't sufficient to move it one more dollar the entire day. So, despite the record high price, failure of the day's action to confirm the strength of the overnight upward move could indicate to the pro that the stock might not be likely to go up much farther. At the very least, the signals are confusing; so the pro would probably leave the stock alone.

In this case he would have made the right decision, for after reaching its new high of 119⅞, Sohio immediately dropped back to 110. A few weeks later it was selling in the low 90s, and before too many months had passed, it had dropped all the way back to 51. Our hypothetical amateur investor, acting for the wrong reasons, would have won; his more seasoned counterpart, acting for the right reasons but not examining the situation closely enough, would have lost; and the truly sophisticated investor, unwilling to risk his money in a dubious situation, would still have all his capital available for a more promising prospect. Quite often this is just what happens.

While virtually all daily newspapers publish stock quotations, their investment usefulness beyond that is limited. For more substantial business news and investment information, two papers predominate: the *New York Times,* offering far-above-average financial coverage, and the *Wall Street Journal,* the vade mecum of the investing public. In many ways the *Journal* is America's best daily; even in terms of political objectivity it merits a higher grade than the *Times.* Certainly the *Journal* is undeserving of the archconservative reputation that it seems to enjoy among people who don't read it. In fact, it is a red-check source for leftish social critics, as John Kenneth Galbraith and Michael Harrington will att st. Right-wing afflatus that might oth rwise incapacitate the *Journal*'s editors is vented noiselessly on its editorial page or—in extreme cases—in the more hospitable environs of *Barron's*, a tabloid weekly that is the *Journal*'s younger sister. Every Monday, *Barron's* publishés a most comprehensive compilation of stock statistics, including dividend dates and past and current figures on corporate profits, something no other newsstand publication offers. Besides its wealth of statistics, which alone justify the 50-cent-a-week cover price, *Barron's* features perceptive articles on market analysis and charming editorials that provide quaint insights into self-righteous business conservatism as it must have existed during the Harding administration.

A handful of biweekly or monthly magazines also cater to the needs of would-be or current investors, but they are all uniformly dreary and suffer from a grievous conceptual flaw: the assumption that anyone who is interested in the stock market is also interested in business and businessmen. If an enterprising publisher were to produce a magazine edited not for businessmen but for investors, a magazine that talked about stocks instead of machines and interviewed speculators instead of executives, he would probably make a fortune. Until he comes along, investors must make do with what's available. *Forbes* deserves special mention, if only because it is so much better than its competitors, though here, too, the editorials provoke laughter rather than thought. *Fortune*, unabashedly edited for well-off businessmen, also publishes useful investment information, as does *Business Week*.

A horde of stock-market advisory services—at last count, almost 3000 of them—fill the void left by the business and investment magazines by offering weekly newsletters telling investors when and what to buy and sell. Since anyone with a typewriter and a duplicating machine can get into the advisory business, it's not surprising that the value of most such advice is marginal. In the aggregate, the performance of the advisors' recommended stocks seems just slightly lower than the performance of stocks in general. Though this is quite a feat, it hardly justifies the price of a subscription, which can run as high as $200 a year—tax-deductible. Back in the depression, delighted congressional investigators unearthed a stock-market advisor who had achieved an enviable track record (and an income of $40,000 a year) by picking stocks on the basis of a between-the-lines reading of the Jiggs and Maggie comic strip in his Sunday funnies. (Don't laugh—the same technique has been used by scholars to prove that Francis Bacon wrote the plays of Shakespeare.)

The only advisory service that this writer knows about that correctly called the 1968 market top is called *Space-Time Forecasting*, published by an elderly couple named Louis and Muriel Hasbrouck. Their letter, which costs $300 a year, declared in late 1968 that "the inflationary run-up in the New York stock market will come to an end over the weekend of December 1." The Dow-Jones industrial average closed December 3 at 985 and then began a long collapse to 627. The Hasbroucks subsequently revealed to *Business Week* that their reputation suffers because investors associate them with astrology. Actually, they abandoned astrology in 1941. Now they base their predictions on recurrent cyclical energy waves and "the changing potential of the electrical energy field of the solar system," predicated on the assumption, in Mr. Hasbrouck's words, that "your mind is an electrical transformer."

More bizarre methodologies probably exist,* but a more common advisory sin is simple equivocation. If an advisor spends four pages a week saying nothing at all, he will

---

* A recent issue of the *Wall Street Journal* profiled the life of Pat Bologna, who has for 48 years been a shoeshine man in Wall Street. Bologna supposedly saved the Kennedy family fortune one day in early 1929 when, while shining Joseph Kennedy's shoes, he made a prediction about the next day's stock market. Kennedy figured that if his shoeshine man was this deep into the market, it was time for the Kennedys to be out. Bologna no longer makes specific predictions, but he does publish a *Yearly Market, Economic and Political Letter* that is highly regarded by (among others) the president of New York's First National City Bank.

never be wrong. Consider this "summary and advice" offered on February 16, 1970 (when stocks were approaching their bottom), by *Moody's Stock Survey,* which sells for $144 a year and enjoys one of the largest circulations of all stock-market tip sheets: "The stock market environment doesn't appear to have all the ingredients needed for substantial price gains soon, although a rally in coming weeks is a possibility. Should this happen, investors can take advantage of it by switching out of stocks whose prospects have diminished into issues more likely to participate in a general market upturn." For those who have difficulty with the prose, here's a translation: "Stocks might go down, or they might go up. If they go up, investors should sell shares that will fall and buy shares that will rise." Few persons could argue with such advice, but fewer still could make use of it.

In fairness to *Moody's,* this was just a bad day. The service does make specific recommendations and keeps an eye on them once they are made. And even though they might equivocate, most advisors these days tend to be rational, even when they're wrong, which is frequent. Many advisory services have been in business for decades; so they must have something worth saying. The better ones should be willing to provide a *complete* record of their past recommendations, so that the would-be subscriber could reasonably assess the value of their advice. And the best of the lot are probably those that provide hard facts on which the investor can base his own decisions. Most advisory services offer free copies or a reduced-rate trial subscription, so that the patient investor—especially if he is willing to write a lot of five-dollar checks—may find one that suits his needs.

Whether he purchases advice or conjures up his own, the novice stock dabbler will soon learn that the process by which investors decide to buy or sell stocks is far from scientific. Despite its name—security analysis—stock guessing hinges heavily on the psychological makeup of the person doing the guessing. For purposes of description, the techniques divide into two broad groups: *fundamental analysis* and *technical analysis*. Fundamental analysis, the older and more established of the two, rests on the reasonable assumption that there is some relationship between the fortunes of a firm and the price of its stock. The fundamental stock watcher will try to sift through all the relevant information by which a company's present and future performance can be measured. This might include the firm's current rate of profit and growth, its past performance, its competitive position within its industry, the state of the economy, the firm's marketing capabilities, prospective new developments and all the other statistical insights that might be drawn from a balance sheet, a profit-and-loss statement, a corporate prospectus or a quarterly report. Fundamentalists will spend hours sifting through these and other documents, jotting down figures, comparing past performance, evaluating management strength and computing net asset values and earnings ratios. (Corporate profits are rarely called profits; "earnings" sounds more socially useful.) The fundamentalist feels that the more he understands about a company, the better is his basis for assessing its potential and thus guessing how its stock will fare.

The fundamental approach is essentially a conservative one. Whether or not he realizes it, the fundamentalist is looking for investments that offer exceptional margins of safety. He seeks stocks that seem palpably more valuable than their current selling price, either because they promise dividends far above the prevailing interest rates or—more likely nowadays—because they promise growth through above-average earnings.

The advantage of investing on the basis of fundamentals is that once the fundamentalist has done his research, he needn't make the effort (it can easily become agony) to watch day-to-day price movements and day-to-day developments. Fundamental analysis locates long-term trends. If his analysis is sound, the fundamentalist can just sit it out—assuming he has the proper reserves of self-mastery and money. (Often his patience runs out first; he sits on what he deems a promising stock for 18 months and watches it go nowhere. The week after he abandons it, the stock skyrockets.) At worst—if he has chosen the right stock and keeps his cool—he shouldn't lose very much.

But there are psychological difficulties. Fundamentalists will agree that almost every company can provide them with more statistical information than they can properly cope with. Corporate bookkeeping nowadays is an advanced form of legerdemain, so that few fundamentalists will agree on which fundamentals are most relevant. Even if they get past this hurdle, they will argue over what the relevant fundamentals *mean*. A *bull* (who thinks stocks will go up) and a *bear* (his opposite) can pore over the same data and reach contradictory conclusions. And in the unlikely event that they agree, the market won't necessarily follow, because, to repeat, stock prices are determined not by statistics but by people. A stock's fundamentals can look unarguable, but if would-be buyers don't like the company's industry, its long-range potential or even its *name*, the stock will just lie there. Years ago a company called Seaboard Airlines invariably rose and fell with the airline stocks, even though its full name was Seaboard Airline Railroad and it was just that—a railroad. More recently, bemused investors watched Southern Gulf Utilities transmogrify overnight into Ecological Sciences Corporation at about the time that Minnie Pearl's Fried Chicken System became Performance Systems, Inc.—a sex change that failed to prevent the company from going into receivership. Of course, strict fundamentalists would deny the importance of such unquantifiable press-agentry. If they can find stocks whose fundamentals make them seem relatively cheap, they are content, because they believe that sooner or later the market will recognize true value and their toil will be richly rewarded.

In the late 1960s one of the most consistently successful devotees of fundamental analysis was Fred Carr, who was in charge of the investing policies of Enterprise Fund during the years when that mutual fund outperformed all others. Carr gained fame as an early and heavy investor in

Kentucky Fried Chicken, one of the fastest-rising common stocks of the last decade. Remarkably enough, Carr's initial commitment in Kentucky Fried was based solely on a reading of the company's prospectus, a document that was available to anyone who cared to send away for it. His technique was elegantly simple: He figured out how much profit could be expected from each chicken outlet (in the fast-food-to-go business, this figure is very consistent) and multiplied it by the number of outlets the firm planned to open during the next two years. The resulting profit figure indicated to Carr that the shares were selling at a low price compared with the finger-lickin' earnings that could be expected in 24 months' time; so he bought. The shares, which first sold at $15, ultimately rose to over $300 each; thereafter they retreated sharply, and Carr left the mutual-fund business.

The devotees of technical analysis, called technicians or chartists, try to avoid the fundamentals. They believe that all the factors that can affect a stock's price are already reflected in the price, and so the best way to locate the trend is to study the price movement itself, usually through charts. Many technicians keep their own charts, laboriously filling them in each evening or each weekend, but for those unwilling to compromise their time even to this extent, scores of technical services offer ready-to-use charts, for one stock or for thousands, airmailed to the subscriber every Friday night. If the technician reads his charts correctly, the market—which chart theory says already reflects the relevant fundamentals—will tell him what to do.

But the technician also faces psychological pitfalls. As with fundamental analysis, different temperaments can interpret identical charts differently; and even when they agree, the market can still drift off perversely in the opposite direction. But unlike the fundamentalist, the technician must keep a close eye on minor fluctuations; and unless he has both the time and the stamina to withstand the daily or even hourly crises that this sort of eyeballing entails, he may come to grief. Beyond this, stock charts, by their very nature, describe only the past. Especially in an area as fickle and as future-oriented as the stock market, one can surely question how relevant past performance is to future performance.

But technical analysis also has some undeniable attractions. Not only does it avoid the ordeal of leafing through such weighty tomes as *Moody's Industrial Manual*, but it also offers an investment technique that requires a minimum of economic expertise. The true technical analyst doesn't want his mind violated by a single fundamental. He reasons that any tidbit of tangible news he hears might prejudice his reading of the charts, which already reflect all the news, giving just the proper weight to each development. *In extremis*, the technician would prefer to plot price movements without knowing what the price is or even what stock he's following. A West Coast stockbroker has actually succeeded at this. His advisory service sends him charts from which both the name and the price of the stock have been obliterated. After he selects the charts that seem most promising, he calls the service to find out what they represent. He's been doing this for years, and at last report he was still active and prospering.

No matter what you may think of such a technique, trading by the charts is far from an occult science; a good deal of common sense supports it. The illustration on page 32 shows a technician's picture of Northwestern Steel & Wire Corporation, a Big Board stock that traded in a well-defined range in mid-1969. As is typical with such charts, the vertical dashes indicate the week's trading limits and the horizontal ticks show the closing prices. Between March and August, as the chart shows quite clearly, the stock never closed above 51 nor below 44. Common sense suggests there must be a reason for such constricted performance over six months. The simplest explanation is that some unknowable investors (perhaps the same people) were willing to buy all shares offered whenever the price went down to 44 and to sell without limit when the price got over 50. For anyone with sufficient capital, this can be a highly profitable activity. But once a stock has established this sort of trading range—here the technicians would call it a *rectangular formation*—it can be expected to move sharply if the price breaks out on either side. In early September, when the stock finally closed above 51, technicians would have rightly assumed that NS&W had given a buy signal. Whoever was doing all that selling around 50 was obviously no longer in the market, and technicians could expect the stock to rise, perhaps to a much higher level. The presumptive explanation is that all prospective buyers and sellers have finally been cleaned out of the trading range; so the stock must move on up to a new equilibrium. In this particular case, NS&W ran right off the chart after its breakout. In October it was selling in the mid-80s.

A host of other chart formations, variously described as *flags, pennants, heads and shoulders, triangles, islands, saucers,* etc., are similarly reliable—or, when they give false signals, similarly misleading. Many defy commonsense interpretation, which would make their use questionable if only they didn't seem to work fairly often in predicting price trends. One reason for their performance might be that chart trading is now quite popular; tens of thousands of technicians are buying and selling stocks every day. Right or wrong, they are staking hard cash on their calculations, and by their very number they can frequently make a stock conform to their notions of what it should do. Unfortunately, the more they rely on the same signals, the less well any of them should profit. Nevertheless, some large investors—notably mutual-fund portfolio managers—even though they may think chart trading is so much numerological gobbledygook, still follow charts religiously, just to get a feeling of what the chart traders are up to.

What most recommends chart investing is that it automatically limits losses. When the technician makes a mistake, it costs him relatively little; when the fundamentalist makes a mistake, it can cost him everything. The technician ponders his charts and determines that if a stock penetrates above $58 a share, it should rise to $70 or so. He buys automatically at the proper moment, and if the stock doesn't immediately conform to his expectations—in

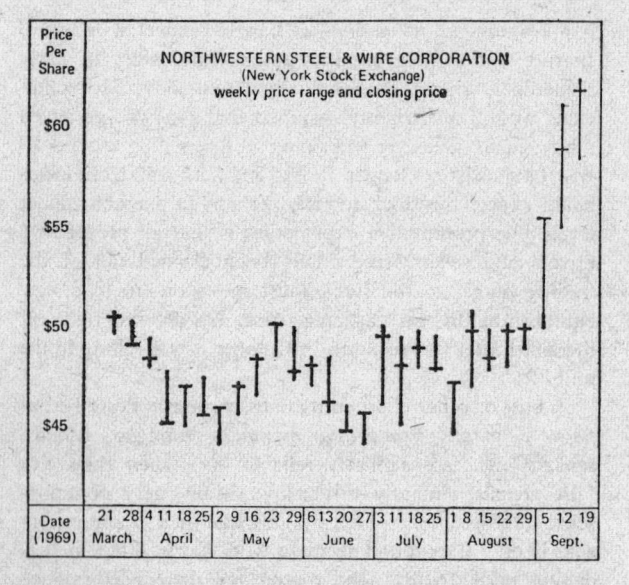

NORTHWESTERN STEEL & WIRE CORPORATION
(New York Stock Exchange)
weekly price range and closing price

other words, if it drops instead of rising—he must sell. He was simply wrong, and he knows it at once. He takes his loss and goes back to the graph paper. Needless to say, chart trading will produce a number of such mistakes, even a disturbing number. But they will be small mistakes. If the technician can limit each loss to five percent or so, he can be wrong four times out of five and still make a profit. If he is right half the time, his profits will be substantial. In other words, the technician enjoys the luxury of being permitted many mistakes.

Though the fundamentalist will make fewer mistakes, the errors he does make will tend to be whoppers; so he can't afford as many. This is due to the difficulties he encounters in limiting his losses. He buys the same stock as the technician at $58 a share, not because its chart looks good but because he thinks it's underpriced. Again, underpriced or not, the stock begins to drop—all the way down to $48. Whereas the technician would have sold the stock already, the fundamentalist can only return to his analysis to see if he miscalculated. If he can't find any errors, the stock has to be a better buy at $48 than it was at $58; so he should probably purchase more. But if the stock then keeps going down—and many do—the fundamentalist will soon find himself in an impossible situation, *averaging down* to take advantage of bargain prices but, in the process, buying ever-larger chunks of an ever-deteriorating stock. Like the red or black roulette player who doubles up after every loss, he may find himself risking thousands to recoup a small bet. At his worst, the die-hard fundamentalist in a losing stock resembles Nietzsche's madman, pleading the sanity of a stock he *knows* is worth $100 in a marketplace of idiots who won't offer $15 a share.

Many investors are unaware that the most cherished barometer of common-stock performance, the Dow-Jones industrial average, was developed as a technical tool. The DJIA, recording the combined action of 30 blue-chip industrial stocks on the Big Board, was the invention of Charles Dow, father of Dow Jones and Company and grandfather of technical analysis. Dow evolved what is now known as the Dow theory, the oldest and most respected technical device for predicting stock-market sea changes. The DJIA's usefulness is far more than technical; it has become *the* popular figure for describing overall market performance. Even though loaded with conservative stocks that are currently out of favor with the Wall Street *cognoscenti*, it's fairly accurate, because the 30 indexed stocks account for much more dollar volume than their modest number would indicate.

The average has often been used as a historical index of stock-market performance, but this is misleading. In a recent ten-year period, for instance, the DJIA had risen only 17.8 percent—but an average of all stocks listed on the Big Board rose 60 percent. Moreover, the DJIA has undergone numerous face-liftings since Dow contrived it around the turn of the century. Curiously enough, only one company listed in the average, General Electric, was a part of the figure when it was devised, and even GE was omitted for a while. Another dropout was IBM, which was discarded in the 1930s. Had it stayed in, it would have pushed the DJIA about twice as high as it now is. Besides the DJIA, a half-dozen other stock indexes provide similar information and lend themselves to similar criticism. Since all market averages are just that—averages—they provide a fix on what stocks in general are doing, but they have little to tell the individual investor, who must buy stocks in particular.

Actually, there's more to technical analysis than simply watching stock charts. Other numerical sequences are also cherished. One with a wide following measures odd-lot trading. The vast majority of stock transactions are made in 100-share units called *round lots*. Units less than 100 shares are called *odd lots*. Because odd-lot transactions involve relatively small sums, they typically reflect the decisions of amateur investors. Based on the historically valid assumption that the small stock trader is usually wrong, many investors scrutinize the odd-lot figures and do the opposite. In other words, when the odd-lot figures show that small investors are buying heavily, then odd-lot followers would begin to sell, on the assumption that the market is fated to decline to accommodate the little people in their quest to lose money.

Until 1966, predictions based on odd-lot theory were right much more often than wrong. The record since then has been mixed. Odd-lotters sold at the top in late 1968 and bought at the bottom in May 1970. Anyone who did the opposite has presumably abandoned odd-lot theory. However, the theory proved dead right in December 1970, when odd-lot sales outnumbered purchases by a record 2.4 to 1—and the market rallied sharply. Contemporary inconsistencies probably reflect changes that have transformed the stock market in recent years. Foremost, odd-lot activity has declined tremendously; it now comprises a scant 7 percent of total trading, compared with 20 percent a decade back. Many small investors have now turned to mutual funds. Others now trade in more economical 100-

share units. And the rest seem simply smarter than the generations that preceded them.

Earlier predictive theories have also gone down the tube. One of the earliest, cited by Benjamin Graham in his *Security Analysis*, was developed by Colonel Leonard P. Ayres of the Cleveland Trust Company in the Twenties. Ayres concluded that stocks should be purchased when the number of operating blast furnaces in America rises above 60 percent, and bonds should be unloaded 14 months after a low point in pig-iron production. This sort of theorizing may seem vaguely plausible when it is set forth, but only because it worked in the past. A future test is needed to ascertain its real usefulness. In this case blast furnaces haven't operated below 60 percent (except during strikes) in modern memory, and pig iron nowadays is nothing more than an antiestablishment euphemism for handcuffs.

In practice all such efforts to develop a surefire formula to beat the market have been doomed to failure. The psychological barriers have seen to this. One man's successful system can be—and often has been—another man's ruin. Moreover, unbeatable formulas embody an economic paradox: Given an infallible system to predict stock-price movements, sooner or later everyone would begin using it, and not everyone can win. Yet the search goes on. An enterprising New Yorker has developed an elaborate theory correlating stock prices with the length of women's skirts. His general rule—don't sell until you see the whites of their thighs—seems to have called the market top in the late 1960s, and popular rejection of the midi dress subsequently signaled a new bull market. Another New Yorker has devised what he calls a "Nausea Index"—an average of 30 Big Board stocks especially selected for "erratic earnings, recurring deficits, poor managements and undistinguished future prospects." When the components of this index start outperforming stocks in general, then, in the words of its compiler, "the market is really sick." A computer, fed reams of statistical data about the top-performing stocks of the last ten years, advised its eager programmers to buy only those stocks whose names end in *x*. An even more recent discovery, the over-the-counter volume index, now tabulated by *Barron's*, has a contemporary history of accurately signaling market tops. The assumption is that whenever over-the-counter stocks are excessively popular, weak speculators dominate the market and a decline can be expected. But it should go without saying that any stock-market technique should be regarded with suspicion if it doesn't have a basis in common sense.

Sad to say, many investors—perhaps the majority—enter the market with no technique at all. They buy one stock on a friend's tip, another because they saw it touted in a newspaper column, a third because their broker says its chart looks good and a fourth because they've heard it's going to split. They might even make money with this mindless approach; after all, the odds are loaded in their favor. But without a single technique applied consistently, they cannot expect consistent results. Rather than investing, they are gambling. The man with one technique consistently applied gets feedback. He will either profit consistently or lose consistently. If he loses, he at least knows his technique is faulty; so he can amend it. And when emendations finally produce what for him is a winning technique, he can expect it to win for him with some regularity.

When the would-be investor finds a technique he thinks will work, he can check out its soundness by making paper transactions—pretending he's investing without really doing so and keeping track of the results as the months go by. Whatever valuable knowledge he comes by this way won't cost him a cent. Of course, it won't make him a cent, either, and, in a way, all the paper transactions in the world aren't nearly as instructive as one real investment, whether it turns out good or bad. It's astonishing how much you'll learn about the stock market once you have a few thousand dollars riding in it. Corporate reports, obscure chart formations, offbeat investment publications, all the detritus of the investment world will suddenly take on an almost cosmic significance when hard cash is on the line. Going in cold is certainly the easiest way to learn about stocks, but it's not the most profitable, because you should do your homework before you enter the market, not afterward. Old-timers insist that real experience is the only teacher, meaning that you've got to lose money before you gain the right to earn some (with the implicit assumption that they expect you to lose money to *them*). But no matter to whom you might lose money, you learn nothing from losing except how to lose. Losing may teach you what not to do, but it doesn't teach what you ought to do. The way to learn to win is by winning, which you're not likely to do unless you learn the rules before trying to play the game.

3. FINDING AND USING A BROKER

Among other things, playing the game requires a stockbroker. Finding a broker isn't a big problem. In fact, if, while experimenting with the market, you have succumbed to ads offering free copies of brokerage-house stock-research reports, you can be certain that brokers are already on your trail. Most of the major brokerage houses greatly expanded their staffs during the high-volume market that ended abruptly in 1968. A good many novices have been let go since then, but boardrooms are still teeming with hungry young customer's men of great vision and small clientele. For the first time in years it's a buyer's market for stockbrokers, and it's probable that from among the glut the would-be investor can find a good one. Good or bad, he should work for a firm with a membership in (or connection with) the major exchanges. All large brokerage houses, and most of the smaller ones, qualify.

There are two breeds of broker: the good and the glib. The good broker is a savvy investor in his own right. Perhaps he doesn't have the money right now (hotshot young brokers, despite all their publicity, aren't paid nearly as well as most investors imagine). Perhaps his personal situation prevents him from taking the risks implicit in any stock-market transaction. Or perhaps he *does* have the money and *is* taking the risks, quietly building up a fortune toward that distant day when he can tell both clients and employer to go straight to hell because he doesn't need them anymore. Whatever his situation, such a man, while he remains a broker, will try to put his customers only into situations he believes in himself. He realizes that his best interest is his customers' best interest. He strives to build his clients' fortunes, because he knows that rich clients generate fat commissions, and fat commissions mean more money to enhance his own fortune. Obviously, good brokers are hard to find. Like good running backs, they fatten too quickly. Why get beat up every Sunday if you own a chain of restaurants, a high-rise or three or an auto distributorship?

Glib brokers are more common. These are men who have small investment sense themselves but who are so good at persuading others of their expertise that they can prosper, like wood ticks, from the constant procession of new hosts with which their peculiar talent provides them. For the investor who can make his own decisions, it really doesn't matter which breed of broker he deals with. All that matters is that his broker follow orders. Actually, the glib variety, properly groomed, is superior at this, because he'll endorse any investment, however irrational, as long as it provides him a commission, whereas the good broker will obdurately and conscientiously oppose a new idea, no matter how perceptive, if it runs against the grain of his own investment sensibility, which is enormous.

The investor in need of stock-market advice must find a good broker and one with experience in down markets as well as up. Joseph Conrad once observed, "Any fool can carry on, but only a wise man knows how to shorten sail." In stock-market terms: An idiot can look like a prophet in a roaring bull market; it's the bear markets that try an advisor's mettle. The investor who must rely on his broker really has no choice but to find a man on whom others have relied successfully. He can ask his friends, his lawyer, his banker, even his doctor. Strangely, doctors are an especially good source; they have lots of money, invest heavily, hear from brokers frequently and seem to enjoy talking about stocks.

For the same reason that General Motors executives drive Cadillacs rather than Lincolns, brokers usually endorse the stock recommendations that are periodically emitted by the firms for which they work. But this doesn't mean their customers should follow suit. Brokerage-house research departments are set up to accommodate big clients who generate big commissions. This includes mutual funds, pension funds, trusts, banks and insurance companies. By the time a brokerage-house report trickles down to the small investor, the big boys have already acted on it (assuming it's worth acting on) and may be girding themselves to sell. Sometimes, too, brokers will offer a special deal on a listed stock, giving customers a chance to purchase it, commission-free, at the current market price or even slightly below. Such bargains should be avoided. Here the brokerage house has picked up a big block of the stock in a private transaction—perhaps buying it from a mutual fund or an insurance company. The transaction was made privately because the seller realized that dumping so much stock on the exchange would drastically depress the price. The brokerage house is trying to end-run the market by distributing the shares to its captive clientele.

Like bartenders and barbers, stockbrokers have finely tuned instincts for their customers' psychological needs. Depending on the client, they can be expected to disgorge a computerlike print-out of unsolicited information or to perform their assigned chores in discreet and competent silence. The novice investor with more money than ideas can expect sufficient tips from his broker to keep him active through retirement or bankruptcy. And the investor who merely wants his orders executed promptly and accurately can find similar satisfaction, probably from the same man. It is the customer himself, through the signals he sends to his broker, who will determine the treatment he gets.

In five years of writing investment articles for PLAYBOY magazine, this writer has received literally thousands of letters from small investors, and a recurrent theme is that the investor is afraid to ask his broker questions. The usual explanation is that the broker seems too busy. More candid correspondents admit that they're embarrassed to betray ignorance. Well, a wise man once observed that for people who don't know who they are or what they're doing, the stock market can be a very expensive place to find out. And an even wiser man, Dr. Johnson, in fact, declared that the best knowledge of all is knowing what you don't know. *Ask* your broker questions. He's *supposed* to know more about the stock market than you do. After all, he spends all day at it, it gives him his living, and he had to study for an exam before he could get into the business. If he always seems busy when you call, maybe he is, but that's encouraging—it means he has lots of customers; so he must be doing something right. Instead of pestering him constantly, try to call at the same time once each week—preferably after the market has closed. Soon he'll get accustomed to this regular chat and consider it part of his job—which it is. As it turns out, most stockbrokers like to talk about stocks. Indeed, that's all they *can* talk about.

Besides talking about stocks, brokers are willing (even eager) to offer loans, in the form of money if customers want to buy stock on margin or in the form of shares if the customers want to sell short. Both concepts are subject to popular confusion. *Margin* is the percentage of the cash value of a transaction that the customer must put up if his broker is to lend him the rest. Currently the margin—set by the Federal Reserve Board—is 65 percent. The investor who wants to buy stock worth $10,000 must bring at least $6500 to the transaction. His broker will then lend him the remaining $3500—at interest, of course—retaining the purchased shares as collateral. Most brokerage houses currently discourage margin purchases on accounts under $2000.

Before the great crash of 1929 margin rates were down to 10 percent (even lower for favored customers) and money was easily borrowed. At today's high interest rates the brokerage house might charge 8 or even 10 percent on the skimpy 35 percent that it can lend. In recent years the margin rate has dipped as low as 50 percent, and the interest rate on broker loans has gone as low as 5 percent. Should these happy conditions once more prevail, small investors would do well to margin themselves to the hilt, to profit from the increased leverage that accrues from working with borrowed money. But unless the investor is dealing in five- or six-figure sums, interest rates are currently so high that margin transactions are barely worth the effort. An additional difficulty is that if you have a margin account, your broker retains your shares. Ordinarily this is a great convenience. But currently, despite years of attempted reform, brokerage-house bookkeeping is so slipshod and broker safekeeping procedures so lackadaisical that experienced investors prefer to keep their shares themselves.

Recent federal legislation, insuring individual brokerage accounts up to $50,000 each, protects against broker bankruptcy, but not against broker ineptitude. When the Francis I. du Pont brokerage house (the firm our friend Perot ultimately bailed out) closed its office in Kuwait in 1970, a local sheik held the du Pont staff hostage until the firm had settled his account. Lacking such authority, most investors resort to other precautions. The simplest alternative is to insist that securities be registered in their own names. In-and-out traders rarely bother to do this, on the assumption they'll have sold before a certificate ever reaches them. But an investor who contemplates holding whatever he's bought for any length of time should request *transfer*—demanding that a certificate actually be issued in his name. Whether he asks his broker to *transfer and ship* (have a certificate issued in his name and sent to him) or *transfer and hold* (have the same certificate stored at the brokerage house) will depend on his own preference. Stock certificates are attractive to look at, and the cost of storage in a bank safe-deposit box is tax-deductible. But even if such certificates are kept at the brokerage house, so long as they are in the investor's name there is small chance they'll be mislaid.

The best alternative, though not generally available to small investors, is the *COD purchase*. Banks and mutual funds pull this off routinely. Here the stock isn't paid for until a properly transferred certificate is actually delivered to the purchaser's bank. Since it currently takes weeks or even months to get a certificate transferred, this has its obvious advantages: The brokerage house has to carry the cost until delivery is made. Banks, incidentally, will also make collateral loans against stock certificates. Such money can't legally be used to circumvent the margin requirement, however, because the borrower must swear he doesn't intend to use the loan to buy more stock. Canadian banks, however, require no such loyalty oath.

While margin purchases may be currently less attractive

Finding and Using a Broker

than they once were, *short sales* deserve more serious consideration. From the earliest days of stock transactions, action-hungry speculators have been eager to profit not only when a stock moves up but when it declines. This is done by borrowing shares from someone who already owns them, then selling the shares in the market. Subsequently, if the price declines, the short seller can repurchase them at a lower price, return them to their owner and pocket the difference. Borrowing shares to sell short is usually no problem, because brokerage houses are literally awash with stock certificates posted as margin collateral or otherwise held on their customers' behalf.

Because stock prices usually fall a lot more quickly than they rise, short selling, properly timed, can be much more lucrative than outright investing. But it's also more difficult and fraught with unpleasant philosophical overtones. To *buy* a share in American industry is a respected and eminently justifiable pursuit. Here the investor is betting on progress and stands to prosper with the fortunes of the economy and of his firm. If he's right, everyone wins. But by selling short the investor is betting on disaster. He stands to prosper only if his firm—or the economy in general—deteriorates. For this reason a great many small investors view short selling as something close to un-American and refuse to have anything to do with it. Only one small-investor transaction in a hundred or so is a short sale.

Many novices think that short selling requires no cash at all, because of the big pile of money that suddenly appears in the seller's account after he shorts a stock. For instance, you decide to short 100 IBM at the current price, say, of $300 a share. Magically, as soon as your order is executed, your account is richer by $30,000 (less commission, transfer taxes, etc.). Suddenly you're wealthy! Why should you have to put up more money, since there's already that much in your account? The answer, of course, is that if everyone could sell short $30,000 worth of stocks without posting so much as a dime in collateral, there would soon be more stocks offered than buyers to purchase them. So the rule is that you must have cash (or unmargined stocks) in your account equivalent to the margin percentage of whatever proceeds you receive from the short sale. In this instance you would need, at the current 65-percent margin rate, something like $20,000 in your account before you could sell short 100 IBM.

Considered from the broker's point of view, this rule makes a little more sense. Assume your broker doesn't have 100 IBM available to deliver to whomever you make your short sale. In this case he'll have to borrow the shares from another broker. To do this he'll have to post the full cash value of the shares—$30,000 in this case, precisely the sum that was credited to your account as soon as the sale was consummated. You may think it's your money, but even your broker doesn't get the use of it until after you've closed out your short position. In addition, he'll have to post additional money with the lender of the shares— *marking to market* is the phrase—if their value should increase. This would come out of his firm's pocket (which is probably empty) if you, the short seller, weren't required to post additional cash yourself. Of course, if your broker *doesn't* have to borrow the stock but can simply use idle shares he's holding for other customers, the economics of the transaction changes dramatically. Here he's getting full cash value for the shares shorted, plus another 65 percent from the funds you must post, and all this money is his to play with, interest-free, for the duration of the short sale. It pays to be big. No wonder Merrill Lynch is prospering while the small houses are going bankrupt.

A happy aspect of short selling is that, if successful, you can withdraw your profits as you go along. The only requirement is that you maintain the margin percentage of the value of what you've sold. If the stock you've shorted begins to drop, you can withdraw your profits as they are made without eliminating your position.

Nevertheless, the short seller faces difficulties that the ordinary investor never encounters. If the amateur buys 100 shares of stock at $20 a share, he knows in advance just how much he can lose. His prospective profits are limitless (the stock might go to $1000 a share), but he can never lose more than the $2000 with which he began. But with a short sale the potentials are reversed. The best a short seller can do is double or maybe triple his money (on a fully margined short sale where the stock he sells drops to zero), but there is no limit to the amount he can lose. If he shorts a stock at $20 and then it goes to $40, he'll lose his $2000. But what if it goes on up to $80 or to $500 or to whatever level might cost him more than he has? This is a remote possibility, virtually an impossibility —stocks just don't shoot from $20 to $500—and even if they did, shell-shocked shorts would find room to bail out along the way. But to the small investor, especially if he is the sort who balances his checkbook every month, the prospect of limitless loss, no matter how remote, is not worth facing.

A highly sophisticated computer study of short selling recently published in the *Financial Analysts Journal* confirms that such large losses rarely—if ever—occur. Instead, the study found, short selling consistently produces *small* losses at a random rate of 8–10 percent a year, a figure that seems to verify the Fisher and Lorie studies discussed earlier. But who needs small losses, especially *consistent* small losses?

Beyond this both the Internal Revenue Service and the Securities and Exchange Commission view short selling less than cordially. Even if an investor should stay short on the same stock for a generation, the IRS denies him the tax shelter of long-term capital gains. Profit from every short sale is taxable just like salary income. For its part the SEC insists that short sales be made on what is called an *uptick* —which means that you can sell a stock short only when it's rising. (Enterprising professionals recently discovered that this ruling applies only to the New York exchanges, which means it's open season for short sellers in such places as Pittsburgh and Baltimore.) To top it off, the short seller must make good—to his broker and ultimately to whoever lent the shares—any dividends that might be paid on the stock he has shorted.

Whether the investor is a buyer or a seller, the sort of instructions that he gives his broker will depend on his investment technique. If he's like most smallish investors, eyeing a stock that he hopes will go up, he'll probably just ask his broker to buy it. This is really a request to buy *at the market,* wherein the broker purchases the number of shares ordered at the best price he can get. The liquidity of the big exchanges is good assurance that such orders—in the quantities in which the small investor will deal—won't be filled at a price differing drastically from the last recorded transaction.

While market orders are by far the most common, there's nothing to prevent an investor from setting his own price, except that if it's very far from the current price, his order won't be filled. If he does name his own price, he's making what is called a *limited order,* which, not surprisingly, is any instruction that has strings attached. By far the most common limited order is known as a *stop,* because its most frequent use is to prevent losses. A stop is an order to buy or sell at the prevailing market price *after* the stock has touched a level the investor specifies. In other words, a stop order automatically becomes a market order when the stop level is touched.

Stops are especially useful to technically oriented investors. In the example of Northwestern Steel & Wire, whose chart is shown on page 32, the technician, once he had perceived the boundaries of the emerging rectangular formation (this was clear by July), could have placed two stop orders: a stop-buy order at, say, 51½ and a stop-sell order at 43½. Thereafter, if he were supremely confident of his technical expertise, he wouldn't even bother to watch the stock's price, knowing that the market itself would trigger his purchase (or short sale) at the appropriate time. He has no certainty, of course, that his buy order will actually be executed at the stop price of 51½; he might actually buy at 52 or 52½. But since any penetration to 51½ is a signal for him to act, he doesn't really care at what price his market order is filled, as long as it's filled right after the 51½ level has been touched. In the example shown, this finally would have happened in early September—and would have made a quick profit of almost $30 a share.

Stops are also used, by technicians and fundamentalists alike, to protect profits. To continue the previous example, once the investor has purchased Northwestern Steel & Wire in the low 50s and watched with delight as it ran up through the 60s in less than a week, he might begin wondering when to take his profits and go elsewhere. To avoid cashing in prematurely, he could put out a stop-sell order a few points below the previous week's closing price. Then if the stock retreated back to his stop level, he would automatically be sold out. Once again the market would be telling him what to do. And if the stock continued to advance, he could keep trailing his stop behind it, changing the stop level week by week, accumulating larger and larger profits until the stock finally reversed. (In this example, a stop trailing just two points below the previous week's closing price would not have triggered a sale until the stock reached the low 80s in late October.) Automatic orders like this are most easily placed in stocks listed on the two major exchanges, where specialists—brokers on the floor of the exchange who are charged with making the market in specific stocks—keep track of all outstanding orders above and below the market.* But similar orders can also be set up, somewhat less effectively, for stocks traded over the counter.

There are many other types of limited order, all equally useful, and a good broker can probably comply with any order he can be made to understand. One that is not used as often as it should be is the *MIT* (market if touched) order, the opposite of a stop, requesting to sell a stock if it runs *up* to a specified level or to buy if the price runs *down*.

---

* The role of the specialists is discussed in detail in Richard Ney's *Wall Street Jungle* (Grove Press, $7.50). The author, alas, is an investment counselor, not a writer. But his murky, disorganized prose conceals a point well worth making: that the stock-exchange specialists are uniquely privileged to profit from inside information. A scholarly article in *Barron's* recently suggested that specialist buying and selling patterns can be an invaluable tool in predicting market performance. One predictive device, based on specialist short selling, proved 70 percent reliable in predicting major market moves over the last decade. For details, see *Barron's* for March 22, 1971.

MIT orders, favored by fundamentalists, are especially useful in getting in or out of a stock at a favorable price. The fundamentalist, with his eye on long-range values, can afford to wait for the market to come to him, rather than chasing it as the technician so often does when his stops are triggered. MIT orders are also useful to short sellers, who are understandably wary of executing a short sale at the market, because the uptick rule might force them to make their sale (in a declining stock) many points below the current level. Limited orders can be circumscribed in time: good for one day, one week, one month or until canceled. As a courtesy, brokerage houses usually send out regular statements to customers listing limited orders that remain unexecuted. Even the canniest investors are human, and these reminders obviate the costly possibility of forgetting to cancel an order.

Brokers, of course, are human, too, and the investor should never forget that they are essentially salesmen, paid in accordance with the volume of business they generate. Thus, they have a vested interest in action, while the prudent investor, like Hamlet, might have an equally strong interest in biding his time. In any case, brokers' recommendations are almost invariably recommendations to buy. Buy-oriented research is infinitely more useful to brokers. After all, almost anyone can be persuaded to buy a stock. To make money from a sell report, a broker has to track down someone who already owns the shares and convince him to unload. So be wary of advice from brokers. They may mean well, and many of them do, but their interests are not necessarily your interests. Depend on your broker to execute your orders faithfully and promptly, and be thankful that you don't have to pay him too much for this valuable service.

4. INVESTMENT COSTS: COMMISSIONS AND TAXES

Compared with the commissions charged in most other investment media, broker commissions are still relatively low. They are assessed on each transaction, which means each purchase or sale of a different stock. The commission rate is almost impossibly complex. It also changes periodically, invariably to the further disadvantage of the small shareholder. Since April 1970 the following *minimum* commission structure has been in effect. No firm may charge less, but some charge more. The rates include a "temporary" surcharge, which, like most temporary taxes, has been extended indefinitely.

Cash Value of Shares	Commission	Surcharge
Under $100	No fixed price	haggle with broker
$100–$399.99	2% + $3	50% of commission or $15, whichever is less
$400–$2399.99	1% + $7	same as above
$2400–$4999.99	½% + $19	same as above
$5000 and up	1/10% + $39	same as above

All these charges are for round-lot transactions—those involving 100-share units. In practical terms this means that the minimum commission on a $400 transaction would be $16.50—equivalent to 4.2 percent. Since the same commission rates apply both for purchases and for sales, the total commission cost, in and out of a $400 transaction, would amount to almost 9 percent. The investor's stock would thus have to increase almost 9 percent just for him to break even. On a $5000 transaction the commissions on each side are only $59, for an in-and-out total of $118; so the $5000 investor will break even if his stock moves up just 2¼ percent. The sliding rate structure reflects the economies of scale that accrue to larger transactions. It's unfortunate, however, that the economics of the marketplace should so patently discriminate against the small investor. Just another instance of the more you have, the more you get.

The investor who trades in odd lots, involving fewer than 100 shares, is even worse off. Odd-lot transactions are computed from a commission base $2 lower than the round-lot rate shown in the table on the previous page, but the buyer must also pay an odd-lot fee of either 12½ cents or 25 cents *per share*. On the Big Board the rate is 25 cents on shares over $55 and 12½ cents on shares below; the break point on the American Exchange is $40. In addition to all this there are substantial discounts for high rollers who trade in units of over 1000 shares, rates by negotiation in transactions under $100 or over $500,000, special odd-lot fees for stocks that sell in units other than 100, small taxes and exchange fees that further add to the cost of each transaction, and a host of other tedious complexities. As a rule it's not advisable to involve yourself in odd-lot purchases of stocks selling under $10–$15 a share, because the odd-lot fee, added to the broker commission, makes the price of admission relatively steep; and it's similarly unwise to invest less than $500 a shot in any one stock, because on smaller purchases the commission will be too high.

Investors are understandably fascinated with the commission structure, because it describes the only investment cost they can calculate in advance. A new and permanent rate pattern has been in the works for years and may already have been announced by the time these words are read. It would be pleasant to speculate that the new rates will reflect the peculiar problems of the small investor, thereby reducing the commissions he must pay. However, if the New York Stock Exchange has its way (usually it does) the low-spectrum rates will be raised further rather than reduced. Robert Haack, president of the exchange, has made the intriguing suggestion that raising broker commissions would actually *attract* small investors, because then brokers "would have an incentive to provide more emphasis and depth in services to the small customer." At the very least this is a tacit admission that small investors are getting shoddy treatment and stale research. It also seems to confirm the observation that discussions of broker commissions are usually fraught with paradox and double-talk. At least in theory, few people disagree with the notion of people's capitalism. The more Americans owning shares in American industry, the better. Widespread shareownership tends to equalize the distribution of wealth, because it passes corporate dividends (and capital gains) on to more and more people. It also lessens the likelihood of revolution, since dissenters would presumably be less likely to mount a massive assault on American industry if they actually owned it.

At least until 1969, the stock exchanges and the government regulators seemed to recognize this. The nature of the brokerage business makes the cost of executing a 10,000-share order hardly more expensive than just trading 100 shares. But commissions were always assessed on the basis of 100-share units, which meant that for a 10,000-share order the brokerage house would make 100 times more money without doing significantly more work. No wonder brokerage houses were falling all over themselves to get business from mutual funds and other large institutional investors. In many instances brokers were losing money on small transactions (usually involving individual investors) but more than making up their losses from their institutional business. In effect people's capitalism was getting a hidden subsidy from the high rollers.

But now all this has changed. A month after President Nixon was elected, the exchanges succumbed to various pressures—mostly from institutional investors—and finally introduced the "temporary" commission structure described above. As noted, this provides a substantial discount on transactions involving more than 1000 shares. Brokers still make money on large transactions but in many instances not so much that they can continue to handle small transactions at a loss. The result has been an increasing unwillingness to take on small accounts. In many cases brokers have been refusing prospective customers if they have less than $2000 to start with. This is a lamentable development, because, carried to its conclusion, it would transform the stock market into a private club for the further enrichment of the wealthy, with the less well-off effectively barred from what has always been the fastest road from rags to riches.

If the securities industry has any long-range sense at all, it would include in its commission structure some means by which small investors are encouraged rather than turned away. As Ralph Saul, former president of the American Stock Exchange, put it, "We must insure that our rate structure doesn't encourage concentration on institutional business at the expense of servicing retail customers." The stock market, after all, is more than just a means of making brokers wealthy. It is the backbone of American capitalism and one of the last surviving affirmations that capitalist democracy is really an open system. If capitalism is to endure, small investors must have access to the nation's stock markets, even if only to lose their money in the process. The brokerage community ought to make every effort not to raise its minimum rates but to lower them. Among today's smallish investors are tomorrow's millionaires, and the more millionaires there are, the more money there will be for stockholders. Donald Regan, president of Merrill Lynch, which, besides being the nation's biggest brokerage house, is one of very few that can boast a social-consciousness, speaks to the same question in a different metaphor: "A shoe manufacturer may lose money on baby shoes, but if you don't make baby shoes, people won't get into the habit of wearing shoes at all."

An interesting and almost heretical solution to the commission quandary would be to infuse into the securities business a breath of the essence of capitalism: price competition. Competition is something that businessmen love to hear praised at chamber-of-commerce luncheons but which they throttle mercilessly whenever it breaks out in their particular industry. The securities business has done better than most. It remains the last surviving major industry where price competition is simply illegal. Minimum broker-commission rates are set by the exchanges themselves, with the SEC's somnolent assent. The Big Board generally calls the tune, and the other exchanges fall promptly into step.

Just before President Nixon took office, the outgoing Justice Department took a parting shot at the securities industry by asking the Securities and Exchange Commission (which supposedly regulates the industry) to abolish the minimum-fee structure altogether. The proposal was elegantly simple: The SEC should immediately eliminate all fixed commissions on transactions over $50,000, throwing brokers into competition for the big institutional investors. The $50,000 cutoff would then be reduced by $10,000 a year for five years, at the end of which price competition would prevail among stockbrokers, just as it already does—with no apparent ill effects—in virtually every other service business.

Needless to say, the brokerage community was not wild about this proposal. The idea has now undergone major surgery, and its latest incarnation calls for price competition only on transactions exceeding half a million dollars —with no provision for future reduction. If the issue weren't so damnably important, one could laugh at such a compromise. But in fact, even this palsied thrust into the netherworld of competitive pricing is not certain to last. President Nixon, for one, is on record deploring the "heavy-handed regulation" of the securities business. To force the brokerage industry to swallow as un-Republican an idea as price competition would presumably constitute a new pinnacle in regulatory heavy-handedness. Competition, after all, does not guarantee profits for everyone. It rewards only the efficient while penalizing the inefficient. That it also benefits the investing public—by permitting the small investor to shop around and thereby purchase more stocks for his money—seems decidedly a secondary consideration.

In the fall of 1970 a coalition of small investors called the National Shareowners Association filed a class-action suit on behalf of everyone who uses the two big New York exchanges, accusing them of monopolistic practices denying small investors "the right to buy and sell securities at the same rate paid by large-lot traders." The suit, among other things, asks the court to insist that commissions be set by competition rather than price-fixing.

However just this request might seem, don't wait up for the decision. City hall, or even the federal bureaucracy, is putty in your hands compared to the New York Stock Exchange. The Wall Street establishment, as apotheosized in the NYSE board of governors, is a self-perpetuating oligarchy that is quite literally the last bastion of moneyed privilege in these United States. It will not topple easily or quickly. But topple it must if democratic capitalism is to survive. If Bernard Lasker, current head of the NYSE's board of governors and a close personal friend of both President Nixon and Attorney General Mitchell, realized how helpful his attitudes are to the revolutionary left, then he would resign tomorrow. But, alas, he doesn't and he won't. At rate hearings in Washington not too long ago, Big Board officials warned that abolition of broker price-fixing would result in "destructive competition," an interesting phrase that apparently suggests that a few more ineptly managed brokerage firms might be forced into bankruptcy.* This, of course, is what competition is all about. Constructive or destructive, the premise that price competition is ultimately beneficial stands as a central pillar in our free-enterprise structure. When it is repudi-

* Even in the absence of destructive competition, at least 80 different brokerage firms were forced into merger or insolvency by the 1969-70 bear market. At least 25 more were indicted or censured by the SEC for various illegal practices.

ated by the stock exchanges themselves, which are in a very real sense the custodians of American capital, one wonders whether the whole body of free-enterprise dogma might be in need of reinterpretation.

The biggest investment expense is not usually brokerage commissions but taxes. But since the individual's rate of taxation can't be determined until the year is over, it's difficult if not impossible to estimate the tax consequences of a transaction when it's made. Despite the new tax laws, small investors will find that their investment profits are taxed in the same old way. *Short-term capital gains*—profits from investments held less than six months—are treated just like ordinary income. You add your short-term profits to your salary income and pay taxes on the lot. *Long-term capital gains*—profits from investments held six months or longer—are treated the same way, except that half of them escape tax-free. In effect, long-term gains are taxed at half your normal rate (or 25 percent, whichever is *less*). With the new law, long-term gains *over* $50,000 a year are subject to a slightly higher maximum tax—32.5 percent in 1971 and 35 percent from 1972 on. Still, anyone who makes such large gains ought to be happy to pay. In addition, profits that escape taxation through the capital-gains loophole are themselves subject to what is called a *preference tax*, which might better be called a "loophole tax."

This tax—amounting to 10 percent—applies only after you have used the capital-gains loophole to escape taxes on investment profits well into five figures each year. The precise amount depends on how much tax you actually pay, but the main point is, if you find yourself subject to the preference tax, you can well afford the high-paid counsel needed to decipher the law, and you can rest assured that the tax you pay will still be a small fraction of your profits.

Unless you are infallible, you will probably incur losses as well as profits. When you pay your taxes, the law requires you to separate investment profits (or losses) into two bundles: long-term and short-term. Short-term losses are the most significant, because they can be used to reduce taxable income by as much as $1000 a year. They should also be the most common, because if you've followed the general principle of taking losses quickly and letting profits run (discussed farther on), you'll frequently conclude an investment year with long-term profit and short-term loss. You will have to pay taxes (presumably at the more favorable rate) on the gains, but you can also use up to $1000 of the losses to reduce your taxable income. For a bachelor in the 50-percent bracket, this represents a tax saving of $500, which makes the $1000 loss a lot more palatable.

Losses over $1000 may be carried forward to future years, and a sizable *short-term tax-loss carry forward,* as it is called, can be a surprisingly useful thing for a young man on the way up. It allows him to dabble in short-term speculations that (in tax terms) might otherwise be less attractive. And as long as it lasts, the short-term tax-loss carry forward allows him to reduce his taxable income, year after year, by $1000, a prospect that gets better and better as he moves into the higher brackets. Of course, it's still better not to have losses at all, but as Bernard Baruch supposedly said, the only investors who never lose are liars.

In the Middle Ages the well-to-do spent much of their time in search of the philosophers' stone—a device that would turn lead into gold. The 20th Century equivalent involves a quest for ways to transform short-term profits into long-term gains. Until a very few years ago this could be accomplished with some consistency, but now the ever-watchful IRS has cracked down so that, other than by holding an investment for the required six months, there is no risk-free alchemy to convert short-term profit into long-term. (Well, virtually none. A few devices available in the commodities markets sometimes turn the trick. These are discussed in part 5.) There *are* several ways

Investment Costs: Commissions and Taxes

to "freeze" a short-term profit and then push it forward into the next tax year or even push it forward indefinitely. Of course, the investor should have compelling reasons before he attempts such shenanigans, and he would probably want to employ competent tax counsel to make sure nothing goes amiss. The best reason would be an anticipated reduction in taxable income. Here the investor would want to push as much short-term gain as possible into the low-income year. (Since short-term gains are taxed just like salary income, they are best taken when salary income is low.)

An extreme example will illustrate: A young executive, unmarried and making $20,000 a year, suddenly finds himself with a huge short-term gain. He bought 500 shares of a volatile over-the-counter stock at 14, and, presto, it went up to 40 in two months. He has a $13,000 paper profit and, after the quick run-up, thinks the shares are overpriced. The "sensible" move would be to sell out, but that would add $13,000 to his salary income. He already pays $6000 a year in taxes, and the windfall profit would bring his tax bite up to $13,000. In other words, the $13,000 in short-term income would result in only $6000 in after-tax profits. To be sure, this is still a good bit of change, but not enough to finance a long-anticipated world tour.

So our man decides to push the $13,000 into the following year. Then he'll take a leave of absence from his job, so he'll have no salary income to speak of. Since the $13,000 will be his only income that year, his tax bite, instead of being $7000, will come to only about $3500, leaving him with the better part of $10,000 to finance his wanderings. He would freeze his $13,000 profit by selling *short* 500 shares of his high-performing stock. Shorting shares you actually own is called selling *against the box*. No collateral is required. Our man would receive the full sale price, minus commission and fees, in a matter of days. At this point he is effectively out of the stock, because whether it goes up, down, sideways or into receivership, his offsetting long-short position cancels the move. If the stock goes straight up (as it often seems to in these cases), he will have forgone the extra profit. But if he is as good a philosopher as he is an investor, he will have learned not to lament the loss of hindsight opportunities.

To finish the deal, the speculator would simply wait for the new tax year and then close out his short position by delivering the 500 shares he actually owned against the 500 he had shorted. Since the IRS considers that a short sale has not taken place until it's closed out, the income is taxable in the new year and—in this case—at a much better rate. For an investor who'd care to drop out of the job market now and then, or for anyone whose income varies considerably from year to year, short selling against the box can be a technique worth knowing about. It's also useful in those mythical years when taxes are scheduled to decrease.

An interesting facet of the 1969 tax revision permits minors to earn up to $1800 a year tax-free. This applies to any income, including stock dividends and capital gains. A man with a child or three can give up to $3000 a year to each, tax-free. Such money could then be invested however the parent wished, all in the child's name. Profits would be taxed as if the kid himself had actually earned them: The first $1800 would escape tax-free, all the capital-gains loopholes would still apply, and profits exceeding $1800 would begin at the lowest tax bracket—14 percent. The rub here is that the money actually belongs to the child. It must be used for his benefit (college, for instance) and *must* be turned over to him when he reaches 21. This is one reason why we have so many wealthy hippies. Social critics who lament parental overindulgence have missed the point completely. These are not spoiled kids but the offspring of crafty capitalist parents who were *using* their children to escape taxation. The fact that the kids might employ the money to undermine capitalism should not obscure the equally antisocial motives that induced the parents to give them money in the first place. In fact, the parents' motives explain the children's. Still, for any parent who anticipates paying large expenses on a child's behalf, it makes good economic sense to invest in the kid's name—always bearing in mind that the money must ultimately belong to the child.

A minor money-maker but one worth noting involves a quirk in the tax law—it might unkindly be called a loophole—that permits up to $100 in U.S. corporate dividends to escape tax-free each year ($200 for a married couple). Dividends over $100 are taxable as ordinary income; so the investor has smaller incentive to receive them. But every investor, especially those in the higher brackets, should set up his portfolio to yield that first $100 in dividend income. For the bachelor making $20,000 or so a year, this is equivalent to $200 in additional salary income; with returns as high as 10 percent currently available, an investment of as little as $1000 can reward him with the equivalent of two or three nights on the town every year for the rest of his life. A small consideration, to be sure, but fortunes are built on small considerations.

5. INVESTMENT GADGETS: PREFERRED STOCK, WARRANTS, RIGHTS, PUTS AND CALLS

Most of the highest dividend payers are not common stocks but *preferred*. Preferred stocks can be likened to interest-bearing corporate IOUs. They are generally issued in peculiar situations, often acquisitions, where the corporation wants to raise money without issuing more common shares. (More common might alienate current stockholders by diluting the value of their holdings.) The company issuing preferred stock promises to pay a fixed annual dividend on each share, and it pledges to pay this dividend —no more, no less—as long as the stock is outstanding. (Dividends on common stock, of course, are not fixed; they rise and fall with the company's fortunes.) Preferred shares are so called because if the company is liquidated, preferred shareholders must get their money back before the common shareholders receive a penny. A preferred stock is thus similar to a bond in that it promises only a fixed income. As with bonds, its market price tends to fluctuate not according to the prosperity of the issuing firm but according to the general interest rate.

This peculiarity is discussed at length in the section on bonds, but for purposes of discussion here, one example should make the point. When investors can get a 7-percent return from U.S. treasury notes, then the preferred stock of a first-rate company, just slightly less creditworthy than the U.S. Treasury itself, might sell in order to produce a dividend of 8 percent. If the share's fixed dividend is $8 a year, then the share itself would have a market value of around $100, because the interest rate determines the price. If the return on treasury notes should decline, say, to as low as 3½ percent a year, the preferred share might then sell to yield 4 percent. At this rate a fixed income of $8 annually is worth not $100 but $200, and the happy man who bought the preferred share at $100 would have doubled his investment. Until mid-1970 interest rates were rising, not falling, while rampant and persistent inflation further undermined the putative security of a fixed income. Preferred shares nosed steadily downward to a point where investors were hardly willing to buy them. At that point, of course, interest rates dropped sharply, much to the delight of investors who had purchased preferred shares when rates were at their peak. Preferred stocks—many of which trade on the New York Stock Exchange—are always worth buying whenever the interest rate starts turning down. But few investors would be willing to risk hard cash on their ability to guess such a turn.

From a corporation's standpoint preferred stock is also unattractive, because the company cannot deduct the dividends it pays to its preferred shareholders. The Internal Revenue Service insists that dividends—whether preferred or common—are not an ordinary and necessary expense of doing business. Interest, however, *is* a legitimately deductible expense, and in the past few years corporations have increasingly raised money through interest-paying securities, which are called *bonds*. As noted, bonds are essentially similar to preferred stock. The company borrows from individuals and gives them a bond as security. The company promises to pay the bondholder a fixed annual interest (the going rate is close to 8 percent) and, after a number of years, to return his money. Since bonds, like preferred stock, represent only a fixed income, their market value also fluctuates inversely with the interest rate. Until mid-1970 bonds fared just as poorly as preferred stock. In fact, while the interest rate regularly reached new highs a while back, the bond market was just as regularly reaching new lows. The total amount of capital tied up in bonds amounted to some $300 billion, and day after dreary day in 1969 and 1970, every bond in the country was worth less than its purchaser had paid for it. But, as we will see in the section on bonds, the abrupt reversal of the interest rate quickly turned many losses into profits.

Many companies circumvented the inhospitality of the bond market by issuing *convertible bonds*. These are ordinary bonds with a fillip: They can be converted into a fixed number of shares of the issuing company's common stock. The investor who buys convertible bonds has the security of a fixed income (though the return is lower t' an that on straight bonds), and he also has the chance of profit if the common stock into which the bond is convertible should rise. Convertible bonds are discussed fully in chapter 14.

Common stock, preferred stock and convertible bonds all have one thing in common: They represent a tangible obligation on the part of the issuing company. In one way or another the investor who purchases them has a stake in the firm's assets. But investors can also make (or lose) money in scraps of paper not backed by corporate assets. One example is a *warrant,* representing the right to buy a share of stock at a fixed price. The best-known warrants are sold on the American Stock Exchange, but a few trade on the Big Board, and the majority trade over the counter. Among the most popular warrants have been those of Leasco Corporation, the computer-leasing conglomerate. Each Leasco warrant represents the right to purchase one share of Leasco common (from the Leasco treasury) at $34.80. At this writing the common stock was selling for around $18 a share; so, technically, the warrant was worth less than nothing. Yet each warrant was selling for around $7. The reason for this is simple enough. If Leasco should quintuple in price (as it has been known to do), the holders of common shares would quintuple their money, but the owners of the warrants would fare even better, since, if the common sells at $100, the right to buy a share at $34.80 would be worth something over $65. In other words, while the common increases by a factor of five, the warrants would increase by a factor of nine or more.

Does this mean that Leasco warrants are a better buy than Leasco stock? Well, they certainly would be if Leasco were to zoom to 100. But what if Leasco only rises to $27? Here investors who purchased at $18 would have made 50 percent. But the warrant, exercisable at $34.80, is still technically worthless. It probably would have risen but not by 50 percent. In other words, it would take quite a healthy increase in the price of Leasco common before the warrant would turn out to have been the better buy. Conveniently, a simple mathematical formula can be used to determine just how much a stock will have to increase in order for its warrant to have been a better purchase than the stock itself. The formula, for which the author is indebted to Daniel Turov, of Walston & Co., is $N = \dfrac{e}{s-w}$, where N is the number we are looking for, e the exercise price of the warrant, s the price of the stock and w the price of the warrant. In the Leasco example the exercise price is $34.80, the stock is selling at $18, and the warrant at $7. Subtracting the warrant price from the stock price yields $11, and this divided into $34.80 gives 3.2 or so. In other words, for the warrant to turn out a better investment than the stock itself, Leasco will have to increase by a factor of 3.2 or better. Anyone who buys the warrant at $7 is betting that this will happen; otherwise, the stock would be more profitable.

Obviously, the lower the N figure, the more interesting the warrant. A study in *Barron's* a while back unearthed warrants whose N was as low as 1.1. Here the common would have to increase by just 10 percent to make the warrant a better bet. Bargain-hunting warrant buyers should beware, however, of two pitfalls: Some warrants are *callable*, which means the issuing company has the right to buy them back (usually for a pittance) anytime it wishes. And most all warrants have an expiration date beyond which they are worthless. Our Leasco warrants, for instance, expire in 1978. If the expiration date is reasonably close, washed-out warrants present interesting opportunities for short selling. In December 1970, as an example, Atlantic Richfield warrants, which expire on September 1, 1972, were selling for as high as $10 each. Each warrant represents the right to buy one share of ARCO stock at $110—but the stock was selling for $60.

For the warrant to be worth anything at all, ARCO would have to double in less than two years. Needless to say, speculators were rummaging all over Wall Street trying to borrow ARCO warrants in order to sell them short, in the reasonable certainty of making $10 a share by September 1972, when the warrants finally prove worthless.

Warrants, since they represent the right to buy something rather than the thing itself, are a breed of option. Options also take forms. *Rights* are identical to warrants except that they are much shorter-lived. Warrants may be good for years or even forever; rights are usually valid for a matter of weeks. Generally a company will distribute rights to its shareholders when it's planning to issue more common stock. When exercised, rights permit the purchase of the new common shares at a small discount. As with warrants, the recipients of the rights can either sell them to someone else or exercise them.

Far more prevalent than rights are *puts* and *calls*. These devices are so useful that they deserve detailed consideration. A put, as any stockbroker will tell you, is an option to *sell* such-and-such a stock at a set price during a given period of time. A call is its opposite: the right to buy a stock at a certain price during a fixed time. Virtually all such options are for 100-share blocks, and they are bought and sold, just like stocks, through your broker, though you can also deal directly with put-and-call specialists in New York. The time period of the option varies from 30 days to one year, but the most popular options run for six months and ten days, to let happy holders of profitable options take shelter in the long-term capital-gains provision of the tax code and to give them a few extra days in which to congratulate themselves as they maneuver for tax advantage.

Many shareowners, to the extent they know anything about puts and calls, view them as gadgets for speculation rather than tools for investment. But in fact they are both. Most of the popular literature on puts and calls discreetly emphasizes the speculative aspect—breathtaking profits and limited losses—but in so doing overlooks the fact that put-and-call options, used intelligently, can be a vital adjunct to even the most cautiously administered investment portfolio.

Put-and-call dealers—firms with whom your broker regularly deals—like to think of themselves as being in the insurance business. Their brochures usually describe puts and calls as "a way to reduce the risk of loss where an investment or speculation in stocks is concerned." There is an element of truth in this. Put and calls *can* be used to minimize investment risk. In fact, the investor can involve himself in near-limitless put-and-call combinations. A *straddle* is a put and a call in the same stock (useful when an investor thinks a stock is going to go but doesn't know which way); a *strap* is one put and two calls; and a *strip*, one call and two puts. The use of the last two is arcane and complex, generally combined with the outright purchase (or short sale) of a block of the same stock in the pursuit of both profit and tax advantage. Novices enter this realm of the put-and-call game only at their peril. And they should beware of becoming so fascinated with insuring stock profits that they wind up with what is known in the trade as a Mongolian hedge—an investment so well insured that both profit and loss are impossible, with the investor's capital gradually dissipating in insurance premiums.

Anyway, the number of investors who actually use options for insurance purposes (the technical term is *hedging*) is highly debatable. After all, there's an easier, cheaper and more foolproof way to minimize loss on investments: Don't invest at all. Most speculators, and even most investors, are less concerned with minimizing losses than with maximizing profits.

For this reason speculators and small investors generally approach the option game from the buy side. That is, they buy calls on stocks they think are going up, and they buy puts on stocks they think are going down. A typical example would be this: Speculator thinks share A, selling at

$50, is destined to go quickly to $75. Instead of buying 100 shares outright (and tying up $5000 plus commissions), he buys a call—through his broker, of course. For $675 he obtains a six-month-and-ten-day call on 100 shares of A at today's price: $50. (Option costs vary tremendously according to supply and demand, price per share, market volatility and other factors, but $675 is a good average for this example. Most of the $675 ultimately goes to an option *writer,* discussed farther on.) If during the option period, shares of A rise, the call buyer can exercise his option profitably. Assuming that A actually goes to $75, our speculator can sell his option (frequently he won't even truck with the actual shares) for a profit of around $1700—after commissions, etc. Not bad on an investment of $675. Of course, if A doesn't move or if it goes down, our speculator has lost all his $675. However, as the brochures point out, he knew his risk in advance. He couldn't lose more than the price of the option. Had he bought the shares outright for $5000, he could theoretically have lost the whole bundle.

On the other hand, he may think that share B, also selling at $50, is overpriced. If so, he buys a put—the right to sell 100 shares of B at $50. Once again, if he's right and the stock plummets to $25, he might make almost $2000. And if wrong, all he loses is the cost of the option.

Put-and-call buyers, in other words, know in advance just what their maximum losses will be, and their profits are potentially limitless, at least for the call buyer. The attractions are obvious, and the price is right, too. However, more often than not, the maximum loss becomes the normal loss, and those limitless profits prove illusory. A plain fact of the stock market is that stocks generally don't go hopping around the board in 25-point increments, even in six months. Prices of most stocks don't change much; when they do change, they wander with treacly and frustrating randomness. For this reason only one in about five options is ever exercised profitably.

This doesn't mean that the profits on the fifth trans-

Investment Gadgets

action won't compensate for the four losses; often they will, which is why puts and calls are such an attractive speculation. Still, those four out of five losing option buyers ought to pause periodically to ponder who is on the other side of all those puts and calls they are dropping their money in. When our speculator bought his put on company B, he paid hard cash for the right to sell 100 shares of B's stock anytime within the next six months plus. Most of that money went to someone else, who was willing to receive 100 shares of company B—and to be paid money for the privilege.

This person was not an option buyer but an option writer. Perhaps he was a portfolio manager handling funds for a rich old lady in Omaha or perhaps just an intelligent investor with a four- or five-figure portfolio bent on nailing down a solid return on his shareholdings year after year. These, generally speaking, are the sort of people who write options. And, generally speaking, they combine their own holdings with the writer's side of the put-and-call game to secure a respectable and consistent return.

As an example, here's how the reader, an investor who's blessed with some money, might use a put option to buy stock below its market price—or to make a hefty profit if he fails to. (For simplicity's sake, this and subsequent put-and-call examples ignore the cost of taxes and, where appropriate, brokers' commissions.) Say that you decide that AT&T, the bluest of the blue chips, selling at $50 a share, is a good long-term buy. You have $5000 to invest. Obviously, you could use your $5000 to buy 100 shares outright. Or you could buy the shares on margin. Or you could buy a one-year call on the stock. That would cost around $575; so for $5000 you could actually buy eight calls, representing the right to buy 800 shares. But this is simple speculation. If you bought calls at $575, AT&T stock would have to go up at least $5.75 a share —in a year or less—for you to break even. AT&T isn't famous for its wild moves. While you're confident it's a bargain for the long pull, you wouldn't want to bet $5000 that it will go up more than 5¾ points in 12 months.

So you decide not to buy an option but to write one. You will write a put. That is, you will sign your name to a contract stating your willingness to receive 100 shares of AT&T at $50 a share (assuming that is the current price) anytime during the next year. This is the backside of the put transaction. Simply stated, someone out there is willing to pay to be able to sell you 100 shares of AT&T stock, at today's prices, during the next year. Presumably, since you're looking for long-term profits, you're quite willing to write such a put, because if the stock is a good buy at $50 today, then it will still be a good buy at $50 throughout the year.

Once you elect to write the put, your broker could take care of the details, but more likely he would bring you in touch with a put-and-call dealer. Since you've chosen a popular stock, this specialist will have no trouble finding a buyer for the put. In fact, put-and-call specialists boast they can place or purchase options in virtually any listed stock, if you're willing to pay the price. You would receive, as soon as your put is sold, about $400 as your premium for having written it. The $400, plus reasonable middleman fees, is what someone else is willing to pay for the privilege of being able to drop 100 AT&T on you, at $50 a share, anytime during the option period. The premium on puts, for several mysterious reasons, is less than that for calls.

To evidence your ability to purchase the shares if they should be "put" to you, you would have to post a margin with your broker. But in this case the margin is much less than the amount required for ordinary transactions. In fact, the margin requirement for put writers can run as low as 25 percent of the market value of the shares, depending mainly on the solvency of the writer. In this case the market value is $5000; 25 percent of that is $1250, but you've already received $400 for writing the put; so all you need is the difference: $850. That's a 17-percent margin. (But subsequently, should AT&T go against you, you would have to deposit additional margin to maintain the 25-percent minimum.)

Having posted your $850, you just sit back and wait. During the next year you may be required at any time to buy 100 AT&T at $50 a share. But this doesn't bother you, because that's precisely what you wanted to do, anyway. However, your cost basis, if the shares are actually put to you, will not be $50 a share but $46, because you've received the equivalent of $4 per share premium for writing the put. In other words, you would be purchasing stock you felt was worth $5000 for only $4600. And if the shares aren't put to you, then you've made $400 in one year on an investment of only $850.

In fact, you could keep writing puts on AT&T ad infinitum, drawing a substantial return on your margin each year, until the stock is actually put to you (in which case you've got it at what is, in your terms, a discount) or until you decide you no longer want to own AT&T (in which case you simply stop writing puts on it).

The only real risk here is similar to the risk taken by the outright purchaser. Like all stocks, AT&T could plummet or at least decline. If it did, the man who purchased 100 shares outright would begin losing money as soon as the stock went below the purchase price of $50. But the man who wrote a put at $50 wouldn't lose a thing until the stock went below $46, because he has his $400 premium to cushion him. Should the stock go below $46, of course, the put writer is also a loser, but he's still $400 ahead of the man who purchased 100 shares outright.

Note, also, that the put writer is better off than the outright buyer in another respect. The buyer ties up $5000 immediately, but the put writer ties up only $850 until the shares are actually delivered to him. The rest of his $5000 can draw interest in the bank until the shares arrive, or it can be used as additional margin on other put-writing transactions. (This last is not an advisable procedure, however, unless you have cash available to meet all your puts. Otherwise, in that worst of all possible investing worlds—a sharply deteriorating market—you may find yourself in the unenviable position of having committed to buy more collapsing securities than you have money to pay for.)

The other side of the option-writing coin is just as straightforward. If you have 100 shares of a stock that you're no longer enchanted with, consider writing a call against them rather than selling them outright. Assume, for example, that those 100 shares of AT&T were actually put to you. This could have happened if, after you wrote the put at $50, AT&T subsequently dropped to, say, $45. The buyer of your put might have put the shares to you then. You would have been forced to pay $50 for them, of course, but since your cost basis was $46, you'd be out only $100. But as it turns out, you were dead right about AT&T's prospects. More time has passed, and the stock is selling at $58. You feel it's fully priced, and you don't care to own it anymore. Instead of selling it outright, you can write a call on it. In this case there's no margin whatever, since you actually own the shares. (If you didn't own them, then you would be required to post a margin of at least 30 percent.)

Once again your broker—or a put-and-call specialist—will find a buyer, this time one who is willing to pay around $700 for the right to buy your 100 AT&T, at 58, for the next year. If the buyer of your option subsequently calls your stock, you'll have to give it up at $58, but you've already received $7 a share premium, which means you're really getting $65 a share. If your stock isn't called and the option expires, then you can simply write another option and pocket another $700. And so on, until you finally unload a stock you didn't want, anyway.

There are marginal dangers in this procedure, too, but the biggest is of the hindsight variety. If you write a call on AT&T at $58 and then the stock instantly shoots up to $100, you will feel a pang of regret when your shares are called away from you at $58. But remember, this was stock that you didn't want, and the alternative to writing a call on it was to sell it outright. In either case you would have given up all the prospective profits. The difference is that by selling the shares outright, you would have given up all those profits for nothing. By writing a call, however, you at least received $700 for your shortsightedness. The other big danger is that you may have been absolutely right in not liking the stock, and after you've written your call on it, the bottom drops out and you feel forced to hold those sinking shares until the option you sold expires. But if the bottom does drop out, there's little chance the call will be exercised (obviously, AT&T would have to go up for the shares to be called); so you could sell your shares before the option expires—and before your losses mount—in the reasonable expectation that the price wouldn't suddenly reverse itself and doubly do you in. Here, too, you have the cushion of the $700 premium you were paid for the call. If you unload your shares before they've declined $7 each, you'll still have a profit—assuming, of course, that the shares don't rise back over $50 before the option expires.

In fact, the biggest drawback to option writing against an investment portfolio is not the possibility of loss but the fact that all premium money from expired puts and calls is taxable as ordinary income. If your tax bracket is very high, the game might not be worth the candle. But for most people, income, no matter what form it takes, is still desirable. And for those who can use more of it and who have cash or a stock portfolio to work with, put-and-call option writing can be a highly rewarding investment technique. Several impressive mathematical studies have shown that while big killings are undeniably made through buying these options, those who write them profit more consistently. This is no more surprising than observing that while you can win a fortune at roulette, you're better off owning the casino.

Once the investor has a grasp of the various elements that comprise the stock market, he can begin to put them to work. If he really craves action, for instance, there's nothing to prevent him from buying a call on a warrant—in essence, purchasing the right to buy the right to buy a stock. Given this sort of double leverage, even a small move in the stock at the end of the option chain can translate into enormous fluctuations in the value of the call. The warrants associated with Tri-Continental Corporation (discussed in further detail in section 2) are a perennial favorite for this technique, because Tri-Continental is a diversified investment company—for all intents and purposes a mutual fund—whose price movement usually parallels that of the broad market averages. Popular feeling that stocks are about to turn is usually accompanied by heavy activity in Tri-Continental warrants.

Buying calls on warrants approaches the apogee of risk taking. Another two-sided technique, infinitely more conservative, is *arbitrage*. This involves the simultaneous purchase and sale of essentially similar securities in hopes of profiting from small price discrepancies. A classic example would involve the purchase of 1000 shares of General Motors at $72 on the New York Exchange and its simultaneous short sale in San Francisco at $72.50. Here the profits, after broker commissions, would be a lofty $38, and the investor would need a five-figure sum to set it up. Not surprisingly, most such transactions are conducted by brokerage houses for their own account; they have the money, they're right on top of price movement, they have their own men on the exchange floors to assure getting the right price—and they don't pay commissions.

Other sorts of price disparity lend themselves better to individual participation. Arbitrage transactions can involve the purchase of warrants or convertible bonds and the simultaneous sale of the stock into which they can be converted, short sale of overpriced warrants and the purchase of the related common stock, purchase of convertible bonds and the sale of a call on the related common stock, and in a proposed merger, buying the stock of the company to be acquired and shorting the would-be parent. This last is a somewhat risky pursuit, since so many mergers seem to go on the rocks, but because of the greater risk, profits (in a few weeks) of 20 to 30 percent are common—if the merger comes off. Incidentally, short sales made as part of an arbitrage transaction are exempt from the uptick rule mentioned on page 45; such sales can be made at any time, regardless of the stock's previous price.

Investment Gadgets

Even quicker profits have been made by investors speculating in *new issues*—stock in companies whose shares are being offered to the public for the first time. The year 1968 was a banner one for such wares. Erstwhile billionaire Perot's company was one example, though his stock took a full year to go from $16.50 to $136. A new issue called Educational Computer Corporation ran from $7.25 to $260 in just four months. In September 1968, when Weight Watchers International went public at $11.25, delighted buyers waxed fat as the shares ballooned to an overstuffed $40 on the first day it was being offered. And Integrated Resources, Inc., ran from $15 to $41.50 on its first day out; it had two full-time employees.

But speculators who pay large markups for unproved new issues do so at their peril. Whenever the performance of low-priced new issues begins to make headlines, it's a certain sign of excessive speculation. A decline, not only in new issues but in the entire market, can be expected to follow. This happened in 1962, after an orgy of new-issue speculation the year before, and it happened again after the 1968 spree. (At the end of 1970 Perot's stock was selling for $67.50, Weight Watchers had shriveled to an emaciated $7.25, Integrated Resources was selling at around $20, and the fourth company had disappeared altogether.) Ironically, small investors didn't get so badly burned in the recent debacle, mainly because amateurs couldn't get their hands on too many of the hot new shares. Brokerage houses generally reserve a limited new issue for their best customers —mutual funds, pension funds and high-rolling speculators —all supposedly knowledgeable investors who had been acting decidedly out of character and whose aberrations were a precursor of disaster to come.

Such speculative excesses are anything but new. In fact, one can trace them back many centuries. The textbook example is the Dutch tulip craze of the early 17th Century. According to a fascinating account in *Barron's*, tulips were introduced into Holland in the late 1500s, and soon afterward every Dutchman was buying them. A furious market for tulip bulbs and tulip futures developed. At the height of the craze the Dutch stock market suspended dealings in securities so as to devote its full energies to tulip trading. By the late 1620s "rare" bulbs were already commanding $80 apiece, but that was just the beginning. In 1634 a farmer traded all his worldly goods for a "unique tulip of regal beauty." Included in the trade was "a farm of 38 acres, cattle and sheep, hundreds of pounds of cheese, lard and butter, all the furnishings of the farmhouse, and a gold drinking cup."

The law of gravity finally prevailed. The large landholders, who had been supplying the tulips all along, had already accumulated most of the nation's real wealth, and in 1637 they decided to pull out the plug. Rare bulbs flooded the market, which, of course, collapsed. Within months bulbs that had sold for $1000 traded for a few cents each. Thousands of speculators went bankrupt, the prisons were awash with debtors, and the Dutch economy entered a 50-year depression.

Just a century or so later came the South Sea Bubble, a speculative excrescence—sparked by the prospective exploitation of the Western Hemisphere—that ranks right up alongside 1929 for the imaginative heights to which it soared. Nineteenth Century economist Walter Bagehot noted some of the new issues that tantalized the go-go set 250 years ago: companies "to fish wrecks from the Irish coast," "to make salt water fresh," "for building of hospitals for bastard children," "for building of ships against pirates," "for making oil from sunflower seeds," "for improving of malt liquors," "for importing a large number of jackasses from Spain" and—most intriguing of all—"for an undertaking which shall in due time be revealed." This last one surely has its contemporary counterparts. Bagehot reports that 1000 eager subscribers lined up one morning to pay two guineas each to get in on the mysterious enterprise. The promoter disappeared that same afternoon.

No matter the era, periodic new-issue benders explain in microcosm why stock prices rise slowly and then fall

Investment Gadgets

sharply. Since it's often impossible to say what a company will be like before it goes public, new-issue buyers operate on the "greater fool theory," which holds that it doesn't matter what you pay for a hot stock, because a greater fool will soon come along to pay more for it. For a time this can work as a self-fulfilling prophecy. People hear that there's money to be made in the stock market; so they buy shares. The pressure of their buying forces prices up. Higher prices generate more publicity, which in turn lures more newcomers into the market, driving prices higher yet. Buyers begin to expect profits from stocks, not because their certificates represent real value but because stocks seem to go up all the time. This kind of thinking —whether applied to common stocks or chain letters— carries the seeds of catastrophe. Someone at the end of the chain, presumably the greatest fool, will someday be left holding certificates for which there are no more buyers. The SEC recently attempted to trace the whereabouts of 504 firms that went public during the new-issue boom of the late Fifties and early Sixties. The SEC couldn't even locate 12 percent of the firms, another 43 percent were known to have gone bankrupt, and 26 percent were currently operating at a loss. The remaining 19 percent were actually running profitably; so perhaps they made some money for those patient and prescient investors who got in, as they say, on the ground floor.

New issues are first sold in the *over-the-counter* market. As mentioned earlier, this is a vast, complex and tenuously related network of dealers who independently make markets in the tens of thousands of stocks that aren't traded on the big exchanges. Not only stocks but most warrants and corporate bonds—and virtually *all* municipal bonds—trade over the counter. At this writing, more than 3000 OTC stocks can be purchased at the prevailing 65-percent margin. The rest you must purchase outright, unless you can talk your bank into accepting your shares as collateral against a loan.

Substantial, conservative stocks are traded over the

counter—most notably, those of the Bank of New York, which has been paying dividends steadily since the days of George Washington—but the vast majority are small, highly speculative issues that don't qualify for listing on the big exchanges. Understandably, some of the best stock buys (and some of the worst) are to be found here. In 1968, the last year for which complete statistics are available, more than 1300 over-the-counter stocks increased by 50 percent or more (97 OTC stocks decreased similarly), and around 50 increased over 1000 percent. To be sure, 1968 was a very good year, and this record won't even be approached when the final returns come in for 1969, 1970 or 1971. But good year or bad, stocks on the Big Board don't usually make 1000-percent moves; the last one to do so was Republic Corporation, and that was in 1967.

You buy over-the-counter stocks through your broker, but beyond that, almost everything about the buying process is different. Over-the-counter stocks take their name from the early days of the New York Stock Exchange. Back then, an investor could go to the exchange and buy some stocks at auction, but to buy others he had to haggle with a banker over the counter. The same conditions still prevail: Listed stocks are bought by auction, OTC stocks by negotiation. That's why over-the-counter prices are quoted in pairs: *bid* and *asked*. The bid price is what some dealer is willing to pay for the stock, the asked price what he is willing to sell it for, and the difference (or *spread*), rarely more than 5 percent, is usually his profit margin.

One of the traditional difficulties in buying or selling over-the-counter stocks has been the lack of centralized and instantaneous pricing information. This is now well on its way to being solved, through a computer network called NASDAQ. (It's pronounced "*naz*-dak" and stands for National Association of Securities Dealers Automated Quotation system.) NASDAQ links brokers with over-the-counter stock dealers, enabling the broker to get quick prices (and other information) for any of thousands of over-the-counter stocks. This is the first serious application of computer technology to the market-making aspects of the securities business, and the results so far have been smashingly successful. It's interesting to note that such an innovation should come not from the centralized and well-heeled exchanges (who could so easily set it up) but from a loose-knit association of thousands of independent securities dealers the nation over.

Usually you pay standard stock-exchange commissions on an over-the-counter transaction. Your broker will buy at the asked price and take his commission on top. There are no odd-lot fees, but your broker might have to pay a slightly higher asked price for small transactions. Many brokers supplement their income by acting as over-the-counter dealers themselves. So if you're buying an over-the-counter stock on your broker's advice, it's wise to find out whether the purchase will involve him as a broker or as a dealer. In the latter case the cost should be lower, but there's the danger that instead of offering good advice, he's just trying to move merchandise.

6. THE PSYCHOLOGY OF SUCCESSFUL STOCK SPECULATION

We've pointed up all the specific guidelines, but it's impossible to overemphasize that successful investment is largely a matter of psychology. Every investor has his own style and his own needs. Well-off executives who are pressed for time frequently prefer to put their capital in the hands of investment counselors. For a fee such men provide professional and supposedly first-rate portfolio management. But even the best investment advisors often fail to recognize that their job isn't over when they've found good stocks. They must then get these good stocks into the hands of investors who can live with them.

The family man who keeps savings bonds in a safe-deposit box and hears noises at the front door at night will probably be miserable owning a volatile over-the-counter stock—even if it skyrockets from the day he puts it in his portfolio. For him every minor reversal will be a portent of imminent disaster. Relief will come only when he's sold out. Conversely, the bachelor who spends his paycheck remorselessly and gets his kicks breaking speed limits in his Aston Martin would be equally uncomfortable with a portfolio of gilt-edged blue chips, even if they were to increase steadily every month he owned them. This man doesn't want stability—he wants action, and he will invariably tinker with his portfolio until he gets it. This is why the investment decisions you make yourself—assuming the proper elements of hard thought go into them—are the most satisfactory. Much more than just profit is involved.

While every investor's decisions will differ with his particular situation, a number of precautions and principles apply to all. The observations in the paragraphs that follow are simple to state. They all appeal to common sense, and if followed religiously, they will almost surely result in long-run investment success. Yet remarkably few investors—

even canny old-timers who know all the rules—have the psychological discipline to act on them consistently.

1. One of the oldest stock-market chestnuts—so hoary that it's been elevated to the rank of a cliché—concerns diversification: Don't put all your eggs in one basket. The assumption is that investing in a broad spectrum of companies and industries minimizes risk. But usually this technique only minimizes profit. The investor who is morbidly preoccupied with avoiding risk should stay out of the market altogether. And the investor who wants to make money should narrow his sights to the very few stocks that seem most promising. Investment writer Gerald Loeb has stated the principle succinctly: "Put all your eggs in one basket—and then watch the basket."

2. Never act on tips, no matter what their source. Only one genre of tip can have any validity: information from corporate insiders. But often even insiders don't know what they're talking about. (A well-known conglomerateur once advised his own mother not to buy his stock—too risky. The stock then ran from $15 to $165.) Even when insiders do speak knowledgeably, to act on their information before it is broadcast at large is probably illegal. There's little reason why tips from any other sources should include profitable advice. Obviously, chance alone dictates that many of them will. But to get a tip, act on it and then profit handsomely is often the most dangerous course of all. Bad tipsters, like bees, will sting you only once, but the tipster whose information pays off may come to seem infinitely wise rather than just lucky. He can hurt you repeatedly.

3. Let profits run; take losses quickly and without self-recrimination. Approach toward losses, rather than profits, usually separates the successful speculator from the ne'er-do-well. To win consistently you must be willing to admit that you will make mistakes—not just a blunder here and there but mistake upon mistake. Once again this is a matter of psychology, but investment success can hinge on it. If

you refuse to admit your own fallibility, you'll be reluctant to take losses, a mental paralysis that continually incapacitates the amateur investor. He sees all losses as paper losses and feels that a paper loss is somehow more tolerable than a real one. After all, the market could turn around tomorrow and give it all back. So he sits on a losing situation, waiting for it to return to where he bought it. This ties up capital, sometimes for years, that otherwise could be working productively, and it guarantees the investor—if he's both patient and lucky enough—that he'll someday break even. The author knows of an undeniably authentic case to confirm this point: an investor who in 1959 purchased 200 shares of U.S. Steel at $100 a share. Steel now sells at around $30. It has declined remorselessly for over a decade. This poor man has been sitting on 200 shares of it for 12 long years, just waiting to get his money back. He has no desire to make a profit—all he wants is to recoup his original investment. Fred Carr, portfolio manager of Enterprise Fund during the years when it was the most successful mutual fund in the country, insists that most individual investors only want to break even. Given the prevalence of instances like this, he may well be right.

The losing investor not only refuses to take his losses, but he takes his profits too quickly. "You never lose taking a profit" is a well-intended but erroneous maxim that has gulled speculators since the Dutch tulip craze. Of course you can lose taking a profit, if you take it too soon and if it has to cover those other inevitable mistakes. Stocks move in trends; once a share starts moving, it tends to keep moving in the same direction. This may be a truism, but it works. Ride along with the trend, perhaps using the progressive-stop technique mentioned earlier, until the stock itself begins to indicate that the move is faltering. If the stock moves considerably, perhaps doubling, consider taking a profit by selling half your shares; that way you have your original capital for other investments and you retain the other half as insurance against a further move. Whatever you finally sell for is additional profit.

Plagued by losses, the unsuccessful investor won't let his

winning stocks work for him. He sees every profitable speculation as a potential debacle. At the earliest opportunity he tiptoes in to steal a miniprofit before the market can take it all back. Overeagerness to grab profits is just as costly as refusal to incur losses. As noted, loss taking is much easier for the technical investor. The fundamentalist, for his own protection, must set some arbitrary loss limit, perhaps 20 percent or so, beyond which he cannot ride with a stock no matter how sound it might seem. Such an approach will surely miss big moves in stocks that crouch before they leap, but it will keep him out of stocks that crouch only to fall on their faces, thus assuring that he'll still have most of his money to bring to the next opportunity. Just as loss limitation is easier for technicians, so do fundamentalists have less trouble in letting profits run. Since they have their eyes on **real** value rather than on the shaky and confusing trail of short-term price action, they are less likely to be frightened out of a good stock on a minor setback. Technicians, for their protection, should refrain from watching the market too closely once they're in a decisively winning position. If they use progressive stops, they should place them 10 or even 15 percent below the market, thus assuring that they won't be sold out too early.

4. Don't try to call the tops and bottoms; go with the trend. When prices are rising, successful investors are buying stocks that losers are selling; when prices are falling, the winners are selling back to the losers. This is because the losing investor buys stocks that look cheap—compared with what they were selling for last month. But anyone who buys a declining stock because it looks like a bargain is implicitly betting that it won't go lower. He is trying to call the bottom. He'd do just as well buying lottery tickets. The successful investor would never have the hubris to think he could pick the tops and bottoms. He knows that if a stock is lower this week than last, chances are it will be even lower next week. That's how stocks move. When prices turn around, as they always do eventually, losing

speculators tend to sell out when they break even and then steadfastly refuse to buy more, on the grounds that prices are now too high. Typically, prices will continue to advance, perhaps for months or even years, until the loser is finally convinced that they're going to rise forever, whereupon he leaps in precisely at the moment when the winning investor is unloading.

5. Average up, not down. At some point in his investing career, every losing speculator discovers the wonders of averaging down. He buys 100 shares of a stock at $30 and then sits on it while it drops to $20. Here it occurs to him that he can now get 150 shares for the same price he originally paid for 100, simultaneously reducing his loss—or at least appearing to reduce his loss. Now he has 250 shares, for which he has paid $6000; formerly the stock had to rise to $30 for him to break even, but now it need go only to $24. If the stock then shoots back to $40, he has made a very wise move. But usually it doesn't. A stock that drops from $30 to $20 will probably drop lower yet. Investors shouldn't sit on declining stocks, and they certainly shouldn't keep sinking money into them while they decline. Averaging up is precisely the opposite technique, and it makes better financial sense, because it goes *with* the trend rather than against it. A winning investor might buy 200 shares of a stock selling at $20. If the stock goes down, he'll get out quickly. Only if it goes up would he add to his position. He might buy 100 more shares at $30 and another 50 at $40. He is buying with the trend, and by pyramiding in reverse (purchasing progressively smaller amounts), he is effectively locking in a profit. After his last purchase at $40, the stock could go all the way back to $26 and still give him a profit— though he'd surely be out before then.

6. Never lament hindsight profits; they are as gossamer and as conjectural as the road untaken. This precept was first enunciated by the earliest articulate observer of stock markets, a Portuguese named Joseph de la Vega, who wrote about the Amsterdam Stock Exchange in 1688,

"Take every gain without showing remorse about missed profits, because an eel may escape sooner than you think." If a stock has been good to you and you decide to cash in and go elsewhere, who cares if it keeps rising after you've sold out? A high-flying stock you no longer own is no different from the other highfliers you've never owned. Despite the practical necessity of cutting losses short and letting profits run, once a stock *has* run, it's both foolish and dangerous to try to squeeze the last dollar from it. An eel may escape sooner than you think. Selling at the top is as problematical as buying at the bottom. The pros are quite content to take their profits in the middle. They leave the fringes for the little people. One of the French Rothschilds, a fantastically successful speculator, wryly explained that he owed his fortune to "selling too soon." One occasionally hears stories about people who bought IBM for the equivalent of 25 cents a share back in the early 1930s and then held on ever after. Virtually all these tales are false. Back in the early 1960s this writer, then a college student, happened to date a girl who was a secretary at IBM's home office and who, by chance, had access to historical stockholder records. A broad core sampling revealed that not one stockholder in a thousand had owned their shares for as long as ten years. Most of the long-term stockholders seemed to be relatives of the firm's founder. Surely many people bought IBM when it sold dirt cheap at the depths of the depression. But just as surely they sold out after doubling or tripling their money —and properly so. How in the world could they know otherwise? Taking quick doubles or triples is honorable and profitable. But to sit on a stock for 30 years in hopes it will turn into another IBM is madness. Not one stock in 10,000 will match IBM's performance, no one can guess which one it will be—and who has 30 years to wait? The anonymous author of *Stockbroker* tells of buying 3000 shares of something called Major Realty Corporation—for 11 cents a share. Three months later it was selling for 65 cents, and the author "sold it so fast it would have made your head swim." A year after that it was up to $17.50—but the author didn't care. He had increased his initial investment by a factor of six in three months, and that, as it should have been, was enough for him.

7. As noted, whatever your investment technique, you must be consistent. Don't buy a stock because its chart action looks good and then, when the price goes against you, hold it because it's now relatively cheap on the basis of the fundamentals or because your brokerage house just declared it a buy. If you don't have a consistent plan, you can't expect consistent results. You may make a profit now and again, but you are staking your money on chance rather than on design.

8. Given a technique to apply consistently, you should enter the market only when it promises to give back more than you risk. Figure that the downside risk in the safest common stock is at least 10 percent. This calculus sensibly recognizes the unpredictability of the market. At the outset every investment ought to be regarded as a speculation. Only when a speculation produces a profit can it be rewarded with the word *investment*. To assume a 10-percent risk in hope of knocking down a 5-percent gain is to fight the odds. With a presumptive downside risk of 10 percent (or more) the investor shouldn't even consider a stock unless it promises profit well over 20 percent. This keeps the odds on his side. If he's right only half the time, he'll still come out ahead.

9. Never risk money that you can't afford to lose. Beyond this you should never commit all your investment funds to make-or-break investments such as puts and calls, where you might blow everything in one mistake. Obviously, if you lose all your money, you won't be able to play anymore. Always allocate enough money to investments that will permit a comeback from the worst imaginable defeat. This may mean being overly conservative with half your stake so that you can take larger risks with the rest.

10. And when you make a good profit, pull some of it out of the market. The ultimate measure of a successful investor is not the size of his portfolio but how much cash he takes home—for good. Assuming relatively consistent success, you can siphon off three-fourths of your net profits each year and still see your investment capital grow handsomely. In addition, you'll be able to enjoy your winnings, which is what the game is all about, or what it should be all about.

Don't think the day of the individual speculator is over. Institutions—mutual funds, savings banks, insurance companies and pension funds—are supposedly dominating the market. Happily for the small investor, the facts don't bear this out. At the end of 1968 the total value of all U.S. corporate stock was $707 billion, and of this, institutions owned only $123 billion—less than 20 percent. The remaining $584 billion was still owned by individuals. True, institutions account for a disproportionate share of the action; recent estimates involve them in half the trades on the Big Board. This means that institutions are generating huge brokerage commissions; whether they're producing comparable profits remains to be seen. At the current rate more than a generation will pass before institutions own even half the corporate shares. Clearly, individuals still reign supreme in the stock market, and they will for a long time to come. This should be especially good news for the beginning investor with a lifetime of bull and bear markets ahead of him. He probably won't make a billion dollars, and on occasion he may lose much more than he bargained for. But over the long run, if he plays his hand wisely and well, he'll not only make money but have the considerable satisfaction of knowing he's a winner at a game that tests his own self-mastery.

II
Mutual Funds

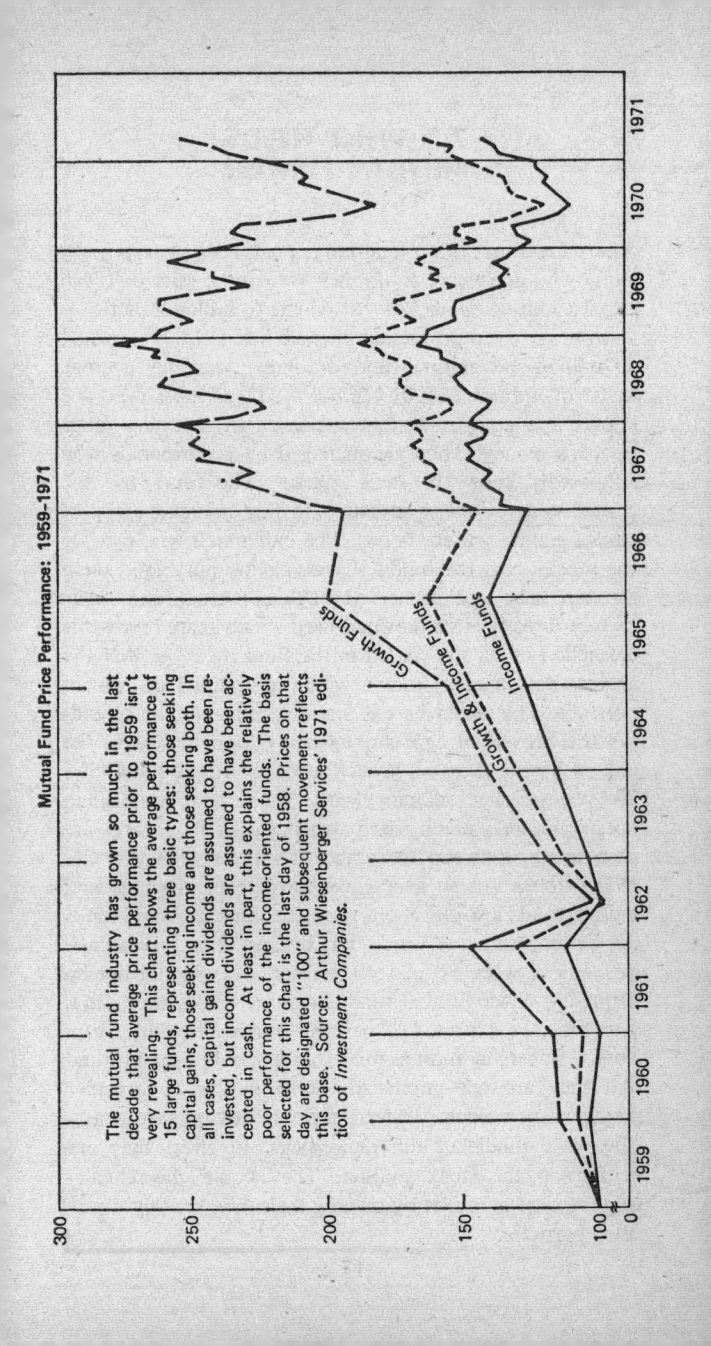

Mutual Fund Price Performance: 1959-1971

The mutual fund industry has grown so much in the last decade that average price performance prior to 1959 isn't very revealing. This chart shows the average performance of 15 large funds, representing three basic types: those seeking capital gains, those seeking income and those seeking both. In all cases, capital gains dividends are assumed to have been reinvested, but income dividends are assumed to have been accepted in cash. At least in part, this explains the relatively poor performance of the income-oriented funds. The basis selected for this chart is the last day of 1958. Prices on that day are designated "100" and subsequent movement reflects this base. Source: Arthur Wiesenberger Services' 1971 edition of *Investment Companies*.

7. WHO NEEDS MUTUAL FUNDS?

Many investors with a long-range point of view, especially those who don't care to do their own stock selecting, lean toward mutual funds. At last count, 6 million Americans —with an average annual income of $11,000—owned 11-million-odd mutual-fund accounts, with an average value of around $4500. *Mutual funds,* as most everyone knows, are companies that specialize in investing other people's money. They are managed by professionals who supposedly know the stock market. The funds use the pooled cash of many investors to buy a broad array of stocks and sometimes bonds. The individuals who provide the money own the fund's shares, having purchased them through their stockbroker, through a mutual-fund salesman or directly from the fund itself. Each share represents a fraction of all the securities the fund owns, so that the shareowners benefit from a widely diversified investment portfolio. The theory here is that diversification, by spreading the proverbial eggs among many baskets, lessens the risk of having them all broken at once. But as the 1969–70 stock-market sell-off clearly showed, diversification doesn't provide much safety when stocks in general are nose-diving. Between November 29, 1968, and May 26, 1970, stocks lost an average of 36 percent in value, and mutual funds lost just about the same amount. Some funds did better and some worse, but by and large the average loss was between 30 and 40 percent. This should not be surprising. Since mutual funds invest in stocks, they can't, over time, be expected to perform much differently from stocks. Buyers of mutual-fund shares should bear in mind that they are not purchasing some unique or oracular management wisdom. Instead, they are buying part ownership in a bundle of different stocks. In effect they are betting on the stock market. They could theoretically achieve similar results by owning their own broadly diversified portfolio.

Who Needs Mutual Funds?

But only theoretically. For an individual to invest his relatively small stake in a diversified portfolio would cost a fortune in stockbroker fees. At the brokerage house, as we saw in the previous section, every different stock you buy is counted as a separate purchase, and commissions are assessed on each purchase. Brokerage fees, in fact, are a sort of inverted income tax: The larger your purchase (i.e., the wealthier you are), the lower your bracket. Not only does the broker's percentage grow as purchases get smaller, but there's a minimum charge of at least $15 per transaction. To spread $1000 among 40 or 50 different stocks would thus dissipate one's investment capital in commissions—rather like the legacy in *Bleak House,* where, after all the legal fees are subtracted, there's no estate left. Mutual funds, by combining the money of many investors, get to buy stocks at rich people's rates: The commission on a large stock transaction can be as low as a penny a share.

Of course, professional management and diversification both have their drawbacks. Professional investors, even if they are paid six-figure salaries for devoting their waking hours to tedious corporate reports, are not necessarily better investors than anyone else, as fund performance in 1969–70 illustrated. And to the extent that diversification reduces risk, it also lessens the chances of large profit. But professional investors do, in the aggregate, perform better than amateurs—at least most of the time—and the people who invest in mutual funds, in the aggregate, are not out to make a killing. They just want to see their money grow—slowly, perhaps, but steadily and in relative safety, year after year. Funds would be a superlative investment, in fact, for anyone who had the perspicacity to sell out when stocks were high and simply sit on cash until the bottom arrived. Of course, not too many investors are blessed with this sort of prescience, but even for folks who cannot divine the future, mutual funds over the years have proved an excellent investment. For the man who couldn't care less about the intricacies of high finance but still appreciates wealth and all the freedom it implies, mutual funds may be the best investment of all. And even the market-wise young pro, confident he can run a few thousand into a small fortune without the aid of outside assistance, might do well to sink a small portion of his hard-earned speculative profits into a well-chosen fund; it won't provide him many thrills, but neither will it break him.

Until a few years ago a strong recommendation for mutual-fund investment was its convenience. There were so many stocks that the chap who was unwilling to spend more than five minutes each Sunday with the financial pages couldn't hope to make an intelligent choice. Investing in a mutual fund, on the other hand, was a paragon of simplicity. All one had to do was fill out a coupon in a magazine or newspaper, and a salesman would soon be calling to talk about the fund he represented. Often it wasn't even necessary to fill out the coupon. The funds were all vaguely similar, making the decision even easier. You just bought one and forgot about it.

But nowadays picking a fund seems almost as difficult as selecting a first-class stock. In fact, the number of funds is increasing faster than the number of listed stocks. In recent years, owing mainly to the astonishing rate of corporate disappearance through mergers and bankruptcies, the number of different shares available on the New York Stock Exchange has actually diminished. Mutual funds, which are not sold on the stock exchanges, have increased in number by several hundred in the last two years alone. Fund assets have multiplied almost a hundredfold since 1940 and now approach $50 billion. Within the past decade the number of mutual funds has doubled; there are now over 800 active and readily available funds, which means that the investor's choice is anything but limited. Mutual funds, in fact, are like orchids. To the outsider they all look pretty much alike. But within you'll find yourself surrounded by a profusion of genera and subgenera, species and subspecies, types and subtypes, all discussed in a language that seems to make sense only to those who speak it themselves. To attempt a comparison of the value offered by several different funds is like trying to nail jelly to the wall.

There's a fund for doctors and dentists (Pro Fund), for farmers (Farm Bureau Mutual Fund), for teachers (NEA Mutual Fund), for airline pilots (Contrails Growth Fund), for Christian Scientists (Foursquare Fund) and even for cemetery owners (Cemetery Care Investment Fund). There are funds that invest only in other funds (First Multifund of America) and funds that invest only in specific industries. Oceanographic Fund, for example, is pledged to invest almost exclusively underwater; International Investors, among others, keeps a fixed percentage of its assets in gold-mining stocks; Life & Growth Stock Fund offers a portfolio of growth stocks and life-insurance companies; Century Shares Trust concentrates on insurance and bank stocks; and Convertible Securities Fund concentrates on—you guessed it—convertible bonds. Corporate Leaders Trust holds only the biggest and best-known companies, making it similar to Founders Mutual Fund, which is rather arrogantly pledged to "full investment at all times in 40 common stocks selected because of dominance in their own industrial classification."

There's a fund that specializes in the sophisticated investment technique, discussed in chapter 5, known as arbitrage (First Prudential Arbitrage Fund); a fund open only to $20,000-a-year-and-over employees of General Electric (it's called the Elfun Trust and has 10,000 shareholders); and there's even a fund for German subscribers to *Reader's Digest*. Since this is available *only* in Germany, American *Digest* fans might want to investigate Vanderbilt Mutual Fund, which "does not invest in liquor, tobacco or drug stocks"—or Provident Fund for Income, which "does not invest in liquor, tobacco, gambling, drug or foreign securities." Mates Investment Fund, the top performer for most of 1968, shuns tobacco and booze and also avoids firms in any way connected with the munitions industry; it may or may not be significant that the fund recently found itself in grave financial trouble and was forced to curtail operations for a while. Followers of Jeremy Bentham's economics will be delighted to see the free-enterprise ideal apotheosized in Competitive Capital Fund, which pits five managers in an intramural battle for investment performance; the fund has been operating since 1968, and already at least four underachieving management teams have been thrown out of the ring. Middle Americans might want to investigate a fund that places "particular emphasis on investments in companies with substantial activities and interests in Kansas and Missouri," touchingly called Heart of America Growth Fund; a similar fund invests solely in companies located in and around Rochester, New York.

Besides the bewildering array of mutual funds, each fund offers a variety of ways in which the investor can purchase it, an equally perplexing number of tricks to be played with the profits whenever they arrive and a surprisingly broad spectrum of charges that the investor must pay for the privilege of getting into the fund in the first place, for supporting those professional managers year after year and—in some cases—for ultimately getting out. The annual management charge and the getting-out cost are not terribly significant to the small investor (in the mutual-fund dictionary, that's anyone with under $10,000 invested), but the entry fees—which consist largely of salesmen's commissions—can be formidable. Most funds charge an initiation fee amounting to 9.3 percent of your investment; some charge less (between 1 and 8 percent) and over 100 funds charge nothing at all. The funds that charge no fee have no salesmen to pay. This makes them all the more attractive to the investor who likes to make his own decisions, but it also means that these self-service funds are more difficult to learn about, though often it's worth the extra effort.

To invest in a fund, you can simply put up as much cash as you care to (though most funds demand a minimum), you can put up some money and declare your intention to pay more within a relatively short time, or you can sign a contract committing yourself to fixed payments over a much longer period, perhaps five or ten years, sometimes with the fillip of an elaborate insurance program to assure that the money will be there even if you are not. There are a few people for whom such contractual agreements may be a good bet, but most investors would do well to avoid them. The funds themselves like to emphasize that the future is unpredictable, and such contract plans will penalize the investor if, when the time comes, he doesn't care to fulfill his commitments. And no matter what the funds say, no investor should sign a mutual-fund purchase contract in which most of the salesman's commissions for the entire term of the contract will be extracted from the first few years' payments. In such arrangements much of one's early "investment" payments go not into stocks but into a salesman's pocket; the SEC—with some justification—is clamping down on such deals.

If this range of choices doesn't seem wide enough, there's also a broad panoply of fundlike institutions—discussed in detail later in this section—that serve the same general purposes but can't call themselves mutual funds because they are differently constituted; unlike mutual funds, these are sold on the stock exchanges just like common stocks. You incur ordinary stockbroker costs to buy or sell them, but market fluctuations sometimes make these special shares available at bargain-basement prices. Like their no-commission cousins, these outfits lack salesmen; so they, too, are more difficult to learn about.

Somewhere in this forest of alternatives there's a fund for almost every type of investor and for almost every investment goal, but the search isn't made any easier by the fact that most information about funds is riddled with jargon and obscure phraseology. The term *mutual fund* itself is part of the jargon, and in some ways it's an unfortunate term, since it excludes a whole class of investment companies that shouldn't be excluded. *Mutual fund* is the popular term for what are properly called *open-end investment companies,* as contrasted with *closed*-end investment companies (the ones sold on the exchanges just like stocks). From the investor's point of view there are two types of open-end investment companies: those that charge commissions and those that don't. The commission funds outnumber the noncommission funds by about five to one, and the two groups comprise about 90 percent of the investment-company business.

Mutual funds are "open-ended" because they create new shares on demand for any investor who is willing to pay for them; then they use this money to make more investments. They will cash in shares (*redeem* them, in financial jargon) whenever shareholders request it. The shares that are turned in simply cease to exist, and the fund's capitalization shrinks accordingly. In other words, the number of shares in an open-end investment company is not fixed; it rises as new shares are sold and diminishes as unwanted ones are redeemed.

Ordinary corporations could never get away with this, because they can't place an accurate value on many of their assets—such as real estate, whose worth depends largely on how eager someone might be to buy it, or goodwill, which is about as tangible as virtue. This is why corporate shares are sold in the various stock markets. The markets permit the investing public to set its own value on what it thinks each share is worth. However, since mutual funds' assets consist solely of stocks and bonds (and usually some cash) and since all these investments have a specific stock-market value at any given moment, mutual funds can compute their net asset value instantly, right down to the last penny. Usually the funds make these computations after the stock market closes each business day, and the figures are published in most daily newspapers. On one afternoon, for example, all the investments and cash in a fund's portfolio might be worth $10 million—quite modest for a fund these days—and the fund might have 2 million shares in the hands of the public. The net asset value of each share (assuming the fund has paid all its bills) would then be precisely $5. Any of the fund's investors could redeem his shares and receive $5 for each; and anyone who wanted to buy into the fund could purchase shares at $5 each—plus (in most cases) the commission, which, doubtless because of its size, is called a *load*. The funds that charge commissions at or near the legal maximum rate of 9.589 percent are called *load funds*. Those that charge somewhat less than the full rate are called *low-load funds,* and those especially interesting ones that charge nothing at all are called *no-load funds*.

A good knowledge of how mutual-fund commissions actually work is extremely useful to anyone who hopes to make an intelligent fund investment. Unfortunately, a discussion of commissions touches so closely on the funds' self-interest that reliable information is extremely hard to come by. We will consider the commission question at some length, but for the nonce it's sufficient for the reader to understand that the commission money he pays when he buys into a fund does not go to the people who run it. It goes to those who sell the shares, usually stockbrokers or salesmen, who often have no connection with the fund itself. The people who run the fund are paid not from commissions but from the fund's investment income. Typically, the fund management takes an annual fee equal to ½ percent of the fund's total asset value. That doesn't sound like much, and for most investors it isn't. If you own $5000 worth of a fund, for instance, you're being charged about $25 a year for all that diversification and professional management. For smallish investors this is certainly a bargain—less, in fact, than the cost of a year's subscription to the *Wall Street Journal*. But if the fund has assets totaling $1 billion (currently at least eight funds exceed that mark), management fees can come to $5 million a year—which ought to buy all the stock experts in the country and still leave a lot left over.

Some funds have belatedly recognized that management costs do not rise directly with the size of the assets supervised, and these enlightened funds reduce the management percentage as the fund grows. Other funds reward management not just according to size but on the basis of how well the fund performs; such an arrangement is commendable not only because it rewards excellence but because it provides the fund managers with an incentive to do more than just lure in new shareholders.

Mutual funds make money for their shareholders in two ways: from dividends (or other income from their investments) and from selling their investments at a profit. Like most companies, funds pay dividends to their stockholders, sometimes quarterly, sometimes annually. Each investor in the fund gets his portion of all the dividends the fund receives from the various investments in its portfolio, after operating expenses (including management's cut) have been deducted. Tax law all but compels the funds to pass such dividend income along to shareholders. The fund pays no taxes on this money, because it simply acts as a pipeline channeling the dividends to its investors, who then pay taxes on it themselves. (But as noted in the previous section, each taxpayer's first $100 in dividends —including dividends passed on by mutual funds—is tax-free, a point well worth the consideration of those who don't currently receive dividend income. Interest income —such as the interest from savings bonds or bank accounts—is fully taxable.)

From time to time a mutual fund will also run up profits or losses when it sells investments from its portfolio. If the fund has held such investments for more than six months, the profits are long-term capital gains. Long-term capital gains, as we have seen, are taxed at lower rates than ordinary income. The mutual-fund shareholder must pay this lower tax on his portion of the fund's capital-gains profits each year. Though the fund has the option of retaining the profits (and paying the tax on the investor's behalf), it usually returns the money to the shareholders in what is called a *capital-gains distribution,* typically paid out each January.

However, funds strongly urge shareholders to accept capital-gains distributions—and even dividends—not in cash but in additional shares of the fund. This provides the fund managers with more money with which to make new investments, and it also gives them an ever-larger pie from which to extract their cut. More important, however, are the advantages that reinvestment provides for the shareholders themselves. Funds usually permit shareholders to reinvest all their capital-gains profits without paying additional commissions. Mutual-fund profits can thus compound in a most rewarding manner, and the fund shareowner who reinvests all his profits is reasonably assured that inflation will not erode the value of his original investment.

More than 70 percent of all fund shareholders elect to take their capital gains in additional shares; the percentage of investors taking their dividends in shares is lower, possibly because most funds still charge a commission on reinvested dividends. Fund shares, incidentally, are not purchased in round numbers, nor even in whole numbers, but in dollar amounts. After deducting the applicable commission (if any), the fund simply credits the investor with however many shares the remaining money will buy —computed down to four decimal places. If the shareholder elects to reinvest his dividends and capital gains, these, too, will be converted into shares to the nearest ten-thousandth, guaranteeing that every penny of the investor's money is always working for him.

Despite such advantages many younger investors have tended to shun the funds in the oft-mistaken belief that they can fare better on their own. In the short run they possibly can. Given a pinch of savvy, almost anyone could conceivably pick a stock that would outshine a mutual-fund investment—for a month, a year or even longer. Not a single mutual fund so much as doubled its investors' money in 1968, but literally hundreds of stocks did. In fact, on the over-the-counter market alone, 52 stocks advanced by more than *1000 percent* in 1968. At least a few investors must have been fortunate enough to own the year's best performer, Diverco, Inc., a company so obscure that diligent research failed to unearth the nature of its operations other than that it was "formerly in the swimming-pool business." The company didn't seem to have so much as a telephone, but it did have lots of tax losses, and these were sufficient to propel it from 1 cent a share (January 2, 1968) to $2.12 (December 31, 1968), for an impressive gain of 21,100 percent. The odds against picking a winner such as this are formidable, even in a good year. Who in his right mind would buy a stock in a company that doesn't even have a phone? And if the odds against making one such investment are steep, the odds against making a series of them—taking the profits from the first stock and sinking them all into a second, taking the proceeds from the second and investing them all in a third, and so on—are impossible. It would be easier to pick a 12-horse parlay, something no one has ever done. The problem with stock pyramids, as with 12-horse parlays, is that no matter how lucky or perspicacious the bettor might be, sooner or later the whole edifice is bound to collapse, and when it does, the ultimate bad bet wipes out the profits from all the previous good ones.

But there *is* a sort of parlay that investors can and *do* make money on, and it's a technique that's at once rewarding and prosaic. The only requirement is patience and the leverage of compound interest. For investors gifted with patience, funds can provide scads of compounding, by virtue of the aforementioned commission-free reinvestment of capital gains. Essentially, compounding means that after the initial investment has produced dividends of one sort or another, the investor then begins receiving dividends on his dividends, then dividends on the dividends on the dividends, and so on, ad infinitum. How this actually works for the fund investor is best understood through an ancient and well-known financial formula called the rule of 72. For a reason that is knowable but not worth knowing, the number 72 divided by the prevailing rate of compound interest will reveal the number of years required for a sum of money to double. An investment that increases at 18 percent a year, for instance, will double every four years—because 72 divided by 18 equals four. Eighteen percent may seem a bit steep, but it's theoretically

Who Needs Mutual Funds?

quite achievable for a good fund in a good year. In fact, in 1968, the last good year on record as these words are written, 18 percent was very close to the gain racked up by the *average* mutual fund. For the entire decade of the 1960s, a period which spans two minor bear markets and concludes in nothing less than a stock-market disaster, the ten top performing mutual funds returned an average of 14 percent compounded.

The funds deserve credit for this performance, but not quite as much credit as one might think. Recall the University of Chicago computer study discussed in chapter 1. This survey showed that the average annual profit (before taxes) on *any* New York Stock Exchange investment held for one month or longer—regardless of what the company was, when the shares were purchased or when they were sold—was 9.3 percent. If a random investment in stocks returns 9.3 percent, it seems reasonable to expect that highly touted and highly paid fund managers can produce somewhat higher. Assuming a perhaps overambitious compound-interest rate of 18 percent, the rule of 72 reveals that a young man could invest a paltry $1000 in funds at the age of 20 and at 60 emerge a millionaire. If he's not willing to sweat out 40 years, he can up the initial ante to $30,000 and watch it run to almost $1 million in only two decades. Of course, this example is wildly theoretical in that it makes several assumptions of a future-predictive nature. The future, as we know, is never predictable. But still the example does emphasize a basic point: that compound interest is not to be derided.

Given the manifest advantages of compound interest, the problem of picking a mutual fund seems to be simplicity itself: The investor should select whichever fund will give him the largest percentage return year after year. This is actually an "iffy," even an impossible, proposition, but it's still what many fund investors (probably a majority of relative newcomers) actually attempt. These investors will confess that they have only one goal: to make as much money as they can in as short a time as possible. Needless to say, a good many funds have sprung up to accommodate them. A decade ago the SEC was worried that mutual funds were being managed too conservatively, but it now thinks the funds aren't conservative enough. Former SEC chairman Manuel F. Cohen expressed his concern in a national business magazine about an increasingly speculative climate that has been enveloping the mutual-fund business, and Cohen's successor, Hamer H. Budge, complained to Congress before the 1969–70 crash about a cult of performance among fund managers who focus on short-term profits in order to make their shares more salable. More than any threatening words, however, the 1969–70 blowout caused a massive reappraisal among fund managers themselves of their investment practices. In the spring of 1970 navel-gazing self-criticism was so common on Wall Street that one could have mistaken a get-together of portfolio managers for a platoon of Red Guards. One result was the widespread acceptance—both in anticipation and in response to regulatory decrees—of sounder and somewhat more conservative investment practices.

But the cult of performance still exists, among fund managers, among fund investors and among investors generally. In fact, if we can believe an interview recently published in the *Institutional Investor,* it has penetrated even the back rooms of the Vatican: Egidio Cardinal Vagnozzi, manager of the Vatican investment portfolio, revealed that "we are, to put it simply, more performance-minded now."

Investors who are not blessed with infallibility usually rely on the evidence of the past when selecting the fund they think will make the most money for them. In other words, they buy funds that have a past or current history of success. Several firms specialize in rating mutual funds periodically—ranking them according to how well they are doing in the performance derby—and whenever new ratings are published, investors fall all over themselves for the privilege of throwing money at the top-ranked funds.

Mates Investment Fund, the one that refuses to invest in the munitions industry, learned the hard way just how anxious the public is to invest in a winning situation. In the halcyon year of 1968, Mates was performing so much better than any other fund that it was literally inundated with investor money—so much so that the fund couldn't keep up with its paper work and had to stop selling new shares. *Mirabile dictu,* Mates Fund actually rejected some $50 million in investor money. On the strength of its top rating alone (Mates Fund is a no-load fund, without commissions or a sales force), its size had grown by a factor of ten in six dizzying months. By the end of the year the fund was so successful that it was almost forced out of business; one of the stocks in the Mates portfolio, a now-grounded highflier known as Omega Equities, had zoomed from $3.25 to $33 in just a few months. Unfortunately, the 300,000 Omega shares that Mates owned were not registered with the SEC. They represented what is known as *letter* stock—perfectly legitimate shares, often originating from corporate insiders who've received them in option deals—except that since they are not registered, they cannot be sold. Being unsalable, they are often available at a large discount from the current market price. A fund could buy them at a discount (these ranged from 20 to 80 percent) and then produce instant profits by entering them on its books at the current market price.

In fairness to the Mates Fund, it was valuing its Omega shares for only $15 when the market price was $27. Still this represented 16 percent of the fund's total dollar value, and when the SEC suspended trading in Omega shares, the Mates Fund had no way to determine the value of its own assets. As a consequence, the fund was forced to stop redeeming its shares—almost an unprecedented event in the mutual-fund business. The fund has since resumed normal operations but without repeating its 1968 growth. In 1969 it lost 23 percent, and in 1970, 39 percent.

The ratings that sparked all the initial interest in Mates Fund are published periodically in some of the financial magazines. As published, however, they are often incomprehensible, and a better source is usually a brokerage-house reference library. Any reputable broker will be able to lend you abundant material from Wiesenberger and

Company, a New York firm that publishes a huge annual compilation of data (including easy-to-read charts) about past and current fund performance. The best of the rating services is probably the Lipper list, published in various forms (including a weekly ranking of the hottest funds) by the Arthur Lipper Corporation, a brokerage house in New York. You can buy the big Wiesenberger book for $40, but Lipper service costs up to $500 annually; so it's best to borrow a broker's copy.

The unhappy experience of Mates Fund notwithstanding, one of the interesting aspects of the mutual-fund performance derby is that success breeds success, at least in the short run. Once a fund rises to the top ranks, it tends to stay there for a while. The reasons for this are obscure, but they definitely relate to the influx of cash from new investors that usually accompanies a high position in the fund-performance list. A high ranking means new investors, and new investors mean new money. Once a fund management is blessed with new money, it is free to buy good new stocks whenever it finds them; it can buy when the market goes down (obviously, this is the best time to buy), and it can count on receiving useful research about hot new stocks from brokerage houses eager to get their hands on some of that incoming cash. Funds not blessed with new money, on the other hand, must dip into their reserves to make new investments or to meet redemptions. If they are fully invested and have no cash (most funds try to keep some in reserve), they must sell old investments, often at a loss or at least at a time when they should not be sold. To the extent that a fund enjoys a steady stream of new money, it will be able to make the sort of good new investments that will keep it high in the rankings, and when a fund stays high in the rankings, it keeps getting more new money. Portfolio managers—the men who actually make the funds' investment decisions—generally admit that a steady influx of new cash is crucially important to their own well-being, financial as well as psychological. It's not simply to appease their egos that fund managers are engaged in a no-holds-barred battle to get into the top ten, or at least into the top 25, on the ranking lists.

Watching all this jockeying, the casual observer might guess that most funds share the same objective: to make as much money as possible for their shareholders. This, unfortunately, is just not true. A great many funds, especially the newer ones and most especially the ones that the reader will be looking for, *do* try to maximize profits —but, by and large, the scope of their investment goals is much broader. Some funds, for instance, are interested only in the preservation of capital—to accommodate investors who have reached that lofty state where their primary concern is simply keeping what they already have. Other funds pursue the maximization of income—for widow and orphan types who must live on whatever they can best squeeze from a fixed sum of money. Most other funds can generally be ranked according to their willingness to take risks.

Since the funds can make money in two ways—from dividend income and from capital gains—the most sensible way to classify them would be to divide them into two groups: income funds and capital-gains funds, which might better be called growth funds. But even here we're forced to add a third category—special funds—to pick up everything that doesn't fall into the first two categories. (Many of the oddball funds listed earlier would qualify as special funds.) Income funds are for anyone who has a specific sum of cash and doesn't want to risk diminishing it in the process of trying to make it grow. But the lure of tax-favored capital-gains profit is so great that even income funds sometimes don't seem terribly interested in income. Of 15 income-oriented funds tabulated by *Fundscope* magazine in 1968, only two paid dividends higher than 5 percent. The highest dividend payer of 375 funds examined is called Keystone B-4 (most funds have more evocative names), and it returned 5.69 percent. Since even short-term treasury notes were then paying around 6 percent, the objective observer must conclude that people solely interested in income shouldn't be dabbling in funds at all.

In fact, the straight-income funds have a relatively small following: They account for less than 5 percent of the mutual-fund business. One of the reasons they attract even this much attention is that the conservative nature of their portfolios makes them relatively safe investments and sometimes, in periods when speculators are disenchanted with high-flying growth stocks, makes them good sources of capital-gains profits as well. The years 1968 through 1970 comprised such a period and embarrassed a great many funds because their declared intentions simply did not reconcile with their actual performance. Funds that claimed to be investing primarily for growth wound up producing nothing but income—and not much of that. And funds set up to invest for income were beset with embarrassingly large capital gains. In one recent year, for instance, Channing Growth Fund "grew" a modest 2 percent, while its conservative sister fund, Channing Income Fund, grew about 13 times faster, increasing the value of its investors' holdings by 25½ percent.

In outfits like the Channing group, the managers run different but similarly named funds designed to achieve different results. (One of the happy aspects of such multiple arrangements is that the managements usually let their shareholders shift their holdings from one fund in the family to another without having to repeat the hefty commissions.) Of nine such management groups this author knows about—each offering one fund dedicated to growth and another dedicated to income—the income funds outgrew their growth counterparts in all but one instance.

But at least they grew. While stocks on the average went up 4 to 8 percent in 1968 (depending on which index you read and how you read it), Manhattan Fund, one of the largest and best known of the growth funds, *declined* 7 percent. As the fund's president, ex-wizard Gerry Tsai, Jr., admitted to his shareholders, "Our investment judgment on growth stocks was faulty. Put simply, we tended to overstay better-known growth stocks." In business, as in life, faulty judgment can hurt. Manhattan's

Hamletlike tendencies to overstay lost it $134 million in profits that it could have taken but didn't. Tsai may be more candid than most growth-fund presidents, but his fund was not alone in its less than meteoric performance. Of 375 well-established funds tracked by *Fundscope* through 1968, 48 wound up trailing the Dow-Jones industrial average. The records for 1969 and 1970 were even worse. A total of 439 funds lost an average of 14 percent in 1969, while the "unmanaged" DJIA was losing only 11 percent. For 1970 the Dow actually increased 3 percent—but the 439 funds lost, on the average, over 13 percent.

Of course, in a falling market, such negative performance is to be expected. In attempting to beat the averages in good years, a growth fund winds up owning just the sort of high-risk stocks that will bring disaster in bad years. An individual speculator, when he senses trouble, can dump his entire portfolio and wait on the sidelines. Many investors do just this. It's a very sensible policy. But a mutual fund, by nature, is more or less committed to full investment at all times. To be sure, many a fund might occasionally have 20 or perhaps even 40 percent of its assets in cash. But you never hear of a fund that's 100 percent in cash, despite the fact that in a falling market cash can be an extremely profitable "investment."

There are several reasons for the funds' reluctance to leave the market. First, there's always the chance of being wrong. What if you're totally out of the market and stocks zoom up? Second, if a fund stayed fully invested in cash for any length of time, it would have no way to justify a high-paid portfolio manager and the ample research staff that backs him up. Money in a mattress doesn't need management. Third—and most important—funds are much too large to go zipping in and out of the market the way an individual can. Liquidity, in fact, was the nemesis of the mutual funds in 1969 and 1970. Ever so many growth funds found themselves sitting on large blocks of thinly traded over-the-counter stocks that could not find a buyer at any price. The stock might be quoted at $7 a share—but that's for 100 shares, not 100,000. In good years there's always another fund to pick up a block of such size, but in bad years there's nobody. During 1970 especially, the growth funds had to eat reams of unsalable paper, watching the price drift a bit lower each week, powerless to act. The alternative—attempting to sell such junk on the open market—would have produced prices quoted in pennies rather than dollars.

8. THE DILEMMA OF SUCCESS

Size is also a fund bugbear for quite another reason. We have seen that success breeds success in the mutual-fund business, but success also carries with it the seeds of ultimate failure. To the extent that a fund's current prosperity lures money from new investors, the fund itself must suffer sooner or later, because it will someday be too large to manage nimbly. The federal laws that govern mutual-fund activities assure this. Most funds aren't allowed to have more than 5 percent of their money in any one company; also, they can't own more than 10 percent of any single company's shares. These restrictions were designed to keep funds from exercising a management role in the companies in which they invest (a role they often exercise anyway), but their real effect is to cramp the style of a fund once it has grown beyond a certain size.

Consider a hypothetical billion-dollar fund. The 5-percent rule says the fund may own up to $50 million worth of any one stock (5 percent of a billion). But most potential investments, especially the smaller, more promising companies, where the biggest profits are often to be made, have less than $50 million in shares—and the fund is limited to owning only 10 percent of them. The result, quite simply, is that as a fund gets larger, it is forced to diversify increasingly or to invest more and more in well-established firms with vast numbers of shares outstanding —the very companies that, because of their large size, usually provide the least action. Common sense indicates that the number of small, hot companies is limited, and even if a large fund elects to confine itself to these, sooner or later it will own as much as it can of them and will have no place else to go. In the process it will also pick up a number of small, promising companies that fail to live up to their promise.

The message should be clear: Once a fund gets past a

certain size, say, larger than $100 million or so, its activities are increasingly restricted. It can diversify by buying an ever-larger number of small-company stocks, it can buy ever-bigger chunks of the large, well-established companies, or it can do both. But whatever it does, it is not likely to keep making the profits that attracted most of its investors in the first place. Year after year the largest funds—those with assets over $1 billion—act most like the Dow-Jones industrial average. Understandably so, because they comprise essentially the same stocks.

Perhaps the most interesting illustration of the dilemma of success is provided by Enterprise Fund, a growth fund headquartered in Los Angeles. At the end of 1968 it was possible to say, without qualification, that Enterprise was the most successful mutual fund in all history. It had been the only fund to rank among the top 25 for six straight years. No other fund has accomplished this feat since 1940, when new legislation changed the structure of mutual funds and meaningful statistics began to accumulate. A $10,000 investment in Enterprise Fund at the beginning of 1963—deducting the 9.3-percent load and assuming that all capital-gains distributions and dividends had been reinvested—was worth close to $70,000 at the beginning of 1969. In the early years of Enterprise, success surely bred success. The fund's assets increased by a factor of several hundred during the period discussed, growing from $3 million to almost $1 billion. Most of that was new money, attracted by the fund's impressive performance.

But from the vantage point of 1971 these new investors can't be very happy. In 1969 Enterprise lost 25 percent, and in 1970, 33 percent on top of that. Investors who had paid over $13 a share to get into the fund in early 1969 found, two years later, that their shares were worth hardly $6, for a cumulative loss of over 50 percent. Ironically, the long-term statistics on Enterprise still look glowing. A thousand dollars sunk into the fund on the first day of 1960 would have been worth close to $4000 on the last day of 1970. The problem is that most investors didn't buy into the fund in 1960. They came in 1967, 1968 and 1969. And for all these the original $1000 is now worth perhaps $500.

What beset Enterprise was not only a bad market but rapid growth to an unwieldy size. The fund's investment philosophy, as articulated by its former portfolio manager, Fred Carr, was to invest in "emerging growth situations" —small firms that promised large success. Even in the best of times, how many such companies exist is open to question. At its peak Enterprise had some 725 stocks in its portfolio, which surely made it less flexible than when it was a $6-million fund and could invest in the most promising 30 of those 725. Carr, in fact, recognized the problems of bigness and divided the Enterprise portfolio internally into a number of different bundles, each tended by a separate manager. But even this attempt at self-imposed smallness may not work, for the 5- and 10-percent rules still apply to the fund as a whole, not to the individual bundles. One thing is certain—no matter how well Enterprise does in years to come, it will certainly not duplicate its record of the 1960s. If its size were to increase that much again, it would wind up owning almost $80 billion worth of securities, which wouldn't leave much for the rest of us.

The dilemma of Enterprise Fund is also the dilemma of the man who wants to invest in funds. Few people would want to buy into a fund with an unproved track record, but a fund with a good track record may have grown too large to sustain its previous rate of success. Most printed information about mutual funds will tell you, in one way or another, that the only real measure of value is how a fund has performed over several years. Unfortunately, this just isn't true, and most of the mutual-fund rating services admit it. After arming the reader with endless pages of statistics about past performance, the services will note, with some coyness, that past results should under no circumstances be construed as an indication of future performance.

9. WHAT TO LOOK FOR AND WHAT IT WILL COST

Despite contradictions such as this, there *are* a few guidelines that would-be mutual-fund investors can follow. First, it never hurts to know how a fund's management is being compensated. Besides the growing number of funds with a sliding compensation schedule (which means that the managers get a smaller cut as the pie expands), some funds, especially newer ones, reward their management on the basis of how well the fund performs in comparison with the broad stock-market averages. This is an innovation that has spread rapidly in recent years, mostly due to the appearance of new funds that needed the lure of bonus payments to attract first-class portfolio management. In 1967 only 16 funds featured incentive arrangements; today the number is over 150. Investors attracted to this device should check the incentive arrangement carefully to make sure it contains a stick as well as a carrot. Some funds have devised a peculiar incentive schedule wherein the managers are rewarded for good performance but not penalized for bad. As an SEC spokesman jaundicedly described it in *Barron's,* "This is a 'Heads I win, tails you lose' policy. And the loser is the investor."

In addition, the potential investor should make sure that all the fine-print terms of the fund—such as those relating to reinvestment of profits, ultimate withdrawal of money, possible charges for getting out—are suitable. The fund's prospectus—which by law must be given to the potential investor before he commits himself—will yield all this information, though in many cases only reluctantly. The prospectus—or an annual report, similarly required by law—will also give the investor a relatively recent glimpse at the fund's portfolio—for whatever that's worth. In a typical growth fund many stockholdings will mean nothing even to the most sophisticated investor; beyond that the information will probably be stale. Funds are required to divulge the makeup of their portfolios twice a year, and most do it quarterly, but this information is usually months out of date before the investor gets it. Anyway, the law permits funds to hide 5 percent of their holdings; so if they're into something really interesting, you probably won't find it.

Another seldom explored fund pitfall is a phenomenon known in the trade as *buying a tax bill*. If a fund decides to make a capital-gains payout shortly after an investor buys into it, he'll find himself owing taxes on profits his money didn't earn. Say you sink $1000 into fund shares, and then a week later the fund declares a 20-percent capital-gains distribution. The net asset value of the shares you own would automatically be reduced by 20 percent, cutting the value of your holding by $200. Of course, you'd also receive that much, in cash or new shares; so you'd still have the $1000 you started with. But you'd also owe taxes on the $200 received. In effect, by poorly timing your fund purchase, you're forced to pay taxes on a return of your own money.

Of course, this is a problem only when funds have capital gains. Currently losses are more the rule, and here this phenomenon works to the new investor's advantage. A fund with large capital losses can use them to offset future gains—so that the new investor profits tax-free. In this situation, instead of buying a tax bill, he's buying a tax credit. The fund can carry such losses forward for up to five years, matching future gains against them. Until the losses are offset, the value of the investor's shares increases—without any tax liability. Many funds now list such losses in their literature. The figure will probably be buried in the back pages, described as "unrealized depreciation on investments" or some similar euphemism. As an example, Mates Fund at one time reported net asset value of $3.23 per share but at the same time showed $2.66 per share in "unrealized depreciation" and another $.43 in losses actually taken. Theoretically, a new investor in Mates shares could come very close to doubling his money without incurring any tax liability whatever.

Obviously this is more interesting to high-bracket investors than to low and more interesting to large purchasers than to small. And despite the recent bad markets, many of the larger funds still have huge untaken capital gains, which sooner or later will prove a tax burden. As an example, Massachusetts Investors Trust, the nation's fourth largest mutual fund, recently had untaken profits of almost half a billion dollars in its blue-chip portfolio. This meant a potential taxable gain of over $3 for each $13 share. Investors contemplating a fund purchase of any size should ascertain whether the fund in question offers tax benefits or tax liabilities. If the latter, it's sometimes possible to ascertain when the next distribution will occur and how large it's likely to be. Then time the purchase to occur *after* the distribution has been made. Most funds declare their profits in early or mid-December, so as not to penalize investors who for tax reasons might want to purchase shares at the very end of the year.

But tax considerations shouldn't loom large in the investment calculus of the potential fund buyer. He's more concerned with how the fund will perform in years to come. All other things being equal, which they never are, it *is* wise to pick a fund with a good track record, though preferably one that hasn't been so good for so long as to bloat the fund to a point where it waddles rather than runs. A good rule of thumb is for the investor to limit his choice to established funds whose assets range between $5 million and $100 million. A fund below $5 million hasn't proved its ability to manage boxcar figures. A fund over $100 million is probably unwieldy. Fifty to a hundred million dollars is best.

Most fund literature tells the investor to pick a fund that's performed well in both up and down markets, but this advice is dubious. The fund itself has probably been through both types of market, but that's no guarantee the current management has, too. A good many portfolio managers lost their jobs during 1969–70. Others, more successful, went on to better jobs—or retired to less demanding work. So don't pay nearly as much attention to past performance as you pay to present performance. That is, once you've decided on a fund or once you've bought it, keep an eye on it; if, over time, you find it's not doing as well as many other funds or if it's not doing as well as stocks in general, then you should consider selling out. Of course, the commissions you will have paid may make this difficult. If you paid the typical 9.3 percent, for instance, unless the fund has increased 9.3 percent by the time you sell, you'll take a loss.

This is one of the big problems with load funds. Not only is the price of admission steep, but once it's been paid, it tends to lock you in. Of course, the investor is free to get out at any time, but if getting out means taking a loss due solely to the salesman's commission, then the investor would have done better not getting in at all. In fairness to the load funds, they *do* lower their commissions drastically on large purchases. This partially accounts for their attractiveness to very wealthy investors (a high-rolling New Yorker recently purchased $7 million worth of load-fund shares), but it's small consolation to the less affluent, who generally have to pay at the top rate. Here's a sample of a mutual-fund commission schedule. It's taken from the prospectus of Fletcher Capital Fund (run by the Enterprise people), but similar rates apply to most others.

Amount of Investment	Sales Charge
$ 500 but under $ 25,000	8.50%
$ 25,000 but under $ 50,000	6.90%
$ 50,000 but under $125,000	4.90%
$125,000 but under $250,000	2.90%
$250,000 but under $500,000	1.80%
$500,000 and more	1.00%

The larger figures are especially interesting in that they are entirely hypothetical—Fletcher won't allow any investor to purchase more than $50,500 worth of its shares. To get the lower percentages, investors must also buy other funds in the Enterprise group. Even the smaller figures in the table are somewhat mythical. In a form of mathematical legerdemain peculiar to mutual funds, the load funds compute their commissions not on the value of the shares purchased but on the entire transaction, commission included. As an example, say you want to invest $1000 in a fund. The commission, a salesman tells you, is 8½ percent—$85. So $85 goes to the salesman and related middlemen, and the rest—$915—buys your fund shares. Suddenly you're not investing $1000 at all. You're investing $915 and paying $85 for the privilege. Long division reveals that $85 is 9.289 percent of $915, and that's the typical commission on a small transaction: 9.3 percent. This is a trivial point, to be sure, so trivial that the funds should consider computing their commissions in a more straightforward manner rather than making potential customers resort to mathematics they haven't used since high school.

Short of writing for a prospectus and recomputing the figures, the easiest way of determining a given fund's maximum commission cost is to consult the mutual-fund listing in the daily financial pages. Many daily papers are woefully skimpy in their mutual-fund statistics, but even the worst usually publish some sort of listing, in which they include several hundred different funds, arranged in alphabetical order, with two prices after each name. In terminology more appropriate to over-the-counter stocks, the two prices are usually headed "Bid" and "Asked." The bid price isn't really a bid at all—it's simply the net asset value per share of the fund for that particular afternoon. That's the price at which the fund will redeem whatever shares it receives that day. The asked price is the price at which it will sell shares, and the difference between the two prices is the amount the investor will have to pay in commissions. From these figures readers can compute precisely what commission they'll have to pay to purchase a particular fund. Nonmathematicians can simply examine the two figures to see if the difference is relatively large or small. If it's large, then the commission on that fund is high, and vice versa. If the two figures are identical, that means there's no commission at all. In other words, the fund is a no-load, and you can buy into it at net asset value. A recent mutual-fund listing in the *Wall Street Journal,* which each business day publishes one of the most comprehensive of all such listings, showed 397 funds, of which 47 were in the no-load category.

It's almost incredible that so many mutual funds can flourish while there is such a gross disparity among their commission structures. In any ordinary business the firm that charged the lowest commissions would very quickly garner most of the trade. But in the mutual-fund business the opposite holds true. The firms with the highest commission rates, as a group, account for a majority of the business. One reason for this is that the mutual-fund product—future performance—is unknowable. A fund that you pay 9.3 percent to get into may, indeed, outshine a similar one that charges no commissions at all. There's no way of telling until after the fact—when the information is too late to act on.

A simpler reason is that high commissions attract good salesmen, and good salesmen sell funds. In fact, it's something of a cliché in the mutual-fund business that fund shares are not bought—they are *sold*. This is by way of establishing the crucial role of the fund salesman and the equally crucial role of the ample commissions that seem necessary to sustain him. Lower the commissions and you will lower his incentive to sell funds. Having reduced his incentive, you will find new fund sales diminishing. We have seen how the absence of new money can curtail a fund's growth, but *in extremis* it can do worse than that. If sales of new shares diminish to a point where redemptions exceed them—that is, if more shares are being cashed in than purchased—then a fund is in bad trouble, because it's forced to sell some of its investments to raise cash to redeem its shares. Funds don't like forced liquidation, because it makes them sell investments they'd prefer to keep, thus forgoing future profits. Moreover, since the redemption rate often rises when stock values are declining, such forced sales usually occur at just the wrong time, making funds sell stocks at the very moment they should be buying more.

In fact, the redemption-sales ratio (relating money going out to money coming in) is the Achilles' heel of the mutual-fund business. The danger of a run on mutual funds, similar to the bank runs that occurred with such disturbing frequency in the Bonnie and Clyde era, has never been real, because continuing growth—and an ever-expanding sales force—has enabled funds to meet redemptions easily out of new cash. That is, in the aggregate, they've almost always had enough money from new sales to redeem the shares of current investors who, for various reasons, want out. But as the fund industry matures, it's at least possible to imagine a day when a relatively large number of investors who might have purchased fund shares long before for the kids' college or for retirement decide to get out. If, as seems most likely, this increased desire to redeem comes at a time when money is scarce, stock values are declining and sales of new fund shares are off, then the funds will be forced to sell many of their investments to raise enough cash to meet redemptions. A wholesale liquidation of this sort—especially nowadays, when monolithic institutions of one stripe or another control a sizable chunk of all investment activity—could cause a stock-market sell-off of major proportions, feeding on itself in a snowball effect as more and more fundholders perceived ever-diminishing stock prices and decided that they, too, should redeem. This is a chilling scenario, but it could take place. We saw a sneak preview as recently as May 1971, when, for the first one-month period in the fund industry's 31-year history, redemptions actually outran sales. The shortfall was a modest $120 million, but Wall Street reacted to the news with unrestrained panic. The announcement of the shortfall was made just after noon, and by the closing bell the Dow-Jones industrials had dropped 17 points. The following month fund sales returned to their historic predominance, but the specter of a massive fund-inspired stock blowoff had raised its head and would not soon be forgotten. If we ever have another 1929-style crash, it will almost certainly be triggered by fund redemptions.

An analogous situation occurred in Japan in the early 1960s. There, however, government halted the potential snowball by creating a state stock-buying company to provide a stable market for the shares the funds were forced to liquidate. A sell-off of this magnitude has yet to occur in the U.S., and the funds have one strong trump card to play if ever it does. Buried in the back pages of most fund prospectuses, the diligent reader will find a provision for what is called *redemption in kind*. This perfectly legal device gives the fund the right, if pressed, to redeem its shares—not in money—but in stock certificates from its portfolio, an alternative that must have seemed highly attractive to battle-weary portfolio managers at the depths of the market sell-off in 1970. But in fact, funds have resorted to it only twice in recent memory, and both instances involved individual high rollers who were trying to abuse fund privileges to their own advantage. In other words, they deserved it. For the average investor, the prospect of such redemption in kind is too remote to bother about.

Moreover, the funds—and the people who buy them—have shown an admirable history of bearing up under pressure. In a report to Congress over 30 years ago, the SEC examined the performance of 40 open-end investment companies (that's all there were back then) during the boom-and-bust decade between 1927 and 1936. Those years were darkened by the worst stock market in American financial history; yet, the SEC discovered, not a single fund went bankrupt, and funds sold $564 million in new shares and redeemed only $142 million in old ones. In other words, sales outran redemptions almost four to one, even during the great crash of 1929 and the subsequent depression. More recently, in the brief market crash of May 1962, when the Dow-Jones industrial average fell 8.5 percent, fund values deteriorated drastically, but people kept buying more; sales were $292 million that month, and redemptions only $122 million. Similarly, sales outweighed redemptions consistently—though by somewhat narrower margins—during every month of the 1969 and 1970 bear market.

One reason for this unflappable investor behavior is that a market collapse tends to lure new customers into the funds—shrewd investors who know a bargain when they see one and less shrewd investors who have been chastened in stocks and reach the belated recognition that they can't do as well on their own as they might have hoped. Ultimately the fact that funds are purchased heavily even in bad market periods is a great credit to the individual investors responsible for the buying. They are bargain hunting and doing it successfully. But to the extent that they do their bargain hunting without the aid of a salesman, they are defeating the funds' case for high commission rates. In fact, for the intelligent investor, the most pernicious thing about mutual-fund commissions is not their size but what they represent. In load funds, as in life insurance, a salesman must be paid whether or not the customer needs to be sold. To the investor who has spent weeks or even months doing just what the fund pundits tell him to do— reading dreary prospectuses, deciphering arcane charts, sitting in a noisy boardroom thumbing through the heavy Wiesenberger books—and then, after all this work, finally settles on the one fund that is precisely right for him, it is rather galling to be forced to give up 9.3 percent of his money to the salesman who just happens to take his order. The investor didn't need to be sold, and the salesman didn't sell him; the fund sold itself. If anyone is to be paid for the sales job, it should be the hardworking investor.

The load funds have an interesting answer to this. (Actually, they have several arguments to support their commission structures, but none as engaging as this one.) The notion is that a mutual-fund salesman must be compensated for *all* his working time—not just the two minutes he might spend writing the intelligent investor's order, but all the hours he wastes telephoning Young Republican membership lists, attending Kiwanis luncheons and making friends at suburban PTAs. The salesman, as the funds see him, is a valuable pillar in the free-enterprise firmament who spends much of his time praising the virtues of capitalism to those oft-neglected 194 million Americans who, for various reasons, do not care to invest. To resist the tide of revolution, the load funds may be justified in taxing those who have the wealth and intelligence to make a good investment, in order to subsidize a pro-capitalist propaganda effort directed at those who don't. But such a campaign seems to frustrate the very elements of choice that are so vital to our free markets. Besides, mutual-fund salesmen spend very little time with the people who really need conversion, and—in this writer's experience—fund salesmen are not particularly incisive defenders of capitalism, anyway.

One of the reasons for this is that price competition, that bastion of free enterprise, is simply *illegal* in the mutual-fund business. Section 22(d) of the Investment Company Act of 1940, which was written with the grateful cooperation of the fund industry, makes it a federal crime to sell a mutual fund at a price less than whatever the fund's distributor decides it should be. In 1968 both the President's Council of Economic Advisers and the Justice Department urged repeal of 22(d), and Senator John Sparkman of Alabama announced that his powerful Banking and Currency Committee intends to consider this as well. But nothing has come of the effort so far. The load-fund lobbyists are strong and well entrenched; still, with this sort of opposition, they are bound to capitulate sooner or later.

10. LOAD VERSUS NO-LOAD

While load funds certainly provide their salesmen with incentives to treat potential customers responsively and cordially, and while the constant influx of new cash generated by these salesmen may help the load fund's performance considerably, the would-be purchaser of load-fund shares must still include the commission cost in his investment calculations. Fund salesmen try to minimize the difference between their funds and their no-load brethren. In the long run, the salesmen will say, it's not the initial cost that counts but how well the fund performs. This is so much garbage. The future performance of any mutual fund cannot be known. But the commission cost, since it is paid in advance, is manifestly knowable. It's the only cost in a mutual-fund investment that you can calculate precisely before you commit yourself. To justify taking the investor's money, the load fund should promise performance not just comparable with a no-load's but *better,* so much better as to compensate for the commission fee and what that would grow to if it were free to compound over the years. Certainly many such load funds exist: Load funds outnumber the no-loads by about ten to one and by twice that if you compare assets rather than funds. But at the starting gate no one can tell which load funds will finish sufficiently in the forefront to justify their commission charges. In terms of what they offer the investor, most load funds have a 9.3-percent handicap to overcome, and the would-be purchaser must weight his bets accordingly.

Until a few years ago fund salesmen—and even the prestigious statistical services such as Wiesenberger—tried to imply that load funds, despite their steep commissions, generally outperform no-loads. This is simply not true and most likely never was. As a matter of fact, a recent tabulation compiled by *Fundscope* showed that even over long periods of time, no-load funds seem statistically a better bet. The study embraced virtually every mutual fund in

Load Versus No-Load

existence during the 1960s and ranked each fund according to how much $1000 invested in it would have been worth if cashed in on the first day of 1970. This sort of comparison properly reflects the load funds' commission bite—as the results indicate. Of the 165 funds studied, only 22 were no-loads, but in terms of performance 15 of the 22 made the top half of the list. Similarly, among the top 25 percent, nine were no-loads, whereas in a random distribution hardly more than half that could have been expected to make the top quartile. Most interesting of all was the bottom of the list: All but one no-load made the top 100; of the 65 worst performers, 64 were load funds. (*Fundscope,* apparently aware where its advertising interests lie, smilingly characterized these results as a random distribution.) Such provably inferior performance is no reflection on the management of load funds, which, especially over long periods, is probably no better or worse than the management of no-load funds. But precisely because management tends to balance out over time, no-load funds (all other things being equal) are bound to prove better performers—solely because of the 9.3-percent head start that their investors enjoy at the outset.

In chapter 8 we discussed how size seems a limiting factor in fund performance. This also works to the advantage of the no-load funds and once again because of the differing manner in which they are sold. The no-load funds, without sales commissions, have nobody beating the drums for them. The load funds, offering fairly attractive sales commissions, have a large and devoted following of salesmen who, at least in the aggregate, do their job. As a consequence, load funds tend to be bigger—and thus less effective. Of the 40 largest mutual funds (in terms of assets under management) at the end of 1970, only one— the T. Rowe Price Growth Stock Fund—was a no-load. Its assets were then under $600 million, making it a relative midget in comparison with the larger load funds, many of which exceed the billion-dollar mark. (The biggest of all, Investors Mutual Fund, comprises $2.8 billion.) Most no-load funds, lacking a sales force eager to promote their virtues, tend to congregate in the $5-million to $150-million asset range from which an investor can reasonably expect maximum performance.

Partisans of mutual funds often spend so much time debating the relative merits of load versus no-load that they lose sight of a larger and more meaningful comparison: how funds of all descriptions compare with other forms of investment, particularly stocks. Unfortunately, the results here are not encouraging. The most recent comprehensive analysis, conducted by three faculty members of the Wharton School of Finance and Commerce, examined the records of 299 funds between 1960 and 1968. The study found that the average fund produced a gain somewhat lower than would have been achieved by simply spreading money equally among all the stocks on the New York Exchange. Most fund studies over the last generation have reached similarly depressing conclusions. The funds are quick to respond that investors can't economically buy every stock listed on the Big Board. This is quite true, but it begs the larger question. Funds *can* buy every stock—but they don't. The reason they don't is not that such a policy wouldn't pay off, since virtually every stock-market study shows that it would. The reason is that such an elegantly simple investment policy would eliminate the need for high-paid management—indeed, the need for any management whatever. The fund would be highly profitable for its investors but much less so for the people who owned and managed it.

The Fisher and Lorie stock-market study, discussed in detail earlier, confirms beyond dispute that an "unmanaged" portfolio of NYSE stocks can prove quite a profitable long-range investment—increasing, in fact, at an average rate of very close to 10 percent a year, which is higher than the average rate of increase for all mutual funds over the same period. When the Fisher and Lorie results were first announced, this writer proposed, in some seriousness, that a mutual fund be set up to take advantage of the study, using computer-generated random numbers to invest in stocks chosen simply by chance from the Big Board list. Such a fund, of course, would have no management expenses other than a few minutes' computer time each day, with the paper work administered—on a cost-plus basis—by the trust department of a bank (a procedure that is already typical in the fund business). If the fund were also a no-load, then it would offer investors the best of both worlds: no sales commissions to pay and no managers to enrich. The fund would be run, in effect, as an investors' cooperative—with the profits going not to middlemen but to the shareowners themselves. I subsequently discussed this idea with the then-chairman of the SEC and received hardly more than a belly laugh in response. The chairman, an honest and realistic man, appreciated the merits of the fund but called it "dangerously frivolous." Especially if the fund proved an investment success (as almost surely it would), it would undermine the credibility of every other mutual fund in the industry, thus doing disservice to the entire investment milieu with whose regulation the SEC is charged.

The investment world is so dreary and deadpan that it could well use a dash of frivolity, which the Chance Fund (as it was to be called) would surely have provided. Moreover, the notion was subsequently vindicated by the recent Wharton study, which declared that "there is much to be said in favor of a new type of mutual fund with minimum management . . . which deliberately duplicates the performance of New York Stock Exchange stocks as a whole." This remains a viable idea, fraught, among other things, with social usefulness; I offer it gratis to any reader who cares to follow it up.

As a matter of fact, one fund already employs this principle, at least in part. Founders Mutual Fund, of Denver, charges no management fees whatever, because it requires no management. The fund spreads its money equally among 40 stocks whose firms are leaders in their respective fields. It has fared quite well with this technique for over three decades. One thousand dollars invested in Founders in 1939 would today be worth over $18,000; its losses in 1970 were less than 6 percent, compared with 16 percent for funds in general. Unfortunately, Founders is a load fund, which means the purchaser must pay a salesman's commission in order to enjoy the privilege of free and unmeddlesome (if not frivolous) management.

Because the no-load funds, even lacking the debatable advantages of nonmanagement, do offer what seems to be better value, and because, lacking a sales force to beat the drums for them, they are more difficult to learn about than load funds, we present here an alphabetical list of well-established no-load mutual funds. All of them have been around for at least eight years, which gives them something of a track record. All are dedicated to growth, which makes them somewhat more speculative and therefore more interesting for the younger investor. And all have performed creditably—or at least reasonably well, all things considered—in recent years. None charge redemption fees and—except where noted—they all permit automatic reinvestment of both dividends and capital-gains income. The list is not a recommendation, nor is it by any means complete. It's just a representative cross section of what's available, and the reader might want to investigate some of these or others not listed. Addresses are included, because on request any fund will send a prospectus or an annual report.

American Investors Fund, 88 Field Point Road, Greenwich, Connecticut 06830, has an especially good record in rising markets. It has been a top overall performer since 1962—but lost 30 percent in 1969 and 30 percent again in 1970. Assets are around $250 million.

De Vegh Mutual Fund Inc., 20 Exchange Place, New York, New York 10005, is relatively small, with assets of around $90 million. Especially considering its size, it has a commendably low expense ratio, which means that its management is diligent in keeping costs down. It also manages to keep losses down, giving up 16 percent in 1969 and all but breaking even in 1970. In fact, in terms of performance in falling markets as well as rising ones, De Vegh seems *the* superior closed-end fund.

Drexel Equity Fund, Inc., 1500 Walnut Street, Philadelphia, Pennsylvania 19101, is both relatively new (1961) and relatively small (around $52 million). It, too, seems something of a fair-weather fund, losing 16 and 20 percent respectively in 1969 and 1970.

Energy Fund, 55 Broad Street, New York, New York 10004, has assets of around $160 million and favors energy-related stocks—coal, oil, uranium and so on. It's been an above-average performer for a decade, even though it lost around 12 percent in the 1969–70 blowout.

Penn Square Mutual Fund, 451 Penn Square, Reading, Pennsylvania 19603, has a respectable long-term record and now boasts assets of around $180 million. It performed reasonably well in 1969 and 1970, giving up 18 and gaining 2 percent. However, its reinvestment program is slightly restrictive; so the would-be buyer should check this carefully.

T. Rowe Price Growth Stock Fund, 1 Charles Center, Baltimore, Maryland 21201, ranks just below De Vegh for all-around market superiority. Price Growth was one of very few funds to make money in 1969 (2 percent), though it lost five times that in 1970. As noted, it's also the largest no-load fund, with assets over $750 million.

Scudder Special Fund, Inc., 345 Park Avenue, New York, New York 10022, has been a top performer for the past decade, though it has been publicly available for only five years. As a matter of fact, it was the top-performing no-load in the *Fundscope* study cited on page 121, though it's 1969–70 loss averaged 19 percent. Assets are $210 million.

One of these seven representative no-load funds, Energy Fund, deserves special discussion, because it is one of the very few no-loads that are also special-purpose funds. The most attractive thing about special funds is that they are very easy for salesmen to sell. A fund designed especially for doctors is presumably easily sold to doctors. And the salesmen of a fund pledged to specialize in oceanography, for instance, can capitalize on the glamour and the prospective riches of an industry that is just beginning, if the expression may be permitted, to surface. But while these funds are easy to sell (that's why almost all of them are load funds—they're a sort of salesman's delight), they are hell to run, as any portfolio manager will attest. Imagine the frustration of supervising a fund pledged to full investment in the fried-chicken franchise business (as an improbable example) and suddenly discovering a genuinely promising company buried somewhere in the computer industry, an industry from which you are excluded by charter. The logic here should be clear: Unless the investor has some unique insight into the future of oceanography or fried chicken, he shouldn't be committing his money to a portfolio that is largely restricted to either. Generally speaking, the more latitude a fund has, the better off its investors are. When the time comes to get into the ocean or the frying vats, your fund will be free to do so, and when both begin to go dry, your fund will be free to get out. To the extent an investor has a genuine insight into some particular industry, he would be better off buying individual stocks he knows about.

Several no-load funds are also hedge funds, but here, too, because of the sales angle, most publicly available hedge funds are load funds. The majority of hedge funds are not publicly available. These are private investment pools in which wealthy investors combine their cash and entrust it to a hotshot manager who can then play tricks with it. Because hedge funds are private, limited partnerships, they don't have to follow the SEC rules. The name comes from their habit of hedging their investment position: At any given time, a hedge fund will not only own stocks, but it will have sold other stocks short. This means it can profit not only when stocks go up but (assuming it has chosen the right losers) when they go down as well. At least theoretically. Keeping a continuing portfolio of both long and short positions has been a key to successful speculation in commodities for generations, but the technique only recently came to the stock market. In fact, the hedge fund is the invention of one man, Alfred Winslow Jones, a former editor of *Fortune* who is now approaching 70 but who is still quite active—and quite wealthy. One of the most interesting things about private hedge funds—at least for those who run them—is that the manager generally gets 20 percent of the profits. If there are no profits, he gets nothing. A hedge fund that Jones runs has supposedly gained over 1000 percent in the last decade; even considering the management fee, this would make it vastly more successful than any publicly available mutual fund.

Because of performances like this, the hedge-fund idea spread rapidly in the late 1960s. Hedge funds are private operations; so statistics are hard to come by. At the peak in 1969 perhaps 300 hedge funds were managing assets of maybe $2 billion. Rumor had it that there were more under-30 millionaires running hedge funds than there were in the entertainment industry. Unhappily, most of these new millionaires forgot—or never had time to learn—the short-selling aspect of their business. During 1969 and 1970 the private hedge funds suffered horrendous losses.*
And in the absence of any profits from which to extract his 20-percent cut, many a youthful gunslinger found himself taking a Trailways back to Little Rock.

But it was fun while it lasted, and given all the action, it's not surprising that a few resourceful souls would try to translate the hedge-fund idea to a mutual fund. Hubshman Fund was first, followed by Heritage Fund, which had actually been around since 1951 but decided to transmogrify into a hedge fund in 1967. A third, Hedge Fund

---

*According to the *Wall Street Journal*, one hedge fund, in which G. Keith Funston had invested $100,000, managed to run $8 million into $300,000 in just 18 months. Mr Funston is hardly an amateur investor. He was president of the New York Stock Exchange for the better part of two decades and still serves as board chairman of Olin Corporation, as well as being a director of IBM, Metropolitan Life and Republic Steel.

of America, appeared a year later, followed by Drexel Hedge Fund, Competitive Associates and others. All but one of these are load funds; so the investor will have to pay standard commissions to get into them, assuming he wants to. Their performance to date has ranged from uninspired to disastrous. Granted, they haven't had the best of markets to work with, but the idea was to make money when stocks were going down as well as up. Parenthetically, Heritage Fund is paid no management fee whatever unless the fund outperforms Standard & Poor's broad market average; this is the sort of meaningful incentive that more fund managements might emulate. However, they'd best not imitate Heritage's performance. The fund failed to beat the S&P average in both 1969 and 1970.

11. DISCOUNT MERCHANDISE: CLOSED-END FUNDS

We noted earlier that the technical meaning of the phrase *mutual fund* excludes a whole genre of fundlike institutions that really shouldn't be excluded. These are the *closed-end investment companies,* oft-neglected elder brothers of the mutual funds. Like mutual funds, they are in the business of investing other people's money. Unlike mutual funds, they have a fixed number of shares outstanding, and they neither issue new shares nor buy back old ones; that's why they're called closed-ends. The shares in these companies are traded on the various stock markets just like stocks. Obviously they don't have any salesmen. You buy them through your stockbroker and pay normal stockbroker fees. These fees, unlike mutual-fund commissions, are extracted at both ends of a transaction (you pay to buy and then pay more to get out), but the commission cost of a closed-end fund is still somewhat cheaper than the cost of a load fund. Moreover, because the market itself determines the price of closed-end shares, they sometimes sell at a discount from the actual value of the investments they own. Frequently, closed-end shares representing $25 assets will be selling for $20.

If you have a huge bankroll, a relatively ambitious means of getting full asset value would be to gain control of the fund and then sell off its holdings. A financier, Floyd Odlum, actually succeeded at this during the depression. He bought controlling interest in a closed-end fund, called a stockholders' meeting, voted the fund into liquidation, then used the profits to buy into another, and so on. But even short of liquidation, the closed-end investment companies selling at a discount seem to offer interesting potential, though investors must bear in mind that such discounts often prove illusory. When the time comes to sell, the discount may persist—or even be larger. Then, too, the closed-end funds occasionally sell at a premium. This means that investors are willing to pay more for them than their net asset value is actually worth—presumably in anticipation of profits to come. At least on the surface, it would seem unwise to pay a premium for such shares, because sooner or later they will again be selling at a discount.

For those who are interested, the *Wall Street Journal* thoughtfully publishes a list of the popular closed-end funds each Monday, giving their market value, their actual asset value and the percentage difference. For those who want to avoid study altogether (never an advisable road to riches), the following five closed-end funds are all sold on the New York Stock Exchange. All have assets over $100 million, all have been in business since 1929 or earlier, all have increased at least 50 percent in market value in the past decade and often sell at a discount from their actual asset value: Adams Express Company, Lehman Corporation, Niagara Share Corporation, Surveyor Fund (formerly called General Public Service Corporation) and Tri-Continental Corporation. As these words are written, all except Lehman and Niagara are selling at discounts ranging from 4 to 12 percent.

Tri-Continental is an especially interesting fund, because its holdings are mostly in real estate and high-powered stocks. As such, it is replete with what market analysts fondly call *leverage*. If inflation or anything else should cause the value of its holdings to take off, the price of Tri-Continental shares themselves—since they sell at a discount from their real value—would move up even more rapidly. This leverage can be compounded through a purchase of Tri-Continental warrants. (Warrants are explained in chapter 5.) In this case each warrant represents the right to buy 3.03 shares of Tri-Continental common, whenever the warrant holder cares to, at $22.60 a share. As long as Tri-Continental shares stay over $23 or so, each dollar increase in a share of common will mean a $3.03 increase in the value of each warrant. A heavily margined purchase of Tri-Continental warrants—financed with borrowed funds—should represent a mutual-fund speculation without peer. The only drawback would be that a minor downward price adjustment in Tri-Continental stock would conceivably wipe you out.

A special subspecies of closed-end investment companies pays dividends that are largely tax-free. This is a situation similar to that discussed on page 111 and grows from the funds' having made a distressing number of bad investments in the past—on the face of it, not an attractive recommendation, but the companies have converted it to the investor's advantage. Since these funds still own stocks in which substantial losses have piled up, each year they sell enough losers to offset their current profits. The funds still pay dividends, but the dividends are tax-free until their total equals the amount of your original purchase. After that dividends are taxed at the favorable capital-gains rate. Some of these funds boast diversified portfolios that seem to promise future profit. Obviously you'll want to think twice before sinking your money into an investment company with a past history of bad choices, but if your tax bracket is very high, the tax-free rewards may justify the risk. The best known of these tax-sheltered dividend payers are Abacus Fund and Standard Shares Corporation. Standard Shares sells on the American Stock Exchange, and the other trades on the Big Board. Both sold off considerably in 1969–70; so one can charitably say that their shares are now cheaper than they used to be. But before buying the closed-end funds, it's a good idea to find out what's in their portfolios; perhaps they're selling at a discount because they're sitting on a bagful of pups. (A *pup* is the opposite of an emerging growth stock: It's an emerging dog.)

Another special breed of closed-end funds is the letter-stock funds. These play a speculative role similar to that of the hedge funds in the open-ended category. As mentioned on page 101, letter stock is unregistered common stock—perfectly legal to own but difficult, sometimes impossible, to sell. It's called letter stock because buyers must sign an accompanying "investment letter" stating they realize the stock is unregistered and that they are willing to face the consequences. This makes the transaction a *private placement*, and neither party need report the deal to the SEC. Until 1969 many mutual funds had large chunks of letter stock in their investment portfolios. Often the stock would come from smallish corporations in need of quick cash and unwilling to go through the time-consuming and sometimes embarrassing ordeal of a public offering of more shares. Instead, they would gladly sell unregistered shares at a discount to a mutual fund, usually agreeing that the shares would eventually become registered and thus marketable.

But when Mates Fund found itself in trouble due to a large holding of letter stock on which no market value could be placed, both the fund industry and the SEC decided to take a closer look at letter-stock investment. The result was that most funds pared their letter-stock holdings down to a 10-percent maximum suggested by the SEC. But at least four funds, all of relatively recent vintage, get around this guideline by specializing in letter stock. All are closed-end funds, which spares them the difficulty of having to compute net asset value every day. They are sold over the counter, and the market evaluates them itself. Since their founding in 1968, all four have fared dismally. Diebold Venture Capital Corporation, originally offered at $20, sold in February 1971 for $6.50; Fund of Letters had dropped from $10 to $2.75; SMC Investment Corporation, from $17.50 to $9.75; and Value Line Development Capital Corporation from $12 to $7. Incidentally, these are all market prices, representing discounts from net asset value averaging 30 percent. The discounts are steep because investors with some wisdom question the evaluations that the funds actually place on their letter-stock holdings. How, after all, do you fix a price on something you can't sell?

The shares the funds owned were risky to begin with, and during the 1969–70 bear market their unsalability compounded the problem. When the market fell off, the letter funds could only sit back helplessly and watch their assets shrink. It may be that the letter funds—and their open-ended cousins, the hedge funds—had a great idea but a poor sense of timing. If this is so, the passage of years might in both cases turn the losses to profits—even large profits. But both fund types are unabashedly speculative vehicles, and it has yet to be proved that the mutual-fund concept can be profitably put to speculative use. Individual speculators tend to concentrate their cash in a very few stocks—frequently in just one stock. But for both legal and practical reasons a speculative fund cannot do this. Thirty different issues is about the minimum that any fund can hold. More, rather than fewer, is the rule.

If individual speculators were forced to diversify their holdings that thin, they probably wouldn't prosper. And on this same basis one must question whether the speculative funds can prosper, either. They must diversify; else they cannot be funds. But as long as they are diversified, they will tend to act like stocks in general. And if they act like stocks in general, they certainly won't double an investor's money every year. Indeed, there will be some years—like 1969 and 1970—when they will cost an investor his shirt. From the vantage point of 1971 it seems safe to say that no mutual fund should be regarded as an attractive speculation—not even those that bill themselves as such. The man who wants to speculate belongs in stocks or commodities—working on his own, not through a mutual fund. Funds are for people who are somewhat less ambitious (or somewhat less greedy) and who are interested in longer-range profits rather than in instant ones.

The most interesting of all the closed-end companies—and perhaps of all investment companies generally—are currently the dual-purpose funds. These are based on an idea that originated in Great Britain, and they might better be called two-for-one-funds. The notion is simple: Some investors are interested solely in income and others solely in capital gains. The dual-purpose funds bring the two together and pool their money. When the investments from the pool begin to run up profits, the income investors get all the income and the capital-gains investors get all the capital gains. In a simplified example, say that widow A, who has $1000 and wants all the income she can get from it, and executive B, who also has $1000 and wants all the growth he can get, join forces. The result is $2000, which is duly invested and, in a year's time, has produced a not unreasonable 5 percent in dividends and 10 percent in capital gains. Five percent of $2000 is $100, and that would go to the widow, who finds she has received a 10-percent return on her $1000 investment. The 10 percent in capital gains amounts to $200, and that goes to the executive, who discovers he's blessed with a 20-percent return. Almost miraculously, both parties are making twice as much as they would if the fund hadn't brought them together.

The dual-purpose funds are obviously more complicated, but that's essentially how they work. Each fund has two classes of shares—income shares and capital shares. When the funds were started (seven are readily available, and all began business in early 1967), investors paid identical amounts for both classes of shares. As with other closed-end investment companies, their shares are traded on the stock exchanges. This means that you must pay stockbroker fees to buy them, and the marketplace determines the price. For some ultimately whimsical reason, the capital shares of six of the seven dual-purpose funds are usually selling at substantial discounts. Like their closed-end cousins, the dual-purpose capital shares are tabulated every Monday in the financial papers. Below is a recent (July 23, 1971) listing of all seven, showing the actual market price of each share, its net asset value and the percentage difference.

FUND NAME	Capital Share Price	Net Asset Value	Percentage of Difference
American DualVest Fund	$ 8.50	$10.86	—21.7%
Gemini Fund	16.75	20.28	—17.4%
Hemisphere Fund	4.12	4.11	+ 0.4%
Income and Capital Shares	10.63	15.02	—29.3%
Leverage Fund of Boston	11.25	16.04	—29.9%
Putnam Duofund	4.88	6.69	—27.1%
Scudder Duo-Vest	6.50	8.97	—27.5%

The discounts, as the table shows, range from 17.4 to 29.9 percent, with one fund—for no apparent reason— selling at a small premium. In the case of the six discounted shares, the figures, as the saying goes, are only half the story. Remember, the capital shares account for only half the funds' assets, and the income shares take up the other half. But the capital-share holder gets *all* the gains from *both*. This means, in the case of Income and Capital Shares, for instance, that while the net asset value of each capital share is $15.02, the capital-share holder also has another $15.02 working for him, because he gets all the capital gains from the related income share, which also is worth $15.02. In other words, on this particular day, the investor could actually buy all the future capital gains from $30.04 in professionally managed stock for the lordly sum of $10.63, plus broker fees. As an executive put it in *Barron's*, "Owning dual-fund capital shares is just like operating on a 40-percent margin—without having to worry about margin calls from your broker."

It's difficult to explain why these discounts exist at all. Given the leverage factor, one would expect that premiums —even substantial premiums—are in order. Some observers, most of them associated with load funds, have claimed that the dual funds are ineptly managed, but this is a difficult claim to sustain. For one thing, the dual-fund managers are known quantities in the fund business (most of them have been successful running other funds), and for another, the record simply doesn't bear this out. Since their beginning in 1967, they have in most cases performed no worse than the average mutual fund and no worse than stocks in general. In recent months they have, in fact, performed a whole lot better. Between the market bottom in May 1970 and mid-January 1971, dual-fund capital shares increased in net asset value by an average of 68 percent. At the same time, Standard & Poor's broad stock-market average increased 25 percent.

Yet most of them have been selling at a discount from the very day they opened business, and six continue to do so as of this writing. A cynical explanation for this peculiar performance might be that the free market, supposedly the gathering place of informed buyers and sellers, is actually peopled by boobs. A more charitable explanation is that anyone who invests is relatively well-off and therefore relatively conservative and that it takes time for new intelligence to penetrate the conservative mentality. The dual funds are only four years old, and in fairness to the investing public, the discounts have been gradually narrowing. By the time this is read, the gap may have closed further. In Great Britain most dual-fund capital shares now sell at a fairly large premium.

Equally interesting is the fact that discounts have persisted in U.S. dual-fund capital shares at a time when they are rapidly disappearing from the other closed-end investment companies. Logically one would expect just the opposite. Ordinary closed-end companies enjoy none of the dual funds' glamorous two-for-one potential. Moreover, ordinary closed-end companies are set up to endure forever, so that their shareholders will always have to go to the market and find a buyer when they want out. The dual funds, however, have a built-in expiration date (between 1979 and 1985, depending on the fund), after which the income investors get their original money back (it ranges from $9.15 to $19.75 a share, depending on the fund)—and the capital-share holders get *all the rest*.

For the younger investors, the expiration dates of the dual funds seem to coincide almost precisely with the distant day when they might most be needing the money. And even if those discounts persist for the next decade (almost certainly they won't), the dual-fund investor is guaranteed to get full asset value—whatever that might be—when the time comes. Of course, he can always get out beforehand by selling his shares in the marketplace. Putnam Duofund trades over the counter, and the rest are listed on the New York Stock Exchange.

To the extent that they have performed poorly in recent years, the dual-fund capital shares also offer the tax advantages discussed on page 111. Capital shares of Hemisphere Fund, decidedly the worst performer among all seven dual funds so far, had a tax-loss carry forward of

Discount Merchandise: Closed-End Funds

$7.05 per share at the time each share's net asset value was only $4.11. This means that net asset value could virtually triple before a new investor incurred any tax liability. It also explains why Hemisphere shares were selling at a premium while most other dual funds were going at a discount. Taxwise, at least, nothing succeeds like failure.

But even considering the tax angle, the question of dual-fund discounts remains a mystery. The two best-performing dual funds, for instance, Gemini and Income and Capital, usually boast discounts greater than their laggard competitors.

One would think that the opposite would prevail. If the discounts reflect investor assessment of the funds' future performance, then those that have done best in the past ought to merit relatively small discounts—or even relatively large premiums. But it doesn't work this way. Income and Capital's discount, in fact, is almost the steepest in the group, despite the fund's superior performance. Even the managers of the funds themselves can't explain this. *Forbes* recently suggested that closed-end funds generally and dual-purpose capital shares specifically lag behind the market, because prices are published weekly rather than daily. However, the lag is not weekly but usually much longer. And it is far from consistent. If it were consistent, the discounted shares would be a foolproof means of making money.

This writer has been a close observer of dual-fund capital shares ever since they commenced operation. The investors who buy them, as a rule, are quite sophisticated. After all, the funds' two-for-one nature, the persistent yet varying discounts, the lack of daily price quotations and the prospect of self-liquidation a decade from now all combine to make a complicated package. Without any solid evidence other than my own observation over four years, I have the feeling that dual-fund capital shares do not lag behind the market but actually lead it in some way. In other words, because the shares appeal to sophisticated investors rather than to amateurs, their price movement—or, more specifically, the changes in their discounts—might somehow be used to get a feeling of where the market is going rather than where it has been. I have neither the mathematical background nor the inclination to pursue such a study, but perhaps some analytically inclined reader might. The result would surely be interesting. It might also make him rich. Whatever the case, I would appreciate learning the results.

Even if they don't conceal the key to predicting the future, the dual-fund capital shares—especially the six that trade on the New York Stock Exchange—seem especially attractive, not only because of their discounts but because the Big Board offers a "Monthly Investment Program" that allows small investors (or large ones, for that matter) to buy listed shares in fixed-dollar amounts. The transaction must be initiated through a broker, but after that it's all done through the mail. The investor simply sends whatever amount he cares to whenever he feels like it, and the stock he's picked is bought for him at the opening price the day after his check is received. This program permits ownership of fractional shares (computed, as with open-end funds, down to four decimal places), so that, as with funds, every penny he spends (less broker fees, of course) goes to work for him. In all stock transactions the brokerage cost makes purchases of less than $300 uneconomical, though if the MIP investor doesn't trust himself to accumulate that much, the program accepts lesser amounts, down to $40 a shot. The MIP also allows automatic reinvestment of dividend or other income, though with the dual-fund capital shares there won't be any, since the income-share holders get all the dividends, and capital gains keep piling up to the credit of the capital-share holders until the fund is liquidated. (Incidentally, the MIP technique can be used to purchase any closed-end investment company—or any stock listed on the Big Board.)

Before the investor rushes out to buy into the dual funds, however, he should be aware that their special makeup provides at least the possibility, in the event of a stock-market cataclysm, that capital shares could become literally worthless due to the funds' prior obligation to give the income investors their money back. The would-be investor should also scrutinize the funds' portfolios to make sure that the funds are investing in the sort of things he can live with. The dual funds are committed to paying their income-share holders minimal annual dividends, and to meet this obligation some of them have relatively large amounts of money invested in income-producing stocks that must be called conservative. To the extent that these investments don't promise capital gains, the capital-share holders will suffer. Most of the funds have resolved their built-in schizophrenia by investing heavily in convertible bonds—a commendably clever solution. The would-be investor should also know that management fees for all dual funds (except Hemisphere and Gemini) are extracted not from capital gains but from dividend income, which means in essence that the income-share holders are subsidizing the cost of management and the capital-share holders are getting a free ride; but it also means that management has an extra incentive to produce lots of income, which, once again, may not work in the best interests of the capital-share holder.

Both these problems should diminish with time. Once the dual funds have grown to a point where they can easily meet their income obligations, which are fixed, they can begin to cater to the dreams of their capital-share holders, which are probably limitless. These dreams might even approach fulfillment, because over the years the double-leverage effect—magnified even further for the investor who gets in at a discount—could conceivably accumulate into a minor avalanche of investment profits, which would redound exclusively to the benefit of the capital-share holders.

Of all the investment-company situations currently available, the deeply discounted dual-fund capital shares seem among the most promising. The younger investor who's willing to accept both the possibility of total loss and the interim vagaries of market caprice might profit handsomely from a well-placed investment—or investment program—in these two-for-one shares. Or he might do just as well (and incur less risk) in most of the other funds discussed: closed-end or open-end, no-load or even full-load. No matter which course the investor takes—assuming he chooses wisely and the market holds up—he'll find, in the near or distant future, that he has been well rewarded for his foresight.

III
The Bond Market

Bond Yields: 1925–1971

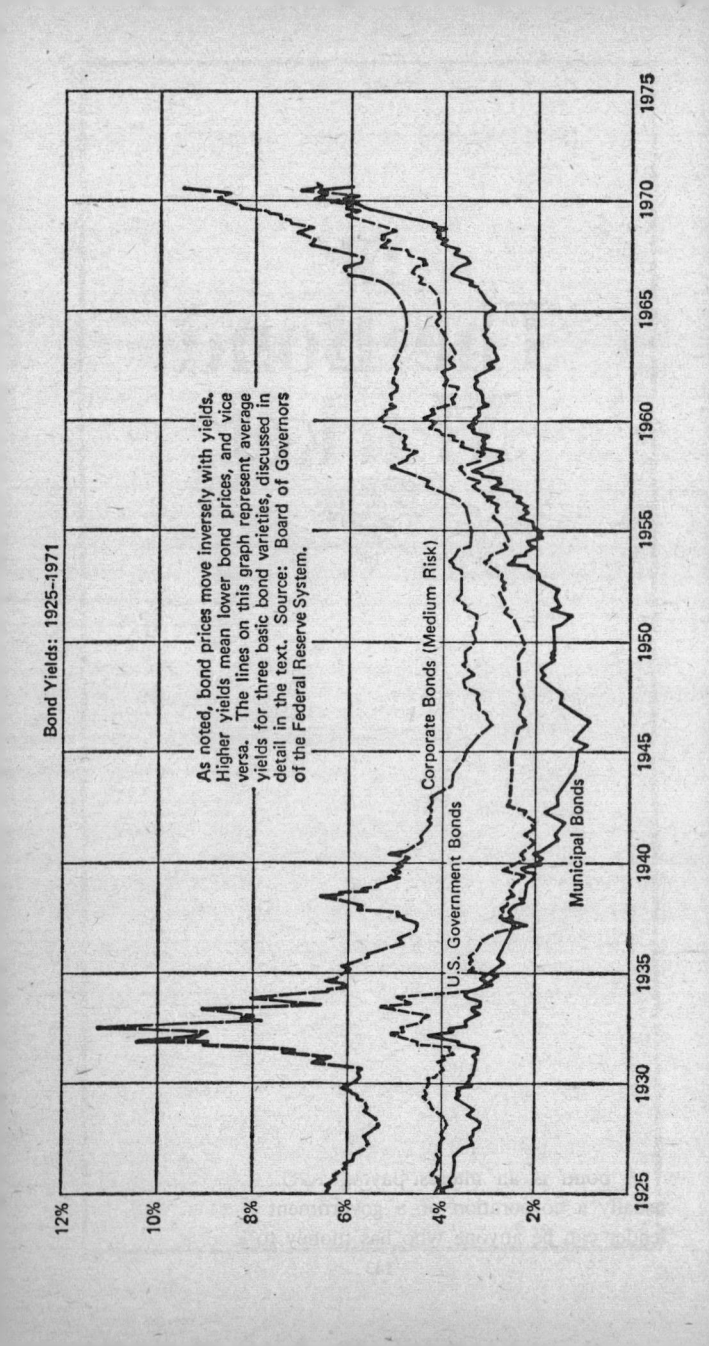

As noted, bond prices move inversely with yields. Higher yields mean lower bond prices, and vice versa. The lines on this graph represent average yields for three basic bond varieties, discussed in detail in the text. Source: Board of Governors of the Federal Reserve System.

12. HOW BONDS WORK

In mid-1970, when the vice-president of a big Wall Street investment firm described the bond market as "a great American tragedy," he was not exaggerating. Day after dreary day every bond in the country enjoyed a market value less than its purchaser had paid for it. The money tied up in bonds was more than sufficient to retire the national debt—and not a penny of it represented profit. The collapse was so total that it could only compare with the great stock-market crash 40 years earlier. Between August 1968 and May 1970, corporate bonds—traditional shelter for widows and orphans—fell an average of 30 percent; municipal bonds—those issued by cities and towns—fell 34 percent. In both cases, this was the worst decline of the 20th Century.

But one man's tragedy can be another's good fortune. The investors burned in the bond crash were mostly those who could well afford it—immensely wealthy individuals and even wealthier institutions. Only recently have smaller investors been drawn to bonds, though their impact has been profound. In 1969 and 1970 the best estimates indicated that individuals were increasing their bondholdings at a rate close to $20 billion a year. That's $100 for every man, widow and orphan in the country. More remarkable yet, these newcomers have already profited considerably, and chances are they'll soon profit even more. Crashes in any market are traditionally followed by bargains. Income rates are now down somewhat from their peaks, but they are still historically high. High interest rates and low bond prices may be offering investors the sort of opportunity that comes but once or twice in a lifetime. At the least, current or would-be investors ought to know what bonds are all about.

A bond is an interest-paying IOU. The borrower is usually a corporation or a government agency, and the lender can be anyone who has money to lend at interest.

The totals involved are astronomical, but for symmetry's sake they are divided into $1000 units. In return for each $1000 it receives, the borrower provides an engraved certificate, therein promising to pay the bondholder a fixed rate of interest (usually twice a year) and to repay the $1000 at the expiration of the contract (the maturity date), which might be 20 or even 40 years off. A few bond certificates represent amounts other than $1000, but these are a tiny minority, and for purposes of discussion it's convenient and not terribly misleading to assume that all bonds involve $1000 amounts.

To sell its IOUs successfully, the borrower must be willing to pay an interest rate sufficiently high to attract money from would-be lenders. In this free-market process, in which borrowers and lenders haggle over prices and finally reach agreement, the ever-changing cost of money—the general interest rate—is established. Once a bond is issued, its rate of return is fixed for life. A $1000 bond yielding 8 percent, for instance, will pay its owner an income of $80 a year, no more and no less, until it matures. But the general interest rate is not fixed. It fluctuates daily, even hourly. And since a bond represents a fixed stream of income, its resale value after it is issued goes up or down according to fluctuations in the general interest rate.

An example should make this clear. As this is written, an investor can purchase for precisely $1000 a 9¼-percent bond recently issued by the Seaboard Finance Company, one of the largest personal-loan firms. This particular bond matures in 1990, so today's buyer is assured of an income of $92.50 a year (9¼ percent of $1000) for 19 years, after which (if he still owns the bond) he'll get his $1000 back.

If he wanted his $1000 prior to 1990, he'd have to sell his bond in the open market in much the same way that he would sell a stock. As with stocks, bonds on the open market are worth only what others will pay for them. In the bond market buyers are usually willing to pay prices that closely coincide with the prevailing interest rate. If that rate were to remain at 9¼ percent, then a bond with an income of $92.50 a year would continue to have a market value of $1000, and the purchaser of the Seaboard 9¼-percenter would break even when he sold. But if the prevailing interest rate were to rise, say, to a stratospheric 12 percent, an income of $92.50 a year would no longer be worth $1000. At 12 percent, $92.50 a year could be nailed down for around $770, and that's just about what the Seaboard bond would sell for. And if the prevailing interest rate should *decline*, say, from 9 percent to a more reasonable 6 percent, an investor would have to pay over $1500 for an income of $92.50 a year. So at this point the owner of the Seaboard bond could conceivably sell for $1500. By a peculiar form of arithmetical alchemy, a three-percentage-point increase in the general interest rate gives the bondholder (in this instance) a loss of $230, while a decrease of three points gives him a profit of $500.

In capsule form this is how all bonds work. Because they represent a fixed stream of income, their market value will fall when the general interest rate rises and rise when the interest rate falls. Thus, while all bonds are worth $1000 on the day they're born and on the day they die, their market value wanders considerably in the interim. For the past 25 years the direction has been largely downward. Until mid-1970 the cost of money had been rising steadily, so that the market value of virtually all bonds had declined to well below their $1000 face value. This was still true in 1971. Depending on which figures you read, you may have to go all the way back to the closing years of the 18th Century, when the U.S. was fighting an undeclared naval war with France, to find comparably high interest rates—and comparably low bond prices.

Top-grade corporate bonds were yielding over 9 percent in 1969–70, and even government bonds were yielding over 8 percent. Older bonds, bearing the lower interest rates, generally sell at the biggest discounts. On the other hand, the older a bond is, the closer it is to its maturity date; and as maturity draws near, a bond's market price will begin to approach maturity value, so that on maturity day—when the bond is redeemed—the two prices are identical. But up to maturity the basic rule still governs: Bond prices move inversely with the general interest rate. This concept is basic to an understanding of the bond market; yet many small investors have trouble grasping it. Those who are familiar with the workings of the stock market have an especially difficult time. In the stock market higher numbers are usually welcomed, because they mean growth, fatter stock prices and bigger profits for stock owners. But in the bond market higher numbers —at least when they describe the interest rate, which is the chief determinant of bond prices—mean *lower* bond prices. As with stocks, lower prices make bonds more attractive to those who don't already own them, but they are hardly cheered by those who do.

The investor who wants to understand bonds would do well to clear his mind of anything he might know about the stock market, because little of that knowledge will apply and much of it will confuse. Years ago amateur investors thought that bonds were like stocks, only safer; more recently the thinking was that bonds were like stocks, only squarer. Both comparisons mislead.

Stocks pay dividends that rise and fall with the fortunes of the firms they represent. Bonds pay interest at a fixed and invariable rate. Stocks represent fractional ownership; so their market value fluctuates with the prospects of the firm owned. Bonds represent simple debt obligation; short of the issuer's being unable to meet its payments (a rare occurrence), a bond's market value bears little relationship to the prosperity or poverty of its issuer. Stocks, like the corporations they represent, are immortal, unless, of course, the company is caught up in a merger or goes out of business. Bonds have to be cashed in sooner or later. Because of the built-in maturity date, almost every bond in the country is sure to be worth $1000 (or whatever its maturity value might be) on some known day in the future. No stock can make that statement.

The stock market is emphatically a market of individual

values. Even in the steepest crash well-selected stocks will buck the trend, sometimes astonishingly. During the 1969–70 crash, while listings on the New York Stock Exchange were losing an average of 35 percent of their value, one stock, Telex, increased 700 percent. Bonds just don't act that way. With very few exceptions, they move en masse, so that the bond buyer needn't be as choosy as his stock-market counterpart. While the stock speculator has to cope with dozens or even hundreds of variables affecting each security he buys, the bond investor has to be right on only one bet—that the general interest rate will fall. Of course, he might also want to choose a bond backed by a firm that seems likely to avoid bankruptcy, he might want to pick a bond that provides special tax benefits, and if he plans to hold it until it expires, he might want to select a maturity date that best suits his personal needs. But within these broad strictures, there are hundreds of bonds that will suit him. All are essentially similar. And, assuming he is correct in his assessment of how the general interest rate will move, all will prove similarly rewarding.

Like all Gaul, bonds divide into three parts: governments, municipals and corporates. Each of the three has its distinguishing features, but as they are discussed in turn, bear in mind that bonds, again like all Gaul, share more similarities than differences. There are also three ways to make money in the bond market, though most bond investments will involve them in combination.

The traditional route to bond profits is through income. Paying $1000 for a bond that yields 10 percent a year will obviously result in an annual profit of $100. In these days of inflation and high taxes, many investors have come to regard income profits as suspect. The big money today is supposedly in growth, and growth is more likely to be found in the stock market. But *growth* is a relative term. When bonds were paying 3 percent a year, the Fisher and Lorie computer study, discussed in detail in chapter 1, showed that stocks, on the average, returned over 9 percent. Surely this was a persuasive case for buying stocks. But when some bonds themselves are paying over 9 percent, the superiority of a common-stock investment—even in the face of inflation—is less clear.

A dominant theme in many Victorian novels is that ladies and gentlemen can fare quite well, thank you, by keeping their money working at 9 or 10 percent a year. In fact, 10 percent is all that's needed to make a man wealthy in less than a lifetime; it will turn $10,000 into $1 million in just under five decades. The problem is that 9- or 10-percent returns will probably not persist—though it *is* possible to buy long-term bonds that guarantee present rates for several decades. Sad to say, this sort of interest profit, from all bonds except municipals, is fully taxable; the bond investor adds it to his salary and pays his income tax on the lot.

He can also profit from capital gains, which are the bond-market equivalent of stock growth. If the interest rate drops to 6 percent, his $1000 bond paying 10 percent might bring as much as $1667 if he sells it. Capital-gains profits such as this are a lot more interesting than a fixed income, and they're taxed at the more favorable rate.

The bond investor can also make what, for want of a better term, might be called speculative profits by resorting to such tricks as buying bonds on borrowed money. Unlike stocks, bonds are regarded as gilt-edged collateral. No matter that bond prices deteriorated for a generation while stock prices during the same period increased perhaps fourfold. Banks, assuming they have the money, are always quite willing to lend up to 90 percent of market value on bonds posted with them as security. (The maximum allowable loan on stocks is currently 35 percent.) For the bond investor interested in capital gains, this favorable loan advantage means he can get a nine-to-one lever working for him.

13. GOVERNMENTS AND MUNICIPALS

Of the three types of bonds, investors tend to know least about government bonds. This is unfortunate, because they boast some interesting attractions. They are easy to buy, sell or borrow against, they pay surprisingly high returns, and in some cases they can be purchased directly from the government without any brokerage fees. While fully subject to federal income tax, the interest from U.S. government bonds is exempt from state and local income taxes. The reason most investors know so little about government bonds probably grows from unfavorable experiences with the one variety almost everyone knows: U.S. savings bonds.

Savings bonds are small-denomination instruments with the size and feel of an IBM card, designed to lure money out of the pockets of small investors and into the coffers of the federal Treasury. They have virtually nothing in common with ordinary government bonds. Savings bonds are registered in the owner's name and are nonnegotiable; this means they can only be sold back to the Treasury. The government promotes this as a safety feature, which, in a way, it is. But it's also a colossal liability, because the bonds' nonnegotiability means they cannot be posted as collateral against a loan. Between the bank and the pawnshop, anything of value can be borrowed against—except savings bonds. In addition to this drawback they offer a lower return than virtually any comparable investment. Not surprisingly, the government loves to sell them, especially in times of inflation. (Savings bonds are the only government borrowing device that directly reduces individual purchasing power on a mass scale; thus, they are an ideal means of damping inflationary fires.)

Unfortunately, when inflation is severe, the government can become overenthusiastic. The current savings-bond campaign, built around the phrase "Take stock in America," is a monument to deceptive advertising. If a private borrower tried to use those words to sell bonds, he would very quickly find himself in court. There is nothing stock-like about a savings bond. In selling a low-yield, non-negotiable debt instrument, the use of the word *stock*—with its implications of equity and growth—borders on fraud.

To the extent that investors have had firsthand experience with savings bonds, they would probably agree that they are poor investments. Inflation has seen to that. Of course, inflation hurts all fixed incomes and, thus, all bonds. But because buyers of savings bonds have to hold on to them till maturity to receive the advertised interest rate, inflation seems to hit them hardest. As an extreme example, $18.75 invested in a savings bond in 1941 would have yielded $25 a decade later. But in 1951 that $25 had a purchasing power, in terms of 1941 dollars, of only $13.75. The net loss over ten long years was 27 percent—plus taxes owed on the $6.25 interest profit, if *profit* can be used in this context. The current return on savings bonds, up to 5 percent, compares almost as unfavorably with today's 5-percent rate of inflation.

A concomitant drawback was first brought to this writer's attention by economist Eliot Janeway. Besides being uncannily correct in his bond-market predictions over the past few years, Janeway has been one of the few financial advisors with the courage to speak loudly and publicly against savings bonds. He points out that virtually all savings-bond investors pay taxes on their interest not as it accrues, which is every year, but in one lump sum, when the bonds are finally cashed in. In this case, increasing affluence and the graduated income tax conspire to penalize the investor even further. He is forced to pay taxes on his savings-bond interest at his current tax rate, which, especially for a young investor, is probably the highest he's ever paid in his life and is almost certainly higher than the rate to which he was subject when the bulk of the interest was actually earned. As Janeway puts it, "The Treasury is getting a double windfall on savings bonds—chiseling on the interest rate it pays and cleaning up on the tax rate it collects."

As usual, the people most victimized by savings bonds

are those who can least afford it. When a rich man buys them, you can be sure he's not doing it to get richer. He might be currying tax favors, setting himself up for an administration appointment or heading a local bond-buying drive that will presumably trickle down to the grass roots. But down among the grass roots are millions of Americans who can't afford to be so charitable. These people might plunk down a hard-earned $18.75—a significant fraction of the average weekly paycheck—in the mistaken belief that they are buying some kind of stock certificate that will grow as fast as the U.S. government. Sooner or later they'll probably get back less value than they gave and still owe taxes on the difference. It's enough to make a buyer suspect not only the bonds but the integrity of the issuer.

All the deceptive transit ads and the free newspaper space could be liberated for more constructive purposes if the government would simply approach amateur investors the same way it approaches the pros, offering an interest rate competitive with the prevailing cost of money. But until this happens, there are only two reasons why anyone should consider U.S. savings bonds: to set up a program of forced savings or to satisfy the patriotic urge.

Forced savings (i.e., buying bonds on a payroll savings plan, where the money is withdrawn before the owner can get his hands on it) is possibly—just possibly—a useful recourse for those who can't trust themselves to save in any other fashion. But anyone who can't manage to accumulate $18.75 at one shot can't be expected to hold on to a bond very long, either. Such a saver, bank tellers will attest, usually cashes in his bond at the earliest opportunity. In the case of ordinary Series E bonds, this is two months after the purchase date. The investor receives only what he paid, with no interest whatever, and in the process penalizes the government much more in paperwork costs than it recouped from two months' free use of his money. This is a remarkable investment in which all parties lose.

Patriotism is a word that stirs different emotions in different breasts. But any investor who is sufficiently sophisticated to know that savings bonds are a bad investment but who persists in buying them anyway because he wants to help his country would probably do better to join the marines. If he deems this excessive, he can compute just how much he wants to lose to his country each year and donate that amount annually to the federal Treasury. This saves paper work on both sides and also provides a tax deduction. Level-headed investors who believe that the cause of their country is best served by the collective enrichment of its citizens will simply avoid savings bonds. Providing government with cheap money only encourages bad habits. When government needs money, it should have to pay the going rate.

Because sophisticated investors, by and large, don't buy savings bonds, the government *does* have to pay the going rate for most of its borrowings, which are represented by government bonds. The most difficult barrier here is nomenclature. The three types of government bonds are distinguishable only by the length of their maturity. *Treasury bills* (sometimes called *certificates*) are bonds with the shortest maturity—no more than one year. *Treasury notes* are bonds issued with maturity varying from one to seven years. Bonds with maturity over seven years are called what they all should be called—*treasury bonds*. The perplexing terminology grows from a congressional edict forbidding any government bonds (except savings bonds) from paying over 4¼ percent interest. No such restrictions apply to notes; so, in good Orwellian tradition, the Treasury has simply declared that any bond maturing in less than seven years isn't a bond at all but a note. Unfortunately, even Newspeak can't solve all the Treasury's problems. Maturities over seven years are out of the question, because these would be bonds and the 4¼-percent maximum hasn't been competitive since 1967. Notes are a possibility, but the Treasury is reluctant to issue them, presumably because the high interest rate needed to sell them would constitute a tacit admission that costly money (and inflation) will be with us for years.

The confusing result is that the Treasury, probably against its better instincts, has been forced by the battle against inflation to raise its cash in the short-term money market, by selling treasury bills. This can be an expensive way to raise money. In the good old days, when the Treasury's main customers were big businesses that gobbled up treasury bills in $1-million lots, at least the paper work was minimal. But by early 1970 the short-term rates were so attractively high that a large portion of T-bill offerings was being picked up by small investors at $1000 a shot. The Treasury was suddenly faced with a back-office bookkeeping problem that made brokerage houses look like paragons of efficiency. Incredibly, the Treasury was spending more to process a $1000 T-bill than a $1-million one, and T-men estimated that the additional clerical expense attributable to small-investor bill buying rocketed the government's actual borrowing cost from 8 to 16 percent.

As usual, the cure was worse than the disease. In February 1970 the Treasury raised its lowest-denomination bill from $1000 to $10,000. At that point the U.S. government found itself in the morally difficult position of offering a risk-free 8-percent return to relatively wealthy investors, with the less affluent being pushed into savings bonds, much less liquid and paying half the T-bill interest rate. This was really an astonishing move, one of those policy decisions that no amount of efficiency explanations can rationalize away. If justice is to be served, the poor should get the bargains, as the rich have a long and glorious tradition of getting by on their own.

The new Treasury policy provoked such a storm of protest from so many quarters that it may have been repealed by the time these words are read. (More recently the Treasury did offer a series of notes, maturing in 18 months, paying 7.79 percent interest and available in $1000 denominations.) But even if the $10,000 minimum persists, T-bills are not the attractive investment they once were, because short-term interest rates have fallen sharply from their 1970 highs. Still they are worth knowing about, not only because rates might soar again but also because T-bills are the only government bonds that individual investors can purchase without going through a middleman and paying the appropriate fees.

The prospective purchaser has his choice of four maturities: three months, six months, nine months and twelve months. All T-bills are bearer obligations: The only names on them are those of Uncle Sam and the issuing Federal Reserve Bank. As with currency, whoever has the bill in his pocket is assumed to be the rightful owner; so the buyer of T-bills will obviously want to take care not to lose them. A safe-deposit box is the usual precaution, and the expense is tax-deductible. Being bearer bonds, T-bills make fine collateral; in fact, they are just about as negotiable as cash, with the important distinction that they bear interest. As with all bonds, the interest rate on T-bills is fixed for life, with the rate on new ones set at issuance according to the vagaries of the money market. In 1970 the yield on three-month T-bills crept over 8 percent; a year later it was around 4.

The standard method of quoting treasury-bill returns understates their yield. Like savings bonds, T-bills are sold at a discount and redeemed at face value. A 7-percent, $10,000 one-year treasury bill will cost its purchaser $9300 and a year later will be worth $10,000. The $700 interest represents 7 percent of $10,000, but in the investor's terms the yield is actually higher—in this case around 7½ percent—since he's really investing only $9300. When rates were at their peak, the huddled masses who queued up to purchase treasury bills in person presumably were unaware that the bills could be bought quite effortlessly through the mails. All that's needed is a certified personal check (or a cashier's check) in whatever multiple of $10,000 the investor chooses, made out to the nearest Federal Reserve Bank, which he can locate by examining the folding money in his wallet. After the discount rate is established, the bank refunds whatever excess was paid when it sends the investor his certificate. (T-bills in virtually any maturity can also be purchased through a banker or a broker, but this involves extra fees.)

The three- and six-month bills are sold every Monday at 1:30 P.M., EST, simultaneously at all 12 Federal Reserve Banks. The nine- and twelve-month bills are sold only once a month; the date varies, but the same procedures apply. Most individual purchasers seem to prefer the three-month bills. These give maximum flexibility (after all, they turn into cash every 91 days) and permit the purchaser to keep rolling them over. Once he gets going, he can send a matured bill instead of a check, receiving in turn a new bill plus the bank's check for the discount difference. For investors who are unwilling or unable to meet the $10,000 minimum, at least one organization has begun pooling T-bill purchases as small as $1000, for fees no higher than $5 per $1000. Details are available from the American Board of Trade, 286 Fifth Avenue, New York, New York 10001.

Banks usually act as the go-between for investors who wish to get into other areas of the short-term money market. High rollers with $20,000 to $100,000 at their disposal can loan out their funds in a wide variety of short-term debt instruments, riskier than treasury bills but paying appropriately higher returns. Among these are Eurodollar deposits (loans of U.S. dollars that have found their way into banks overseas), bankers' acceptances (complex commercial IOUs that banks frequently resell to individuals), federal agency notes (short-term IOUs issued by government-sponsored corporations or agencies), commercial paper (IOUs that big corporations and finance companies issue to meet current cash needs), and municipal notes (short-term IOUs issued by cities and towns—and paying tax-free interest). Anyone with cash enough to get into these deals should have the banking or brokerage connections needed to set them up.

One precaution: Short-term debt instruments, be they treasury bills or any of the other notes that can be purchased through a banker or a broker, are *not* a long-term investment medium. They are an attractive short-term repository for idle cash when rates are high, but when the short-term rate dips below 5 percent (as it has at this writing), T-bills are no more attractive (and considerably less convenient) than an ordinary passbook savings account. Short-term instruments such as treasury bills are simply a temporary shelter wherein the investor can sit on ready cash and knock down a decent interest rate until the storm clears in stocks, bonds or whatever other investment medium he might be drawn to.

He might be drawn to treasury bonds or notes—the ones that mature in more than a year. As already mentioned, they *do* exist and most are available in $1000 denominations. But since the government hasn't sold many to the public in recent years, the usual way to purchase them is through a private dealer. The market for seasoned government bonds—which is what these older issues are called—is similar to that for over-the-counter stocks. Individual dealers make the market, and their profit usually comes from the spread between their buying price and their selling price. Since they don't like to truck with the public, the prospective buyer usually has to go through a stockbroker or a banker—and pay a fee. The going rate for a single bond purchase is $20, no matter what the price, but the investor ought to shop around, because the figure can vary widely from one institution to another. On large transactions, the commissions diminish to one-fourth of 1 percent.

As with most bonds, each government bond or note is available in either bearer or registered form. Bearer bonds, like treasury bills, don't have the owner's name on them. But unlike treasury bills, they pay semiannual interest. Each bond will have one or more coupon sheets attached to it, and every six months the owner clips off a coupon and deposits it at his bank just like a check. Registered bonds, like savings bonds, have the owner's name on them. Here there are no coupons to clip; interest arrives through the mail. Either way, it's paid twice a year. Since most bond transactions won't be made on the precise day on which interest is due, the new buyer must pay the seller his proper share of the accrued interest; this is automatically added to the sale price.

A preference for bearer or registered bonds is largely personal. Bearer bonds are marginally more negotiable; juice men, bookies and even pushers have been known to accept them. But they are also riskier and, because of the coupons attached, more of a nuisance. Banks and trust funds strongly prefer the convenience of registered bonds: There's no record keeping, the certificates are much easier to stack, and they don't have to be shuffled through and clipped periodically. The big buyer of bonds might share this preference, and the average small purchaser has other important things to worry about. However, he would be wise to insist that his certificates, whatever their form, be issued and delivered to him. Brokers offer to provide safekeeping for customers' securities, but their offices are so disorganized these days that the safety factor is debatable.

Government-bond prices are quoted daily in the *Wall Street Journal* and in the financial pages of most other major newspapers. (The best source of government-bond information—in fact, the best source of facts on most aspects of the bond market—is the *Weekly Bond Buyer*, published every Monday at 77 Water Street, New York, New York 10004. At $96 a year it can hardly be called a bargain, but for serious investors it's probably worth the expense; for big-timers, there's even a daily edition.) Currently about 75 different government-bond series are available, with maturity ranging from next year down to the end of the century. Prices are quoted per $100 face value, even though there's no such beast as a $100 treasury bond. The reader has to multiply by ten to produce the real-life figure. Worse, quotes are in dollars and thirty-seconds of a dollar. In other words, 67.16 means 67-16/32, which really means 67½, which *really* means $675. This system supposedly saves newspaper ink.

Government bonds are identified by coupon rate and maturity date: 4¼s74 describes the 4¼-percent bonds maturing in 1974, as distinguished from the 4⅛-percent bonds or the 3⅞-percent bonds that come due that same year. A hyphenated date such as 3¼s 83-78 describes 3¼-percent bonds that mature in 1983 but are callable as early as 1978. This just means that if the government cares to, it can redeem the bonds early (call them in)—an unlikely possibility these days, since this would have the Treasury borrowing money at a high-rate percentage to retire a series of bonds paying lower rates. Government-bond quotations are usually accompanied by a percentage figure that describes the bond's yield to maturity, a computation reflecting the fact, already noted, that a bond selling for less than its $1000 face value will not only bear interest but will also give the owner a capital-gains profit if he holds it until it matures. A recent quotation for the government's 4-percent bonds of August 1972, for instance, showed them selling at 93.10—about $933 apiece—with a yield-to-maturity figure of 7.88 percent. This indicates that the $40-a-year interest until August 1972, plus the $67 profit when the bond pays off, would equal a net return of 7.88 percent a year on the $933 invested.

Yield-to-maturity figures are a convenient means of comparing bond values, but they are mildly misleading because they combine interest profit and capital-gains profit without reflecting the different tax consequences of each. A deep-discount bond yielding the equivalent of 8 percent to maturity is obviously a better buy, in tax terms, than a bond selling at a lesser discount but offering the same equivalent yield. In the case of the discount bond, much of the investor's ultimate profit will be taxable at the more favorable capital-gains rate.

Would-be suicides might take note of the fact that many government bonds issued before March 4, 1971, are acceptable at face value in payment of federal estate taxes. Some of these "flower bonds" are currently available for $700 per $1000 bond, which means the wily decedent can pluck a posthumous profit of around 40 percent if he plays his hand properly. Not worth dying for, presumably, but something to think about when advising a dowager aunt.

Bonds issued by the U.S. government—including ordinary bonds, notes, treasury bills and even savings bonds—are properly regarded as the safest of all investments, since it's the government that pays both interest and principal whenever they are due—and, you'll recall, the government prints the money.

Most of the safety of government bonds, plus higher returns, is available in what are known as *government-agency bonds*. Like the short-term agency notes mentioned earlier, these are issued by organizations that are somehow related to the federal government. Among them are the Federal Land Banks (which make mortgage loans to farmers), the District Banks for Cooperatives (loans to farm cooperatives), the Federal Home Loan Banks (mortgage loans to savings-and-loan associations), the Export-Import Bank (loans for foreign trade), the Inter-American Development Bank (loans south of the border), the International Bank for Reconstruction and Development (better known as the World Bank, where Robert McNamara now works), the Tennessee Valley Authority (which sometimes borrows money to finance its power plants), the Farmers Home Administration (rural finance), and the Government National Mortgage Association (more mortgages). Of all these, only the last two are clearly and fully backed by the credit of the U.S. government.

Much discussion centers around whether the government would bail out bondholders if any of these quasi-official bodies were to default on their IOUs. During the depression, when so many farm mortgages were forced into foreclosure, the Treasury *did* step in to help the Federal Land Banks. Presumably it would do so again. But because the government doesn't have to, bonds issued by these organizations pay a slightly higher return (perhaps ½ percent more) than their cousins issued by the Treasury. As with government bonds, the interest on agency securities is exempt from state and local income taxes.

In terms of tax exemption, nothing beats municipal bonds. These are issued by local governments. The name implies only cities, but states, villages, mosquito-abatement districts or any nonfederal governing unit can use them. They offer lower returns than government bonds—the current rate is around 5 percent—but they provide a unique appeal: The interest they pay is totally exempt from federal income tax. If the bondholder lives in the state where the bond was issued, the interest is also exempt from state income tax. And, for some unfathomable reason, municipal bonds issued in Alaska and Hawaii before they became states are exempt from all income taxes—federal, state and local—no matter who owns them. The speculative potential of municipal bonds is somewhat circumscribed, because there's no tax advantage to purchasing them on borrowed money. The Internal Revenue Service, with reasonable justification, feels that individuals shouldn't be allowed to deduct interest costs on loans financing the purchase of a tax-free income.

Obviously the attractiveness of this sort of income increases with one's tax bracket. For the man who pays only 15 or 20 cents in taxes on each additional dollar he makes, tax-free income has little value, but when he begins giving up 50 or even 60 cents on the dollar, then the prospect of tax-free money becomes more alluring. Yet not all that glitters is gold—perhaps for the best, since gold ownership is illegal for Americans. Municipal bonds are fraught with difficulties that aren't encountered in other bonds. First, while most municipal bonds offer similar interest rates, there's such a bewildering array of them, in varying denominations and maturities, that it's often difficult for buyers and sellers to get together. Municipal-bond prices are not quoted in any of the financial papers because if such quotes were published, there would be no room for anything else. At last count, 92,000 government units had municipal bonds outstanding. Typically, each series of bonds might have from ten to thirty maturity dates, so that if municipal-bond prices were quoted like those of stocks, there would be something on the order of two million items to account for.

The real reason municipal bonds aren't quoted is not their vast number but the fact that the bonds themselves seldom come to market. Investors tend to buy them as they are issued and hold them until maturity. Those that *do* come to market are handled like seasoned government bonds, by private dealers who make their profit the same way grocers do—selling at a higher price than they've paid. As with the grocery store, the profit margin on slow-moving items has to be substantial. Until mid-1970, municipal-bond prices had been plummeting so drastically that few dealers were willing to sit on big inventories. In this sort of environment municipal bonds begin to resemble exotic pets—easy to buy but difficult to sell. However, now that the interest rate has fallen back, dealers stand to profit from their inventory; they are more willing to expand and, therefore, more willing to buy.

The municipal bonds that dealers offer to buy or sell are listed and priced daily in a thick azure document called the *blue list*. Stockbrokers usually have access to a copy, and it is through a stockbroker that the small investor usually purchases municipal bonds. The typical broker's fee is $5 to $20 per $1000 bond, regardless of the price the bond is selling for; as usual, the rates diminish on larger purchases. The broker contacts the appropriate dealer and buys at the dealer's asking price. The same procedure and fee apply for sales, except that these are made at the dealer's buying price, which (on small transactions such as this) might be 5 percent lower. While virtually all municipal bonds exist in $1000 increments, such certificates are difficult to buy or sell individually; $5000 denominations are more common, and $10,000, or even $25,000, is the preferred unit. Most brokers who are concerned with more than just getting their commissions will rightly advise that purchases under $10,000 a shot are a mistake.

The perfect investor in municipal bonds would be someone like Mrs. Horace E. Dodge. This amiable lady, now deceased, sank her entire auto inheritance, some $59 million, into municipals, assuring her a tax-free income of several million dollars a year and liberating her even from the annoyance of having to fill out a tax form every spring. The new tax laws have slightly diminished the attractiveness of such an investment for the select few who might be able to afford it, but the point is the same: It usually takes an enormous fortune to justify an investment in municipal bonds. A youthful investor, even if he has this kind of money, would probably want to do something more exciting with it.

14. CORPORATES AND CONVERTIBLES

Corporate bonds are issued by established (sometimes not so established) companies to finance new plants and equipment. Like butterflies corporate bonds have been classified into all sorts of confusing subcategories, but from the investor's point of view there are only two types: straight bonds and convertible bonds. With a few important distinctions, straight bonds are similar to governments or municipals: They pay semiannual interest to maturity, whereupon the owner retrieves the principal. Convertible bonds have all the same features, with one important extra: They can be exchanged, at any time the bondholder wishes, for a fixed number of shares of the issuing company's common stock.

Straight corporate bonds offer most of the advantages of long-term government bonds and generally attract the same sort of clientele. Because no corporation is deemed as creditworthy as the federal government, corporate bonds generally pay a slightly higher return—usually ½ to 2 percent higher—than comparable government bonds. This makes them that much better an investment for income seekers who are willing to assume the concomitant risks, which are slight. Obviously some corporations are riskier than others, and these have to pay more to borrow money. Two New York firms make a living grading corporate bonds (municipals, too) in accordance with the creditworthiness of the issuer. Like grades in a college for draft dodgers, the ratings range from triple A to C; all the ratings are highly conservative and much more useful to bond issuers than to investors. Most brokerage houses subscribe to one or both rating services; so the grades are available to anyone who cares to seek them out.

Corporate bonds are bought and sold just like common stocks, through a broker. The legal minimum commission is $2.50 per $1000 bond, and the diligent investor might still be able to find a firm willing to do business at that low rate. (A comparable transaction in stocks might cost $20–$40.) But just as hospital fees rise during an epidemic, so have brokerage costs risen with public participation in the bond market. No brokerage house *has* to charge the minimum, and despite the lip service they like to pay to the cause of people's capitalism, brokers seem ever less willing to do business with small investors on the same terms they offer big ones. Typical fees on small transactions now range from $5 to $10 per bond.

The biggest problem facing the individual who's interested in corporate bonds is not the fee he has to pay (even $10 per bond is only 1 percent) but the arm twisting and arguments he has to endure before he can convince his broker to accept an order. Most brokers loathe bonds. The bond experience of many is confined to the knowledge that the sales commission is tiny. Worse, bond investing tends to discourage the in-and-out trading that sends stockbrokers to Europe every summer. When a customer buys a deep-discount corporate bond selling at $640 and yielding the equivalent of 9 percent until it matures 20 years later, chances are that he'll hold it until maturity. After all, his profit is guaranteed. Had he sunk the same money into stocks, he would surely trade more frequently, probably generating a minor jet stream of sales commissions in the process. As one brokerage-house official lamented candidly in the *Wall Street Journal,* "Bonds tend to tie up the customers' money."

Many bonds permit the issuing corporation to redeem them early for a price slightly higher than the maturity value. As noted earlier, this call privilege is hardly a privilege as long as the general interest rate remains higher than the rate prevailing when the bond was issued. In days when the interest rate was more stable, the call privilege gave the borrower an element of protection. If the interest rate were to decline significantly, he could call in his bonds and issue new ones at a lower rate. But at today's high rates, any drastic decline in interest costs would mean huge profits for investors who have purchased discounted bonds. The prospect of having their bonds called away at prices much higher than they paid shouldn't prove too disturbing.

Bonds issued prior to the early 1960s are generally more likely to have less desirable call provisions than bonds issued since then, but these older bonds are generally the ones selling at the greatest discounts, because they were issued when interest rates were low. The net effect is that the investor who buys bonds for less than their face value shouldn't be overly concerned about call provisions. Only when the interest rate drops back substantially, to a point at which he might find himself buying bonds at or above their face value, should he be more careful lest he find himself paying $1100 for a bond that the issuer can retire early for $1000. Newspaper bond quotations provide no information about the callability of corporate bonds; so the best source is a brokerage-house reference library or the Moody's and Standard & Poor's rating services.

Newspaper quotations of corporate bonds generally leave a lot to be desired. Fewer than 1000 of the great multitude of corporate bonds are traded on the big New York exchanges, and only these are quoted daily in the press. Here's a typical quotation from a recent issue of the *Wall Street Journal:*

67⅜ 54 Am T&T 2⅞s87 46 56⅞ 56 56 —2½

The format and symbology are similar to those for stock quotations, and the imaginative reader ought to be able to deduce that this bond was issued by American Telephone and Telegraph, that it pays interest at a rate of 2⅞ percent per $1000 bond and that it matures in 1987. As usual, the price figures have to be multiplied by ten before they make sense. The two figures before the name represent the high and low prices for the year—in this case, $673.75 and $540. The 46 after the maturity date is the number of bonds (in $1000 units) sold that day. The next three figures are the day's high price ($568.75), low price ($560) and closing price (also $560). The final fraction is the change from the previous closing price, showing, in this case, that the bonds lost $25 each, which is quite a lot for any bond to give up in one day. The interest-rate figure of 2⅞ percent doesn't sound like much. It means that the bond returns $28.75 a year, and investors who are mathematically inclined can compute that, since the bond could be purchased for just $560, the return, in the purchaser's terms, would be around 5.12 percent. This, of course, doesn't include the $440 profit the investor is sure to make if he holds the bond the 17 years to maturity. The $440 spread evenly over 17 years means an extra $26 annually. Added to the $28.75 interest, this gives an annual return of $54.75, which means this bond is actually offering 9.9 percent a year, a respectable return by almost anyone's standards.

It's instructive to compare this AT&T bond with its companion common stock, which is the most widely held of all corporate shares. As these words are written, $565 (counting taxes and broker fees) could purchase 10 shares of AT&T common or one AT&T 2⅞ bond. The bond investment would yield $28.75 a year, the stock investment $26. And in 1987 the bond investment is sure to be worth $1000. Not too many Wall Streeters would be willing to bet that 10 shares of AT&T common would perform similarly. The multitude of investors who have purchased AT&T stock for its putative security might consider switching into AT&T bonds.

On the day the telephone bond just mentioned was selling to yield 9.9 percent, most other comparable bonds were offering less than 9 percent. An interesting aspect of the listed bond market is that the sharp-eyed reader of the financial pages, if he is blessed with a calculating machine or a penchant for long division, can often discover solid, high-rated bonds yielding perhaps a full percentage point above the prevailing rates. If his broker is quick enough, he might then buy an authentic bargain of a sort that is rarely available in the stock market. Bernard Baruch owed much of his early fortune to a sharp eye for such price disparities.

They exist because the listed market for bonds is gossamer thin. A day's turnover in a typical bond on the New York Stock Exchange might involve 10, 20 or perhaps 35 $1000 units. Institutions still dominate the bond market, and in institutional terms, 35 bonds is an insignificant number. You can bet your life insurance that Prudential (or any other big bond buyer) is not about to dump 5000 bonds into a market that can handle 35 a day. Institutional transactions are conducted through big private bond dealers—the same ones who handle municipal and government bonds. Surprisingly enough, many small-investor transactions are handled this way, too, because a good broker will know where the bargains are and often can get a better price by avoiding the exchanges. This works well for the investor, but it makes the listed bond market somewhat mythical. Sure the newspaper quotations represent real transactions, but real transactions made at a time when the same bond might have been selling elsewhere for $20 higher or lower than the listed price.

The one breed of corporate bonds that trades widely and well on the New York exchanges is the convertible bond. As noted, convertible bonds pay fixed interest to maturity just like straight bonds, but they can also be exchanged, at the holder's option, for a predetermined number of shares of the issuing company's common stock. This means that "converts" (veterans accent the second syllable) can act like stocks as well as like bonds.

The use of convertible bonds as a corporate money-raising device increased twentyfold during the 1960s. At the beginning of the decade converts were being issued at a rate of only a few hundred million dollars a year, and some of this was privately placed (sold direct to insurance companies or mutual funds), so that the public couldn't get at it. By 1969 convertibles were appearing to the tune of $5 billion a year, and the public was very definitely involved. Corporations like to issue convertible bonds because investors like to buy them—so much so that they're usually willing to settle for a lower interest rate (perhaps 1 or even 2 percent lower, depending on the specifics of the deal) in return for the conversion privilege and the vision of limitless riches that usually accompanies it. So far the corporations have got the better of the deal.

From their point of view convertible bonds are a cheap way of selling stock at high prices without hurting anyone's feelings. A corporation might sell $50 million worth of convertible bonds, and as long as its stock keeps rising, investors will gradually exchange the converts for stock. When the maturity date finally rolls around, all the bonds will have been converted and, presto, the corporation won't have to repay the $50 million. More typically, when a company's common stock has risen to such an extent that its convertible bonds are selling far above maturity value, the firm will call the bonds, in effect forcing the bondholders to exchange them for common shares. In either case the net result is simply that the company has sold more stock, thereby diluting the holdings of the pre-bond stockholders.

But this assumes that stock prices are rising. When prices are falling, it's quite a different story. In the bear market of 1969 and 1970 the speculative public took a saturating bath in the convertible-bond market, mostly from buying converts on the assumption that they are just like stocks only safer. The logic goes something like this: If the value of the related common stock were to rise, then the bond, being convertible into a fixed number of common shares, would rise, too. If the value of the underlying common were to fall, then the value of the convertible bond would stay the same—or at least not fall as much—because the convertible bond also pays fixed interest, which means it has value as a straight bond. Convertible bonds, as a popular observation had it, are like stocks with a theoretical floor underneath them. But safety in the bond market is a relative term. When stock prices and bond prices began falling simultaneously, that theoretical floor looked like an open elevator shaft. Losses of 30 or even 50 percent in less than a year were all too typical.

An understanding of the intricacies of converts is best achieved through a real-life example. In the summer of 1967, RCA sold $160 million worth of convertible bonds yielding 4½ percent interest and maturing in 1992. When the bonds were first sold, the prevailing interest rate was somewhat over 5 percent, but RCA got by with 4½; investors were willing to accept a lower return in exchange for the conversion privilege. In this case each $1000 bond can be exchanged, at the bondholder's option, for 17 shares of RCA common stock. RCA common was then selling for around $52 a share; so conversion wasn't profitable (17 times $52 is only $884). Yet the bonds began changing hands at $1050 each. The year 1992 was a long way off, and since stocks were rising, buyers valued the conversion factor considerably. For a while their optimism seemed justified. RCA stock rose, and so did the market value of the convertible bonds. For each dollar increase in the common, the bond, representing 17 shares, rose $17. Just a few months after it was issued, the bond was selling for $1235.

But that was as high as it got. Investors began to realize that inflation is as bad for companies (and thus for stocks) as it is for people. The stock market—RCA included—entered a long decline. Inflation also worked on the bond market. Interest rates rose; so bonds declined, too. At the bottom of the market, in May 1970, RCA common was selling for under $20 a share and RCA converts for around $650. Anyone who bought in at the peak price of $1235 was out almost 50 percent of his investment and had good reason to question the carpentry of that theoretical floor. More recently both the stock and the bonds have recovered somewhat, but they have a long way to go to match their 1967 levels.

The convertible-bond debacle may have been abetted by an obsolete cliché: that bonds and stocks tend to move in opposite directions. In the Twenties and Thirties this was certainly true. When stocks were going up, bonds were falling, and vice versa. Even into the Forties, knowledgeable investors with a well-developed sense of timing used this simple rule of thumb as a painless and elegant means of making money. But, like many devices, it became obsolete during World War Two. Since then stocks and bonds have sometimes moved in concert and sometimes at odds, but they have always declined together. Every major bond-market decline in the past 25 years has been accompanied by an equally major sell-off in stocks. Convertible bonds partake of the more volatile elements of both stocks and bonds; so investors shouldn't be surprised that converts can fall even more quickly than they rise.

The investor can approach convertible bonds from opposite sides: He can treat them like stocks or like bonds. Either way they present intriguing possibilities. As a straight bond, a convert has value determined by the prevailing interest rate. And as a bundle of stocks, it has value determined by the price of the stocks themselves. Not surprisingly this is called the *conversion value*. A moment's thought will reveal that a bond will rarely sell below its conversion value, because whenever it does, investors can make a risk-free profit by purchasing the convert and simultaneously selling however many shares it can be converted into. As discussed in chapter 5, this purchase-sale technique is called arbitrage. Big brokerage houses (which don't have to pay commissions) profit consistently from arbitrage operations and, in the process, assure that no convert will sell below conversion value for very long. As a matter of fact, whenever a convertible bond has had a substantial increase due to a rise in the underlying common stock, most transactions in the convert will involve profit-taking bondholders selling out to arbitrageurs.

The RCA convertible bond mentioned a moment ago can be exchanged for 17 shares of RCA common. If RCA common ever rises above $59 a share, the converts will sell at more than their face value of (17 × $59 = $1003). Thereafter, as long as RCA continues to rise, the minimum market value of the converts will be determined by the value of the common. If the common goes to $60, for instance, the converts will be worth at least $1020 (17 × $60); if the common goes to $100, the converts will be worth at least $1700. So in terms of potential profit, purchasing a convertible bond at or near its conversion value is just like purchasing the underlying common stock. As long as the bond's price is determined by the common, the bond can't fall any faster. But while the rewards are the same for both common and convertible, the convert offers four very important advantages. First, the brokerage fee, for the man who shops around, will be three or four times cheaper on the purchase of a convertible bond than on the outright purchase of the associated number of common shares. Second, the margin rate (the amount the investor can borrow, using the purchased shares as collateral) is twice as favorable. Third, interest on the convertible bond, while it varies from case to case, is usually higher than the dividend rate on the underlying common stock. And last, in case of crash or bankruptcy, the convertible bond is still a bond with value as such, whereas stocks can turn out to be no more than scraps of paper. The message of all this is that the purchase of a convertible bond selling at or near conversion value isn't really a bond investment at all. Instead it is a sophisticated and potentially rewarding way to speculate in common stock.

Converts begin to resemble straight bonds when they are selling far below their conversion value. As the price of a stock declines, so will the market value of any related convertible bonds. But as the decline continues, sooner or later the converts will reach a level comparable to their value as straight bonds. When the prevailing interest rate on corporate bonds is 9 percent, the market value of a convertible bond might decline until the bond is priced to yield 9 percent, but thereafter it won't sink much lower, even if the common should drop from $200 to $10. This is the "theoretical floor" mentioned earlier. It's theoretical, of course, because no one can guarantee that the interest rate will remain at 9 percent. If the interest rate rises, down goes the floor. But when converts sink to the straight-bond level, the conversion factor, whatever it's worth, is being thrown in gratis.

Obviously the best time to buy converts is after they've fallen—when all hope has been abandoned and both stocks and bonds are selling at their lows. As long as the convert is selling at its straight-bond value, the risk is no more than that entailed in an ordinary bond purchase, and the prospective rewards seem considerably greater. Almost 1000 corporations—from AMK to Zapata Norness—have convertible bonds (or their close cousins, convertible preferred stock) outstanding. Even though stocks and bonds have both recovered from their lows, a surprising number are still selling close to their value as straight bonds. (Younger, less seasoned companies—at least a few of which will surely take off if the stock market stays healthy—are more likely to issue convertible bonds than straight ones, because it's easier for them to raise money that way.)

Details on all convertible bonds, including estimates of straight-bond value and computations of how much each would be worth if converted into common stock, are published monthly in *Moody's Bond Survey,* which can usually be found within maroon loose-leaf binders on a stockbroker's bookshelf. From this information the interested investor might want to evolve a checklist of converts selling at or close to straight-bond value and then determine which of these offer the most attractive common stock and which are closest to conversion value. (The nearer a convert is to its conversion value, the sooner will it rise in sympathy with its underlying stock.)

It should be obvious by now that bonds can fulfill different goals for different investors. Convertible bonds selling at their conversion value are as risky and potentially as rewarding as any common stock—even more so if purchased on full margin. Converts selling near their straight-bond value are as sound as a regular bond investment, with the added possibility of distant profit if the underlying stock should revive. Straight bonds themselves, with their current high yields, offer guaranteed returns virtually unparalleled in anyone's memory, plus the prospect of handsome capital gains whenever interest rates return to lower levels. When bonds are offering 8, 9 or even 10 percent—returns that compare favorably with the average performance of common stocks over the past 44 years—they are certainly no longer the sole province of widows, orphans or insurance companies. Bonds should be part of the portfolio of every investor, even the gutsiest.

15. SPECULATING IN BONDS

Strangely, the bonds that appear to be the stodgiest are probably the most interesting for the nervy bond speculator who is willing to assume large risks for the prospect of proportionately large rewards. The borrowed-money leveraging technique, already mentioned briefly, works only for straight bonds: corporates, governments and the higher-paying government-agency bonds. Here the investor gets no tax preferences and no convertibility, just the chance to make (or lose) a real pile.

Rather hypothetically, here's how the leveraging transaction would work. With the general interest rate heading downward, a speculator with $5000 concludes the cost of money will go lower yet, which means bond prices will rise. His first step is to set up a credit line with a bank willing to accept bonds against a collateral loan. Most banks will oblige, but the speculator would do well to shop around for the best rate. His first instinct—to approach a tried and true local banker—ought to be repressed. Like conventioneers, banks do things out of town that they'd never dare at home. To reduce lending rates at home would mean discriminating among favored customers. Better to charge a uniform high rate at home and then lend idle funds at a discount to trustworthy strangers. The peculiar result is that Manhattanites can often find better loan accommodations in Los Angeles, while at the same time, Angelenos are discovering they have a friend at Chase. Interestingly enough, the best out-of-town banking connections are often rural banks; they sometimes have more money to lend than their city cousins.

Assume that our speculator finds a bank willing to lend him $45,000 at 9 percent a year, against $50,000 worth of bonds posted as collateral. Here the bank is financing 90 percent of the transaction; even 95 percent would not be unusual for government bonds. His credit line secured, the speculator purchases $50,000 worth of 8-percent bonds. Commissions on a transaction this size would be minimal—$100 to $200, depending on the number of bonds involved. The speculator pays his broker $5000 (plus commissions), and the bank pays the remaining $45,000 when the brokerage house delivers the certificates. In effect, the speculator has bought all the action from $50,000 worth of bonds for a little over $5000. The interest cost on the collateral loan will amount to $4050 a year, but the bonds themselves pay 8 percent—$4000 a year. So the net cost of carrying the loan is a lordly $50 per annum, tax-deductible. This is very close to being what speculators happily call a *free carry,* difficult but not impossible to achieve these days. And note that even if the borrower had to pay as high as 10 percent on the bank loan, the cost to him would still be a manageable $500 a year, also deductible.

Having bought his bonds, the investor need only wait. If the interest rate remains constant, he can maintain his position indefinitely, at a cost of $50 annually. Of course, if the interest rate rises, he'll soon be in very serious trouble: His collateral will diminish in value, and he'll have to post more cash or sell out at a loss. In fact, if the interest rate rises as much as one percentage point, he'll be wiped out. However, he has projected that the interest rate will decline, and if this occurs, he will profit handsomely. A 2-percent decline in the general interest rate—from 8 to 6 percent—will give his bonds a market value well over $60,000. He could sell out, pay his brokerage fees, repay the $45,000 bank loan and emerge with around $20,000. Not bad on an investment of just one-fourth that. Note well the arithmetic here. If the interest rate *increases* from 8 to 10 percent, our speculator loses $10,000. But if the rate drops from 8 to 6 percent, he makes $15,000. Such odds should appeal.

Even given such favorable figures, not too many people will be willing to assume the risks implicit in this sort of transaction—and for good reason: Money can be lost this way just as quickly as gained. But it should have a

Speculating in Bonds

special attraction to risk takers who are familiar with the workings of the stock market, because it follows one of our fundamental rules of stock speculation: betting *with* the trend rather than against it. In stocks the successful speculator soon learns never to "call the turns." He won't buy into a declining market in the hope that it will reverse direction tomorrow, because he knows that stocks reverse themselves infrequently; so to bet on a turnaround is to bet against the odds.

The more cautious investor, drawn to bonds because of their high yields, finds himself in a less justifiable position. Everyone desirous of a fixed income seems to have his own price. Some will be lured in at 7 percent, some at 8, more yet at 9 and 10. But all of them, once they become bond owners, find themselves in just the role they should avoid in the stock market. As new bondholders, they are unanimous in their expectation that the interest rate will turn down tomorrow. If they didn't expect the interest rate to reverse itself immediately, they would do better not to buy—to sit on their cash and await higher returns. So, to the extent that they are attracted to bonds solely by their high yields, individual bond buyers are trying to call the turns.

But, to repeat, stocks and bonds are different. The most fascinating aspect of the bond market, from the small investor's point of view, is that there he *can* call the turns, with astonishing regularity. We have already discussed the stock-market cliché that the small investor is always wrong. Professional stock players scrutinize what are known as the odd-lot statistics, measuring the activity of investors (invariably amateurs) who buy and sell fewer than 100 shares at a time. When the odd-lot figures show small investors buying heavily, the pros take it as a time to sell; and when the odd-lotters start selling heavily, the pros begin to buy. Over the years this simple technique has produced more profits than losses. The rationale for its success is that when small investors go on a stock-buying bender, the market is intoxicated with speculative excess and likely to stumble; and when small investors are so disenchanted that all they want is to sell out and go elsewhere, then the bottom is close at hand.

The bond market turns this upside down. In the words of Sidney Homer, partner of the nation's biggest bond house and éminence grise of the Wall Street bond fraternity, "The public is extremely well heeled and extremely interest-conscious." Small-investor money is drawn to bonds only when interest rates are rising. The public still brings its remarkable ability to buy at the top and sell at the bottom, but in the bond market the result is not disaster but distinction. High interest rates mean low bond prices. The small investor's instinct for the top gets him into bonds at the very bottom. In fact, when interest rates are in the doldrums, the market belongs entirely to professionals—big institutional investors who, like stamp collectors, spend much time exchanging esoteric scraps of paper among themselves. But when interest rates approach peak levels, amateurs get interested. This was true three times during the Fifties, it was true in the "credit crunch" of 1966, it was true at the peak in 1970, and it seems true today. As one bond analyst hypothesized to a *Wall Street Journal* reporter, "The figures suggest that the little guy is the final source of money reserves and that when he comes into the bond market, it's because prices are about to bottom out." When prices *do* bottom out, of course, the little guy profits handsomely.

IV
The Collector Investments

Price Performance of Collector Items: 1925–1971

As this section makes abundantly clear, any generalizations about price trends in the collector world are heroic and fraught with ambiguity. The price performances charted here are average figures for three broad collector areas where sales are frequent enough to permit graphic depiction. In no case should these average figures be construed as anything but very rough orders of magnitude, with the additional caveat that no single collectors item will ever conform to "average" performance. In every instance, items charted are rare and desirable pieces that have long been cherished by discerning collectors. Technical data: 1925 has been selected as base year, with average prices during that year designated "100". Subsequent increases (or decreases) reflect the 1925 base. Art price performance computed from figures presented by Richard H. Rush in a lecture at the New School Art Center, New York City, in March 1967, and updated by the author. These figures reflect the price action of the paintings of 125 western-world artists whose works are collected internationally. Stamp and coin averages are from the author's records. Each reflects the continuing price performance of six internationally recognized rarities.

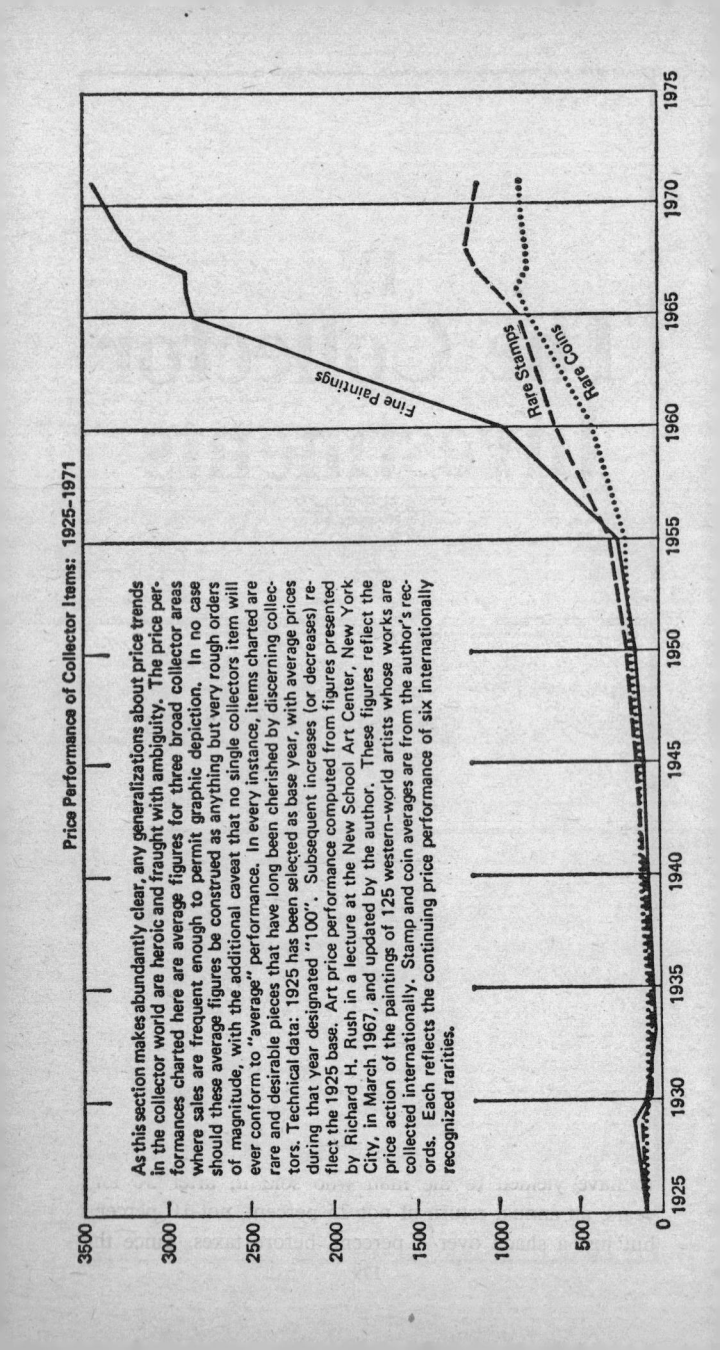

16. THE COLLECTOR MENTALITY

The recent sale of a single postage stamp for a world-record $280,000 blew minds on Wall Street. Whenever stocks are falling and inflation raging (and especially when both occur at once), the investment potential of collector's items—stamps, coins, paintings, rare books, autographs, antiques and all the rest—seems especially promising. In this instance the facts had all the allure of lucre. The stamp was the fabled "penny magenta" of British Guiana, the only one known to exist. The seller had purchased the stamp in 1940 for a mere $42,000. And the buyer was not one of your nutty millionaire stamp freaks but a syndicate of eight hardheaded businessmen, most of whom wouldn't know a rare postage stamp if it came to them on a corporate report.

"If you think the stock market was running wild with speculation in 1968 and 1969," rhapsodized *Forbes* magazine, "take a look at what's going on in postage-stamp collecting." Rare stamp prices, the magazine's experts declared, "have been rising year to year, without pause, at an annual rate of between 10 percent and 25 percent. What these figures mean is that prices have been going up somewhere between 150 percent and 800 percent every decade. Thus a $10,000 stamp today could be expected to be worth somewhere between $25,000 and $90,000 by 1980. . . . In 1960 it might well have gone for somewhere between $100 and $400."

These statistics must have titillated the palates, if not the wallets, of *Forbes*'s stock-worn readers. But unfortunately, as we will see shortly, the *Forbes* figures are simply not true. The penny magenta itself, had anyone cared to examine the details of its history and then consult a compound-interest table, would have been found to have yielded to the man who sold it, after 30 long years, an annual return of not 25 percent, not 10 percent, but just a shade over 5 percent, before taxes. Since this was considerably less than the yield then available from bank savings accounts (not to mention tax-free municipal bonds), small wonder the seller decided to bail out.

The term *collector investment* can embrace literally anything that collectors are fond enough of to pay for. An exhibit of Dürer engravings alongside a well-mounted showing of fossilized dinosaur droppings would illustrate quite clearly how collector tastes range from the rarified to the ridiculous. In the 18th and 19th centuries, a man of means could tie up a fortune in a showing of birds' nests. This hobby, like many of the birds themselves, has all but vanished from the earth, though the lavish and well-wrought cabinets that wealthy nest nuts commissioned to display their treasures are now highly sought—in fact, they are collector's items. More recently collectors have bid avidly not only for dinosaur dung but for barbed wire, millstones, baseball cards, old golf clubs, horse-drawn fire engines, player pianos, even woodpecker holes. A cursory reading of one issue of *Collectors News,* a marvelous monthly newspaper originating from the mid-American communications mecca of Grundy Center, Iowa, reveals hard-cash markets for (among other things) used streetcar transfers, empty beer cans, Kewpie dolls, erector sets, orgone boxes, stagecoach passes, brass doorknobs, railroad timetables, chauffeurs' badges, Felix the Cat figurines, Pennsylvania drivers' licenses, Captain Midnight giveaways, dining-car silverware, Shirley Temple memorabilia and pink porcelain pigs.*

Any of these, or any of the myriad other collected items, could turn a profit for the person fortunate enough to secure sought-after objects cheaply and then doubly fortunate to locate an eager and well-heeled buyer. But such profits would be windfalls. By any reasonable definition, an "investment" ought to be repeatable; so this section will confine itself to collector pursuits where, all question of profit aside, investments can be made *con-*

---

* A more recent ad reads, "Wanted: Memorabilia of anything, regardless of condition."

sistently. Even ruling out Felix the Cat and the pink porkers, we are still confronted with a vast and intimidating junk heap. Convenience dictates the division of the universe of collector investments into five arbitrary and certainly arguable categories, each characterized by a large international collector following, a well-dispersed and generally competitive network of dealers and auction houses and annual sales figures amounting to many millions of dollars.

In our categorization, *antiques* will include not only furniture but decorative or dinner-table silver, porcelain, and utilitarian objects of all descriptions, so long as they are over 100 years old. *Art* includes paintings, sculpture, drawings, engravings, prints and anything else produced by artists for the enjoyment of art lovers—a market, incidentally, wherein annual sales exceed $1 billion worldwide. *Literary material* consists of autographs, letters, books and manuscripts. *Stamps and coins* are just that. The rest comprises vintage autos, cultural and ethnic artifacts, firearms, paperweights and all the other seriously collected items, whether objects of art or objects of utility, that don't fit the previous categories but which, taken together, involve tens of thousands of collectors and staggering annual sales. We will discuss each of these categories in some detail and then examine ways the would-be collector-investor—assuming he's not intimidated by the many pitfalls involved—might go about assembling a collection for fun as well as for profit.

But before we can discuss the prospective rewards, which are problematical at best, we must consider the risks, which are very real. Journalistic inadequacies, epitomized by the *Forbes* report, are just one difficulty confronting the would-be collector-investor. To the outsider, especially if he believes his newspaper, collector's items might seem a delightful and painless way to make money. Not only are the profits gratifying, but in the interim, while they are abuilding, there's the intangible but significant thrill of possession. You buy a Rembrandt etching for $600, hang it in your library for a few years, then sell it for $1500 and buy two more. What could be easier? Well, as it turns out, many things are easier—flying an unrestored Fokker D-VII through the hand-forged eye of a colonial cobbler's needle, for instance.

The absence of accurate, factual reportage would be enough to deter most investors from buying stocks or other paper securities, but in the case of the collector investments this is just one of half a dozen difficulties. Hard buy-and-sell prices, for instance, of the sort investors can find daily for stocks, bonds, commodities or mutual funds, are usually lacking. When they can be found, examination often proves them deceptive or meaningless. Worse, the market for many collector's items is as weak and as thin as last night's drinks. To sell a high-priced art object, an investor must wait many months to get it included in a decently cataloged auction sale. The alternative is to take a beating in a quick transaction with a dealer. Except for the buyer at auction, commissions are high. Indeed, the investor in securities or real estate, accustomed to paying commissions from 1 up to perhaps 7 percent, could easily regard the prevailing 15–20 percent auctioneer's commission as prohibitively high.

Transactions with private dealers, whether purchases or sales, involve markups that make even this look cheap. Add the undeniable need for expertise, in an area where experts don't come cheap and rarely agree, and you have an investment medium that, despite all the glamour, can hardly be regarded as an easy way to make a killing. In fact, taken as a group, the collector investments are a fine way to *lose* money. Given great good luck, uncommon prescience or a sublime combination of both, profit—even enormous profit—is always possible. But it is nowhere near as commonplace as ecstatic journalists would lead the novice to believe, and it is certainly not as easy as collectors and dealers would indicate.

The journalists' shortcomings are most easily explained by analogy: For centuries a recurrent old wives' tale held that porpoises push drowning men to safety. In several documented cases this actually happened. But recently cetologists discovered that porpoises just like to push things—life jackets, logs, anything that floats—and they push without regard to destination. For every drowning man nudged to safety, half a dozen more were surely pushed off the continental shelf. Only the survivors returned to tell, and therein lies the difference. We read about the Renoir purchased for peanuts in the 1920s and recently sold for seven figures because that is news. But we don't read about the other 19th Century "masters"— Sir Lawrence Alma-Tadema, for instance, or Jules Lefebvre or Pierre Puvis de Chavannes or Sir Edwin Landseer—all of whose works once commanded six-figure prices in turn-of-the-century dollars but now sell for a few thousand or a few hundred. Even among living artists one can find instances like Bernard Buffet, the middle-aged boy wonder whose stark lines fired the imagination of a generation of interior decorators and whose works fetched $10,000 or more in the early 1960s. Of the ten Buffet canvases auctioned in 1969, seven sold for under $2500 and only one even approached five figures. We don't read about things like this because, somehow, they are not news. Surely it's a commentary on contemporary capitalism to observe that investments generally, and collector investments specifically, are the last area of human endeavor where the good news gets all the publicity and the bad news languishes in neglect.

Imagine yourself a newspaper reporter assigned to write something on the investment potential of, say, rare books. You know more about bourbon than you do about books; so you do the obvious. You go through the microfilm files of the *Wall Street Journal* and the *New York Times* and locate a few reports, invariably about record-setting sales. Then you look up a rare-book dealer or two in the Manhattan Yellow Pages. (Most dealers in rare anything have their main galleries in New York or London and possibly a branch in Houston or Los Angeles.) When you reach a dealer, you are greeted with a telephonic orgy: "Best investment in the world. . . . Doubling every three years. . . . Nobody's buying stocks anymore. . . . We're all getting rich." If you're an especially ambitious reporter, you might call a few big-time collectors—and hear the same spiel. Certainly you have a consensus, and the consensus makes colorful copy. Better, it comes from the experts; so who can deny it?

Well, no one can deny it. No one else knows anything about it. But, unhappily, the experts are the least objective sources imaginable. The Wall Street comparison would have an investment analyst assessing a company's stock-market potential solely by talking with executives of the firm and its major stockholders. Of course they think it's good. Their whole lives are tied up in it. A rare-object dealer is rather like a grocer; he doesn't care which way prices are heading so long as he has customers. His profit comes not from inventory appreciation (after all, rising prices mean he'll have to pay more to restock) but from the markup on each item he sells. The more goods he can move, the more profit he can make. If an investment rationale brings additional customers into the store—especially *new* customers—then he will certainly try to create an investment rationale. This is not to imply that dealers are venal, just that they are human.

Collectors are the worst offenders of all—and understandably so. They are probably the most misunderstood minority group on God's earth. Like acidheads or homosexuals, they live in a hostile and intolerant world, and their personalities can unfold only in communion with their own kind. Thus the incredible proliferation of collector magazines, collector societies and collector correspondence clubs. (As an example, there's a club—and a quarterly magazine—for people who collect books about stamp collecting.) Fate forces the typical collector to spend most of his life in the company of noncollectors. In a moment of weakness he might try to explain to outsiders the ineffable joy he derives from plunking gold coins into little Plexiglas holes, from lovingly contemplating the cream bindings of his French first editions, whose uncut pages can never be read, or from caressing the silky-smooth and somehow sexual hemispheres that comprise his collection of Clichy paperweights. But such explanations are rarely understood. The listener nods wanly and tries to change the subject. Depending on the seriousness of the collector's commitment, his outsider communicant will regard him as a harmless and doddering eccentric or as a highly advanced case of galloping anal fixation.

Reluctantly the collector turns to the investment rationale: "This is my paperweight collection; I get a charge out of it—also, it appreciates 30 percent a year." Here is an explanation with which noncollectors can identify! Eccentricity becomes shrewdness; madness assumes a method. Blowing half one's paycheck on an old campaign button suddenly becomes justifiable, even in the wife's eyes, because the proceeds from that very button will someday cover a year of little Arthur's college. Of course, it seldom works out this way. When he reaches college, poor Arthur will find himself working weekends in a head shop, because dad is not going to liquidate a lifetime accumulation of Republican-primary campaign buttons just to subsidize his son's radicalization. Dad will die with his collection intact. Heirs will fall all over themselves in their haste to sell it, only to discover that it's worth a good bit less than it cost. The heirs will blame the dealers, the auctioneers or even the collector fraternity itself, but in truth the blame is theirs alone. They—the noncollectors—by their callous unwillingness to understand the collector mentality, forced a sensitive soul to resort to hypocrisy just so they'd leave him alone.

Quite literally, the collector mentality extends beyond the grave. Despite the enormous tax advantages that accrue from bequeathing a profitable collection to a public or semipublic institution, many serious collectors insist, in their wills, that their holdings be auctioned off or otherwise privately dispersed. The explanation, when there is one, is that the deceased owner wants other collectors, perhaps collectors yet unborn, to share the joy that he has known. Thus the last will and testament of the late Frank Hogan, an important autograph collector: "I do not deem it fitting that these friends of many happy hours should repose in unloved and soulless captivity. Rather, I would send them out into the world again, to be the intimate of others whose loving hands and understanding hearts will fill the place left vacant by my passing."

Reflection will reveal how hypocritical the investment rationale actually is in the eyes of a serious collector. Above all, the collector doesn't want the things he collects to increase in price. Price increases would mean he can add fewer and fewer items to his collection; his happy hours would boast proportionately fewer friends. The collector's interest, in fact, is precisely the opposite of the investor's, which is the main reason why collector's items are so difficult to approach from an investment standpoint.

The very phrase *collector-investor* is schizophrenic. The investor wants steady, heady appreciation. The collector wants prices that are both stable and *low,* and he will do everything in his power to keep them that way. Moreover, his powers here are not small. His instinct for his own kind will have brought him in touch with the other collectors who share his particular interests, and he and his compatriots will make sure they are not bidding against one another when a mutually desirable item appears at public auction. If an official catalog or magazine speaks for his pursuit, he and his correspondents probably write it—and set the prices if there are any. His group will know all the major dealers in the field, and if any one dealer begins to raise prices too exuberantly, he will soon find himself without customers. And if a well-heeled and unknowledgeable newcomer enters the lists in hopes of making a quick killing, the collectors can do him in much in the same way stock-market insiders gun down amateurs trying to poach in their preserves.

17. WHAT TO COLLECT FOR PROFIT

Properly forewarned, the reader is invited to enter the thicket. Literary materials are a good departure point, being a subject few people know anything about. The collection of literary materials—manuscripts, autographs, letters and especially books—has historically been a preoccupation of persons of literary taste. Now, however, well-heeled university libraries are also murking up the market, and they sometimes run prices up to dazzling levels on the theory that Virginia Woolf's letters to her husband, for example, are worth more to unborn generations of Ph.D. candidates than they are to a Dallas computer-software magnate. *Fortune* recently estimated that 70 percent of rare-book sales are now made to universities and museums, compared with 40 percent in the early 1950s. This bodes well for investors, of course, because it means the available supply of desirable material is diminishing, so that what remains will command higher and higher prices. (To a greater or lesser extent, institutional buying puts similar pressure on all the other collector's items.) According to one index, collectable books generally increased in value by a factor of five during the last decade. In other words, if a hypothetical rare book was worth $1000 in 1960, it is worth $5000 today.

First editions have always been treasured by book collectors, but very old works (virtually anything before 1550 or so) and early non–first editions of very great writers (Shakespeare, for instance) are also valued. As a general rule—which also holds true for most other collector pursuits—value is determined by demand, rarity, condition, historical importance and beauty, very roughly in that order. Rare-book prices fluctuate wildly, and, despite popular impression, they can go down as well as up. John Galsworthy, for instance, an author who was lionized several generations ago, is now less highly regarded—the BBC's *Forsyte Saga* notwithstanding. A so-so first edition of his little-known *Island Pharisees* (1904) sold for $1375 in 1930; a much better copy, inscribed by the author, went for $60 a generation later, at about the same time a first-edition *Vanity Fair* ($3000 in 1929) fetched $350.

Despite the academic pretenses, the last thing a collector would do with a rare book is *read* it, because this would surely diminish its value. In all the collector areas, condition crucially affects value. First editions of Boswell's *Johnson* (1791) sold at auction in 1968 for $400 or so and today bring over $500. But in 1969 a copy in its original binding with pages uncut (obviously never read) sold at auction in London for over $3000. This was the finest copy extant, as the price tag—about seven times the then-current market—clearly showed. Scholarly research can also affect values. Shortly after the University of Indiana published a definitive bibliography of the prolific writings of Daniel Defoe, bookworms began to note increases in the prices of his works. The Indiana scholarship, in the words of one expert, "by removing the element of doubt, pushed the value of books in the accepted canon sharply higher." After all, collectors can't know what they are buying until someone has told them so.

Literary works from the preprinting era are also cherished, especially by universities. A 13th Century manuscript of the Apocalypse sold for $180,000 in 1958 and ten years later fetched half a million. Hand-copied books from before 1450 or so, especially those that are replete with illustrations ("illuminations") have increased perhaps threefold in the last ten years. Needless to say, these are all one-of-a-kind items, and not too many are left.

Medical and scientific books, seriously collected only in the last 40-odd years, have risen perhaps tenfold in two decades, probably because there are so many wealthy doctors and engineers to collect them. (As befits the current economy, values now have leveled off.) Original works of enduring consequence are the most sought after. Ten years ago the edition of a Leipzig scientific journal wherein Einstein first published his theory of relativity (1916) was worth $45 or so. Today it sells for over $600.

What to Collect for Profit

Newton's *Principia* (1687), surely the greatest scientific work of the 17th Century, sold in first edition for around $500 in 1952 and is worth upwards of $10,000 today. Similarly, Copernicus's revolutionary *De revolutionibus* (1543) jumped from $1000 to $30,000. But Darwin's *Origin of Species* is off from its 1968 peak of $840.

Lavishly illustrated old books seem to command especially high prices, oftentimes because they can be split up individually and sold as art. *Connoisseur* magazine estimates that 70 percent of the old atlases sold at auction are transmogrified into interior decoration. William Blake's Illustrations for the Book of Job (1825), which sold for $1725 in 1966, last year fetched $4200—at a London print sale. A copy of Balzac's *Chefs d'oeuvre inconnus*, for which the illustrator happened to be Pablo Picasso, sold in 1966 for $1820 and fetched $6000 in 1970. Pierre Redouté's *Les roses*, a three-volume botanical work from the 1820s that is regarded as one of the great masterpieces of the color-printing art, sold for $1500 in 1953 and $24,000 in 1968. Most dramatic of all was the record realization of $216,000 for a first edition (surely not to be split up) of Audubon's *Birds of America*, a collection of 448 hand-colored plates that the purchaser, Chicago dealer Kenneth Nebenzahl, claims to be "the best copy in existence." A less fine edition sold for $51,000 in 1966.

Modern books form a subcategory of their own. Besides first editions, this includes finely printed works, usually in limited, numbered and signed editions, produced solely to gratify bibliophilic desires, which seem insatiable even in the absence of institutional competition. The fad for collector editions came of age in the 1920s, died abruptly with the depression and came back strong in the last decade. Today more than a dozen publishers make a handsome living producing little else. Despite what seems to be a rigged market, such books, especially the earlier illustrated ones, have fared quite well in the last decade, increasing by a factor of five or so.

Among modern books originally sold for reading rather than for collecting, first editions predominate, and their value generally varies with the stature of the author. Sudden changes in his literary status can trigger equally sudden reactions in the collector value of his works. Books that become fad hits years after publication—*Lord of the Flies* and *The Sot-Weed Factor* are good examples—are sought in first edition by collectors who speculate that the author's new importance might endure. The film *Lawrence of Arabia* caused the value of first editions of T. E. Lawrence's *Seven Pillars of Wisdom* (1926) to double. This, incidentally, is a scarce item, worth (in fine condition) perhaps $2500. Similarly, an author's death can rekindle collector interest. This happened with Hemingway and Faulkner and more recently with John O'Hara, whose *Appointment in Samarra* (his first book) sold for $7 in the early 1960s and recently commanded $75.

Of the modern poets, T. S. Eliot ranks supreme. A first edition of *The Love Song of J. Alfred Prufrock* (1917) fetched $100 ten years back and is now worth three times that. William Butler Yeats enjoyed an especially big run-up in the mid-1960s, but collector focus more recently shifted to Dylan Thomas. Thomas's *Eighteen Poems,* published at 50 cents in 1934, now brings $300. Most eagerly sought in England now are the early works of Samuel Beckett, who, if the London *Times* can be believed, is "perhaps the greatest literary figure of our times." His *Proust* (1931) sold for $35 three years ago and recently commanded $250.

Important children's books in good condition have always fetched premium prices, because they are difficult to find. Heinrich Hoffman's *Slovenly Peter* and Lewis Carroll's *Alice in Wonderland* both sell for $25,000 in first edition; *Pinocchio,* however, sells for less than $1000, and most children's books, including many that will surely be classics of tomorrow, fetch much less.

In all the collector investments, newcomers are well advised to confine themselves to as narrow a specialty as possible—preferably a subject that already appeals to them. A novice bibliophile with a gourmet bent, for instance, might want to begin assembling a first-class showing of cookbooks. He will soon find that these have suffered similar ravages as children's tomes, with older items especially difficult to locate in pristine condition. Historical figures from Lafcadio Hearn to Henri de Toulouse-Lautrec have authored cookbooks, and a first-edition showing of these would surely be a treasure. Other bibliophilic topics that command specialized collector attention include astrology, automobiles, airplanes, Christian socialism, homosexuality, horses, investments, pornography, snakes and war, to name but a few.

Magazines are a risky speculation. They are produced in quantity and invariably boast more sellers than buyers. The first issue of PLAYBOY, for instance, is generally thought to be quite valuable, because dealers have asked up to $125 per copy. But these same dealers will rarely offer more than $25 to a potential seller. For the record, only the first 14 issues of PLAYBOY have any special collector value, with retail offerings ranging between $100 (volume one, number one) and $12 (volume two, number two). Old movie magazines, especially those involving Shirley Temple, around whom a fanatic collector cult has swirled for decades, sell between $2 and $100. Perhaps the most widely collected of all magazines, *National Geographic*, has no speculative appeal whatever, because the crafty National Geographic Society saved all its plates and reprints old issues as need arises.

Early comic books, once thought to contribute to the delinquency of minors, wound up contributing to the enrichment of the few delinquents who saved them. Comic collecting came of age in the 1960s, gathering scholarly magazines, hard-cash buyers, national associations and many of the other trappings that characterize a serious and enduring collector pursuit. Last year, when comic collectors convened at the Statler-Hilton in New York, over 2000 of the faithful showed up—a mammoth turnout for any collector confab. Typically, first editions are the most valuable. The first *Superman* (1938) now sells for $300; *Famous Funnies* (1934) also brings $300, and

Batman (1940) $150. All these, recall, originally sold for a dime, and all could have been bought for under $50 five years ago. Some non–first issues, sought by collectors to complete full runs, are also valuable. The 44th *Terry and the Pirates,* for example, sells for $40, and the 328th *Donald Duck* brings $6. For those who think they might have a fortune tucked away in their parents' attic, Brooklyn's Grand Book Center publishes a catalog listing 15,000 comics at prices between 50 cents and $150. These are offering prices, of course. Purchase prices, assuming a buyer could be found, would be much less.

The collecting of signatures, letters and other historical material was once confined to history buffs but now seems to have gathered an investor following as well, perhaps because of pronouncements such as that of New York autograph dealer Charles Hamilton (he who sold the Jackie Kennedy letters), who recently told an eager *Business Week* reporter that "prices for fine American autographs have increased twenty-five times since 1960." This would be true only if you define a "fine American autograph" as one that increases 25 times in a decade. Most signatures, while they have fared well, haven't done nearly this well.

Novice autograph hunters still have visions of wealth as they root through Aunt Hattie's trunk, never realizing that five or a dozen searchers have probably been there before them. As in all the established collector areas, the possibility of making a significant find these days is virtually nil. Back in the 19th Century it was still possible. A Britisher discovered his milkman wrapping butter in Boswell's correspondence with Dr. Temple, and an American collector retrieved a valuable Button Gwinnett autograph (one of the signers of the Declaration of Independence) blowing across his front lawn.

Today's collectors buy their autographs through dealers or at auction. Reliable estimates place 5000 serious collectors in the U.S. alone, and annual sales worldwide are guessed to be $20 million. Institutions are into this market, too. Autographs of John Howard Payne, author-composer of *Home, Sweet Home,* sold a few years ago at around $100 each until Brown University decided to add him to its collection of musical Americana. Today the same items, when they appear, command $500–$750. Similarly with George Bernard Shaw, whose letters were easily obtainable a decade ago for $30 each and now—partly because of large-scale institutional buying—fetch $300.

Autograph prices depend on the fame of the signer-writer, the scarcity of his signature and the content of the letter, if any. All historical signatures have collector value, but if the signature is of a famous personality on an interesting letter, the price increases enormously. Notoriously scarce are signatures of Franz Joseph Haydn, Edgar Allan Poe (himself an autograph collector) and William Shakespeare; only six Shakespeare signatures are known.

Most popular with American collectors today are Revolutionary War material and presidential signatures. Many speculators, not only in autographs but in stamps, prints and other collector areas, are anticipating a run-up in Revolution-related material to coincide with the celebrations planned for 1976—the 200th anniversary of the Declaration of Independence. Jefferson, so intimately associated with the Declaration, seems especially favored. A similar boomlet occurred in Civil War memorabilia on its centenary ten years back but failed to reach the proportions that greedy speculators had anticipated.

Presidential letters have always been a favorite, and recent increases have been nothing short of breathtaking. Typical, according to Bruce Gimelson, a young dealer from suburban Philadelphia, is a letter signed in the field at Valley Forge by General George Washington, written to a French soldier who was interested in joining the Continental army. A collector bought this letter for $2250 twelve years ago and sold it in 1968 for $10,000. Today it's worth over $15,000. Lincoln signatures, which exist in quantity on officers' commissions that somehow filtered out of the War Department years ago, jumped from $25 to $400 during the same period.

Contemporary presidential signatures are among the scarcest, because of the advent of the Autopen, an automatic letter-signing machine. President Kennedy, for instance, used such a device almost exclusively after he joined the Senate in 1953; in toto, he went through 14 different machines. Gimelson reports he has seen over 6000 Kennedy signatures, of which only 100 or so were actually hand-signed. A real Kennedy signature would be worth $150 or more, but very few exist, since apparently Kennedy rarely signed his name; only one canceled check bearing his signature is known. Hand-written Kennedy letters on White House stationery are the rarest of all such documents for 20th Century presidents; Dwight D. Eisenhower is runner-up. The rarest of all in-office presidential signatures is that of William Henry Harrison; he held office only one month and was mortally ill for much of that time.

Nonsignature historical memorabilia is also collected, but here the market is much too thin and the objects much too scarce to permit any definitive investment judgments. As an example, in May 1969 a broadside copy of the Declaration of Independence, which Congress printed by the ream but of which only 19 survive, was purchased for $404,000 by Ira Corn, the Texas capitalist who is best known as founder-patron of the Dallas Aces bridge team. But less than 18 months later another copy turned up, and this one found no buyers at $150,000. A lock of George Washington's hair (reddish brown, for those who are interested), with accompanying documentation, recently sold for $750.

Forgeries plague all the collector investments, but they are especially common in the world of autographs and letters. A prolific Frenchman of the last century supplied a prominent collector with no fewer than 20,000 fakes in eight short years, including letters (all in French) from Judas Iscariot, Alexander the Great, Aristotle, Cleopatra and Lazarus (this one dated two years after his resurrection). Contemporary collectors are somewhat more sophisticated, but the possibility of clever forgery still exists.

Most high-priced autographs will carry not only a dealer's guarantee but a pedigree of sorts, tracing the collections in which it has previously reposed or the circumstances under which it was discovered, a policy that also prevails in other collector areas.

As always, prices can swing both ways. Until the 1920s or so, collector taste leaned not to presidents but to signers of the Declaration. In 1924 the very same Button Gwinnett letter that was earlier found drifting across a collector's lawn sold for $51,000. (Strangely, Gwinnett isn't the scarcest of the signers; that honor goes to Thomas Lynch, who died young, but Gwinnett is the most expensive.) Today this letter reposes in a Philadelphia museum, but if it would reappear on the market, it would certainly not reach $30,000.

Art is usually regarded as the premier collector investment and for the last 20 years or so has certainly lived up to its billing. Prior to 1950, art prices (and those of many other collector investments) closely followed stock prices. A privately compiled index charting the price movement of the works of 125 internationally known artists, starting at a base of 100 in 1925, peaked at 165 in 1929, had fallen to 50 by 1933, did not reach 100 again until 1945 and stood at 150 in 1950. Anyone vaguely familiar with the history of stock prices will recognize the close similarity to the meanderings of the Dow-Jones industrial average. In retrospect 1950 looms as a watershed year in American social history. The country was on the verge of two unprecedented decades of prosperity, wherein new millionaires would pop up like wild flowers after a desert rain. Even those with less than millions would find the time—and the money—to devote to collector's items and especially to art. (More recently the same transformation has overcome western Europe and Japan. Germans are now big buyers of American pop art, and Japanese are active in the rare-book market.)

Between 1950 and 1960 the art index increased by a factor of six, while the Dow-Jones industrials, during the greatest bull market in American history, only managed a triple. Between 1960 and 1970 the art index quadrupled again, while the DJIA just lay there. Of course, any art-price index is misleading. While the stock averages reflect huge sales of identical items exchanged every weekday of the year, a representative work of art may come to market only once or twice in a lifetime. Better pieces have the habit of leaving the market altogether, while, to a much lesser extent, new discoveries and new favorites take their place. As a result, any generalization about art-price trends should be taken with a whole shakerful of salt.

The most serious and widely regarded charting of art-price movements is an ongoing collaboration between Sotheby's (pronounced *Suth*-er-bees), the huge London auction gallery, and the *Times* of London, whose coverage of art-world developments is without peer. (A few years ago Sotheby's acquired New York's vast Parke-Bernet auction galleries—the correct pronunciation is Ber-*net*—creating an international cartel that is rather the IBM of the auction world.) These *Times*-Sotheby indexes, as they are called, attempt to plot price movements in dozens of different art categories. The compilers rightly stress that precision is impossible and that the figures should be taken only "as rough orders of magnitude," a caveat that often gets lost in journalistic transcription, possibly because the public is so hungry for digestable information about art profits and possibly, too, because the indexes are expressed in specific numerical quantities that belie the compilers' warnings. The indexes have only been in existence for three years; so they have been extrapolated back into the past, conveniently depicting the post-1950 period during which prices shot up so dramatically. (A stock-market analogue would be to decide, in 1970, to concoct a growth-stock index for the last 20 years and to select, as components of the index, those stocks that had grown the most; the result would be wonderful to behold, but its relevance to the course of stocks in general would be less striking.)

Still, the *Times*-Sotheby indexes are a beginning, and since they are all we have, we must make the best of them.

They are the source of many of the price generalizations made earlier and will be cited frequently in the paragraphs that follow. But readers must bear in mind that they are a far from perfect measuring rod. Their after-the-fact nature, plus their overrepresentation of museum-quality masterpieces (in the art world, a "masterpiece" tends to be anything that sells for six figures or more), means that they might overstate the performance of run-of-the-gallery works by a factor of three or five. Still, even granting such overstatement, the figures are impressive. The T-S indexes show that since 1951 (base year for all the figures), French Impressionist paintings have increased in value 17 times over, 20th Century paintings 21 times, old-master drawings 22 times, British paintings 9½ times, Italian paintings 7½ times, and old-master paintings 7 times. (This last figure will surely console the man who purchased Bassano's *Flight into Egypt* for $645,000 in 1960 and sold it in 1970 for $240,000.)

American works are not indexed, since they rarely get to London, being largely a preoccupation of U.S. collectors. However, American works have risen tremendously in the last decade, perhaps by a factor of ten or so. Most knowledgeable observers think this is just the beginning. A significant sale of American paintings held at Parke-Bernet in March 1969 seemed to herald a whole new era of collector interest and high bidding. American taste for art has traditionally followed European fashion ("aped it" might be more precise), but now American collectors are becoming both more chauvinistic in their taste and more confident in their judgment. Then, too, American works are considerably cheaper than their Continental counterparts. Whatever the reason, Americans seem on the verge of becoming leaders rather than followers in the art world. And regardless of the soundness of their instincts, they certainly have the money, as recent prices confirm. Perhaps even more revealing, European museums are now serious buyers of American works.

Paintings by American "old masters"—John Singleton Copely, Charles Willson Peale, Gilbert Stuart and Benjamin

West, for instance—actually declined in value during the early 1950s. Works that then sold for a few thousand dollars now command six figures. (American "Prairie Painters," notably Frederic Remington and Charles Russell, have fared almost as well.) West's *Portrait of John Eardley-Wilmot*, which recently emerged from the hands of the subject's descendants, fetched $86,400—then an auction record for an American master—when sold at Sotheby's in late 1970. An interesting feature of this canvas, which would have sold for perhaps $2500 fifteen years back, is that its background shows *another* lost painting by West, this one an allegory of peace, included in the Eardley-Wilmot portrait because its sitter was associated with the treaty that finally settled the American Revolution. The lost canvas, like so many other masterpieces of American art, probably reposes, unappreciated and neglected, in somebody's grandmother's attic. American art, being such a newly fashionable field, still offers opportunities for significant discovery.

The Eardley-Wilmot price record lasted all of one month. Current auction record for an American work, a figure that might be shattered by the time these words are read, is $210,000, paid by an anonymous collector for Thomas Eakins's *Cowboys in the Badlands* in December 1970 at Parke-Bernet. Eakins may well be the greatest artist America has ever produced, but this is still a startling realization for a painting that is far from a masterpiece. Indeed, what most commends *Cowboys* is its western subject matter—now very much in vogue—and the fact that it vaguely resembles a Remington. Underbidder on the Eakins canvas was the appropriately yclept Armand Hammer, board chairman of Occidental Petroleum Company. At the same sale Hammer paid $205,000 for a Stuart portrait of George Washington—similar to the face on our dollar bill. This transaction also raised eyebrows, because once again the work hardly qualifies as the greatest thing an American artist ever set to canvas. Much of Stuart's livelihood came from knocking off portraits of Washington for post-Revolutionary patriots; he actually produced scores of them, all strikingly similar—and this one isn't the best.

When each of these canvases was sold, collectors in the bidding audience burst into spontaneous applause—presumably their way of saying that if *these* paintings are worth six figures, many other American works are worth much, much more. After the sale Lawrence Fleischman, director of New York's Kennedy Galleries, a major dealer in American works, opined that before too long a made-in-America canvas will fetch over $1 million. Eakins's *Gross Clinic,* for instance, a grisly insight into 19th Century surgical procedures that now reposes in Philadelphia's Jefferson Medical College, would surely exceed the million mark if auctioned tomorrow.

At the same sale works by much more minor American artists also garnered surprising prices. A harbor scene by Edward Redfield, which had sold for $225 in 1935, brought $2500. Landscapes by semiabstractionist John Marin, a significant artist but hardly a household word, all sold well into four figures; a Marin beach scene that had changed hands for $850 in 1945 reached $7000, and a summer landscape ($500 in 1944) sold for $5250. A watercolor of nymphs and satyrs by an artist named (right hand up!) Pop Hart brought $950; it had sold for $120 in 1953. However, a Ben Shahn watercolor from his series on the Sacco-Vanzetti trial, which had sold for $4000 in 1968, fetched only $4500, probably because it was reoffered too soon after its previous sale.

Many art lovers, whether collectors, speculators or both, have turned to print collecting as a cheaper substitute for the real thing. A print can be any printed picture, but the collector market is largely confined to those that are produced under the artist's supervision. Many come signed, either by hand or in the plate, an embellishment that adds 25–100 percent to a print's value. Print dealers seem an especially cliquey group, and by and large they caution against buying prints for investment—despite the fact that prices have increased dramatically in recent years. Abraham Lublin, now head of a huge print distributorship, recalls that in 1949, when he started selling graphics in the 42nd Street subway station, "you couldn't wrap up a loaf of bread in them and give them away." Today the woodcuts Lublin jokes about fetch $250 each, and his firm's sales exceed $3 million. The print boom really began in the mid-1960s, fueled in part by large-scale entry of contemporary American artists into the print market. Robert Indiana's red, green and blue *LOVE* poster, for instance, now seems to grace every third bachelor-girl apartment in urban America.

But prints have their problems, too. Those of James McNeill Whistler, he of "Mother" fame, may never regain the popularity (and the price tags) they commanded 50 years ago. Prints are also easier to forge than originals, and unless the novice collector has done his homework, he'll have no idea how many of a particular print exist. At Parke-Bernet a Renoir went for just $100—because it was from an edition of 1000. If it were scarcer, of course, it would be much more valuable. Condition is also a factor. The Kennedy Galleries recently showed two Rembrandt prints from the same plate. An early impression, pulled before the soft copper wore down, was offered at $15,000. The other, a much later (and therefore fuzzier) impression, was $4500.

In the world of sculpture Giacometti stick figures regularly sell over $100,000, but Renaissance sculpture, the sort of things William Randolph Hearst was importing to San Simeon, seem highly undervalued. Edward Cave, head of the works-of-art department at Parke-Bernet, suggests this is because there has been scant scholarship in the field. Collectors thus tend to avoid it. Many fine pieces of Renaissance sculpture are now available at around one-tenth what they fetched in the 1920s. Tapestries are a similar case but even more dramatic. Pieces that sold for $10,000 in the gilded era now find no buyers whatever. Museums have all they need, and few private collectors have the space or the inclination to display them.

Fine antique furniture is a work of art in its own right.

Great furniture shows superb workmanship, the artist's eye for form and the craftsman's attention to detail. The French pieces from the golden age of the Kings Louis generally command the highest prices. In this era the development of the medieval guild system, the appearance of exotic woods from newly exploited colonies and the emergence of a taste-conscious and affluent (not to say decadent) aristocracy conspired to produce works of furniture—virtually all of them commissioned to order—that were regarded almost from the day they were made as the quintessential masterpieces of the cabinetmaker's art. (Of course, the 18th Century produced a lot of junk furniture as well; the fine pieces came only from those who had both taste and wealth, and even when new they were far from cheap.) During the French Revolution, when the sans-culottes were burning every vestige of aristocracy that didn't conveniently fit the guillotine, the furnishings from Versailles were carefully set aside, eventually to be auctioned off by the state in what was surely the most dazzling furniture sale in all history. The current record furniture item, incidentally, is a Louis XVI writing table that would have shown up in the Versailles sale had not a Russian princess managed to smuggle it out of Paris at the height of the Revolution. It was purchased by an Iranian oil magnate at Christie's in mid-1971 for $415,800. The previous auction record for a single piece of furniture was only $176,400—for a Louis XVI marquetry commode that *did* come out of Versailles.

According to the *T-S* indexes, fine French furniture increased in value by a factor of five over the last 20 years, though it has only managed to double in the last decade and has recently retreated somewhat. Other 18th Century furniture has done better, increasing sixfold during the 20-year period. English and American pieces have fared less well, increasing by factors of 3 and 3½ respectively, though this lagging start may promise greater increases to come.

American collectors would probably do well confining themselves to the British and American pieces already available here. Fine American works—not your cobbler's benches or thrift-shop bric-a-brac but the quality walnut or mahogany sideboards and highboys crafted in 18th Century Philadelphia or Newport—increase every year. Many of these are as rare—and almost as expensive—as their French counterparts. Recently a Queen Anne armchair from a famous Philadelphia cabinetmaker brought $27,500, at a time when the British pieces from which it had been copied sold for only a few thousand and similar American pieces, not from Philadelphia, could be had for a few hundred. Many observers feel that American Queen Anne pieces are now as fully priced as their French counterparts and thus won't go much higher. Experts at Parke-Bernet note increasing interest in American Federal- and Empire-period furniture, styles that taste makers have so far neglected. Here, at least, the price is right, and good pieces can sometimes be found at prices comparable to the contemporary equivalent.

Among dinnerware and similar items, silver pieces are the most widely collected, because they are both durable (unlike glass or porcelain) and useful. Despite a recent speculative sell-off, British silver ranks premier. Since the days of Chaucer, British goldsmiths and silversmiths have marked their works in a special code (called a *hallmark*) that not only dates each piece but also identifies the maker, thus assuring authenticity and making hallmarked objects more collectable. Eighteenth Century pieces are the most popular, because earlier works are few and derivative and late ones impossibly ornate (though Victorian silver is certainly increasing in popularity, as a successful sale at Sotheby's in 1970 indicated). The 18th Century works were produced in uncomplicated shapes that appeal nowadays, and the number of different styles is limited. Many different examples of any given type survive, which allows collector-investors to follow price changes.

For the last 20 years the T-S indexes show 18th Century English silver up by a factor of 8½, off considerably from the peak two years back, but a good showing nonetheless. Perhaps the silver sale of the decade was held in 1970 at

Sotheby's, in London, when the magnificent collection of Mrs. Charles Plohn, an American, was dispersed. (Ironically, this sale was directly related to the stock-market blowout. Mr. Plohn was a principal in a medium-sized brokerage house, and the proceeds from the missus's silver were direly needed to shore up the firm's finances—a vain effort, as it turned out, since the company folded anyway.) In an extensive review of the sale the *Financial Times,* London, added up the price of 36 of the best pieces (£119,248—about $285,000) and then pored through old auction records to see what Mrs. Plohn had paid for them. The purchases, all made between 1953 and 1961 had cost £39,093—about $86,000. Mrs. Plohn, in other words, had tripled her investment in 12 years—far from the T-S index standard, but a record that her husband's brokerage house would surely have envied.

American silver, such as it is, is a less desirable investment, partly because it only finds a market on these shores. The *sine qua non* of any American silver collection is a piece by Paul Revere. While no better a craftsman than many other colonial silversmiths (most of whom were self-taught and none of whom turned out works anywhere approaching Continental quality), Revere has had, in the venerable personage of Henry Wadsworth Longfellow, the world's most enduring press agent. A silver porringer (easy to mistake for an ashtray) bearing Revere's rectangular logotype would fetch $12,000 today; an identical porringer, just as old and just as well made but lacking the Revere emblem, would bring perhaps $150. Needless to say, such disparities offer rich opportunity for forgery. Even experts can be confused, which is why so many Revere pieces carry a pedigree. Many American collector-investors have recently turned to pewter. American 18th Century pewter is probably as good an investment as silver. It's also lower-priced and (many would say) more attractive.

Chinese porcelain—especially animal and human funerary figures from T'ang-dynasty graves (roughly A.D. 600–900)—is in a class by itself. According to the T-S indexes, T'ang funerary objects have actually increased 60 times in the last 20 years. This is such a staggering multiple that it's best expressed in a real-life example. In 1950 a 28-inch T'ang horse (originally intended to accompany a Chinese aristocrat on his gallop into afterlife) was offered at Sotheby's and failed to meet its reserve price of $120. In retrospect the owner couldn't have been too disappointed. In 1969 a virtually identical figurine sold at Parke-Bernet for $30,000. Perhaps significantly, an earlier boomlet for T'ang figurines boosted prices tenfold during the 1920s. Then it collapsed. And around the turn of the century, 17th and 18th Century oriental porcelains were in vogue. Pieces that then sold for $10,000 are now available for a few hundred.

Overall, oriental porcelain has increased 25 times during the last 20 years, a performance that can't easily be explained. Vastly increased collecting habits by newly wealthy Japanese and nonmainland Chinese is one reason, and the lure of legal difficulties another; smuggling priceless art objects out of Red China has its James Bond elements after all. Most significant, perhaps, is that popular Chinese pieces wear well in a contemporary setting. The glaze and coloring of T'ang porcelain, for instance, is similar to the warm and rather sensuous effect achieved by popular girl sculptor Frank Gallo.

English and American porcelain—the sort of painted statuary figures that decorated turn-of-the-century mantels—have not done so well. Even the best collector items are up only four times. French porcelain actually sells at a much lower level than prevailed 40 years ago.

Coin prices are just now recovering from the aftereffects of an enormous speculative bender that almost destroyed the coin world in the late 1950s and early 1960s. Back then every other American was sifting through pocket change looking for scarce dates and mint marks. The Whitman Publishing Company sold hundreds of thousands of those little blue coin albums. Speculators were "reinvesting" profits even before they were made. Fly-by-night dealers, linked to nationwide teletype "coin exchanges," bought and sold coins by the roll, by the bagful, even by the carload, seemingly unaware that if a coin exists in carload lots, it can never become rare or enduringly valuable.

The Great Koin Kraze (as serious numismatists call it) collapsed under its own weight when a handful of big-time speculators made the tactical error of trying to cash their paper profits. A horde of novice collector-investors shortly thereafter received what numismatists regarded as their very just deserts, and coin collecting returned to the engrossing (and sometimes profitable) hobby that it is.

Serious collectors avoid pocket coins. This is not the stuff of which an interesting collection is made, and coins that have seen circulation are usually scuffed and scarred and thus less desirable. Collectors prefer coins *uncirculated* or even *brilliant uncirculated* (still being original mint luster), a preoccupation that obviously has its counterpart in other collector fields.

The premier item among U.S. coin collectors is the 1804 silver dollar, a piece that has provoked much controversy among coin students, few of whom can agree on why only four examples should exist. One of them sold in 1954 for $8000, resold in 1960 for $28,000 and sold again in 1963 for $36,000. Last year another one—from the archives of the Massachusetts Historical Society, originally from the collection of President John Adams, America's first serious coin collector—fetched a world-record $77,500 at Stack's, New York's biggest coin dealership. The impressive gains scored by this rare item are extreme, but they do suggest something of the uninterrupted price advances that have accrued in genuinely rare coins.

From an investment point of view the interesting thing about coins and stamps is that in most instances they are not unique. Depending on condition, each stamp or coin variety has its own value limits, so that when one example fetches such-and-such a price, a collector will be able to estimate the worth of whatever similar ones he owns. In fact, sales are frequent enough to enable dealers and independent observers to publish price catalogs similar to a used-car dealer's blue book, a periodically revised price guide to enable buyers and sellers to get a feeling of the market.

A long run of these catalogs arms the collector-investor with unique insights into the price performance of stamps and coins. But unfortunately, until very recently, this information was never fully exploited. Now, thanks to a computer study published just a few months ago, we can make hard-fact observations about postage-stamp price trends over the last 20 years. (And, by extension, about price trends in other collector areas.) Using catalog valuations (which don't reflect actual retail prices but do reflect long-term price *changes*), an organization called Mardis Industries International, Bement, Illinois, has studied 2117 collectable U.S. postage stamps—all in unused condition, which investors generally prefer. This total embraces virtually every U.S. stamp, and many different subvarieties, issued up to 1940.

The result, alas, gives the lie to all the ecstatic reportage about rare-stamp prices increasing 10 to 25 percent a year. It also makes one wonder how the other collector investments would stand up under similar high-intensity analysis. The 2100-odd U.S. stamps studied over the 21-year period from 1949 to 1969 increased, on the average, at a rate of 5 percent per annum, compounded. (Over a shorter period, between 1964 and 1969, the performance was somewhat better: 10.5 percent. But this reflects an era of rampant inflation, which if "deflated" by a 4–5 percent loss in dollar purchasing power would also approach 5 percent.)

Those who invest in postage stamps will quickly counter that the 5-percent performance figure is meaningless, since it includes the dawdling performance of loads of common stamps that only fools (and collectors) would buy. True, except that the rare stamps—the very ones that big-time investors favor—haven't done significantly better. The upside-down airmail stamp, for example, one of the most popular stamps among well-heeled philatelic "investors," and an item that garners headlines every time a copy sells for $30,000 or $40,000, increased at a rate of 8.4 percent. Not a bad return, to be sure, but a far cry from the 25 percent we have been reading about.

As it turns out, of all 2117 stamps in the Mardis study, only *one* returned over 15 percent. This particular item, a coil stamp (for vending machines) issued in 1929 to celebrate the 50th anniversary of the light bulb, increased at a rate of 16.2 percent. But it isn't a rare stamp. Almost 134 million were issued, and it now retails for $4. Any investor looking to make significant profits here would have been forced to hold more copies than the market could bear.

Worse, of the entire list, only 39 (counting the light-bulb item) returned 10 percent or more, and of the 39, more than half were what collectors call *government reprints*—sort of nonstamps, many of them not even valid for postage, printed for souvenir seekers at the Centennial Exposition in Philadelphia in 1876. Altogether, only a few thousand of these have survived; they are so scarce as to be all but unobtainable. In a given auction year no more than half a dozen of each will come up for sale. And of the rest of the 10-percent performers, most were so common and so low-priced that anyone who bought them in the quantities needed to justify the investment could never unload without destroying the market. One of the top 19th Century items, for instance, was the two-cent Columbian commemorative, well known to anyone who had a childhood stamp collection. A staggering 1.5 billion copies of this stamp were printed, and unused examples now retail for around $2, up from 40 cents two decades ago.

Even an experienced collector of U.S. stamps, poring over the list of top performers, would be hard pressed to explain why the winners won and why the losers lost. And if after-the-fact explanations could be drawn, no one in his right mind would have believed them 20 years ago, which is when investors should have bought these stamps. We might soon read a news item about an Ohio grandmother who purchased 1000 copies of the light-bulb stamp

40 years ago at the post-office price of $20 and who recently sold them for $4000. But if we do, we must resist the temptation to think she had some unique insight into the stamp-investment world. She was not prescient, just very lucky. And so, too, one must reluctantly conclude, are most of the other "investors" who make windfall fortunes in the collector world.

There are many more collector pursuits than can be discussed in a brief section or even in a not so brief book. We have concentrated on the major ones, paying special attention to fields where investment profit, if far from certain, is at least possible. Before we turn to investment *techniques,* here, in the interest of completeness, are capsule appraisals of a random selection of similar but less important areas.

Oriental rugs, at least those made before 1850 or so, have become an increasingly popular investment, though they have a long way to go to reattain the prices that prevailed in the 1920s. Most of the magnificent royal carpets of yesteryear are already in museums (such as the one that recently slipped out of the Rothschild collection—for $600,000); so collectors content themselves with the distinctive peasant varieties produced by different Arabian towns and tribesmen. Strangely, the U.S. is the primary source of these rugs, which were imported by the boatload around the turn of the century to decorate the mansions of railroad magnates. In comparison with other art areas, price increases have been modest so far (a realization of $200,000 for 21 carpets in a Sotheby sale in late 1969 was reckoned "astonishing" by a rug-trade journal), and collectors feel that prices have nowhere to go but up. Typically, smaller carpets—more portable and more hangable —command proportionately higher prices.

Automobiles: The record auction price for an automobile is currently $59,000 (sold by Parke-Bernet, of course) for a 1936 585C Bugatti, a streamlined coupe of which only three examples exist, but as is true in most collector areas, private sales have probably exceeded the auction record. One classic-car buff has rejected offers of $65,000 and $100,000 for his brace of Duesenbergs. Even Edsels have been quoted at $5000, but no transactions at that level have been recorded. Like Bugattis, Edsels somehow inspire camaraderie; there are two Edsel-owners clubs and a national convention in the offing.

Barbed wire is a recent collector pursuit that supposedly commands 10,000 devotees, mostly in Texas and points west. As is typical in new collector fields, the hobby was given a big boost by the publication of a semischolarly book, *The Wire That Fenced the West*, by Henry D. McCallum (University of Oklahoma Press, 1965). Eighteen-inch barbed-wire strands have reportedly changed hands for as much as $140 each, but at this point barbed-wire collecting is still in the "I'll give you two of this for one of that" stage, which means that it can't yet command serious investor attention. (Stamp collecting, however, was at roughly the same point 100 years ago, and many pioneer collections were subsequently worth fortunes.)

Old weapons have done well in recent years, though it's difficult to credit one widely publicized estimate that values increased 1000 percent in 1970 alone. The high prices that characterized one of the major weaponry sales of the year reflected not so much the market in general as the astonishing quality of the material offered. A matched set of two pistols and a rifle (never fired, of course), with original case and equipment, from the Napoleonic master Nicolas-Noel Boutet, France's greatest gunsmith, fetched $103,320, more than double the previous record. Writing about this sale, *Auction* magazine commented that "the market for fine arms could not be stronger, having seen as rapid development over the last five years as any other field in the art world." (*Auction*, incidentally, while it still betrays its origins as a house organ for Parke-Bernet, is the best single source of information about happenings in the collector-investor world. It's published monthly, from September to June, for $12 a year, at 980 Madison Avenue, New York, N.Y. 10021.)

18. HOW TO COLLECT FOR PROFIT

Most outsiders think that every collector's goal is to assemble a complete collection—of whatever it might be. But as with so many popular impressions, nothing could be less true. A complete collection is actually a collector's nightmare, because nothing more can be collected into it. It is no longer a collection at all but a museum piece. Most collectors instinctively avoid areas where completion is even faintly possible. If wealth and longevity should conspire to bring a collection dangerously close to completion, the collector will marshall every energy to postpone such disaster. Instead of desiring simply one of everything, he will seek the finest example extant or delve deeper into the scholarly arcana of the field in search of correlative or corroborative material or other imperceptible (but highly collectable) trivia. And if all this fails, he will simply lose interest and start a different collection.

That prince of contemporary collectors, Josiah K. Lilly, of Indianapolis, heir to the vast Lilly drug fortune and free all his life to indulge his even vaster collector idiosyncrasies, was once offered, by one of his rare-book scouts, a complete collection of first editions of all the works of every author who had ever won a Nobel Prize in literature. The price was right and the books were in magnificent condition, but Lilly rejected the offer. "A splendid idea," he reportedly told his bookman, "but I'd rather do it myself." Whether Lilly accomplished this noble feat is not known. He died a few years back and left, among many other effects, the finest collection of U.S. gold coins, unused U.S. postage stamps and lead toy soldiers that had ever been assembled. The coin collection, virtually complete, went to the Smithsonian in a special tax transaction whose details have never been revealed. The toy soldiers are still in private hands. The stamps were dispersed at auction and realized over $4 million.

Lilly's stamp collection sold for much more than he paid

to put it together. In other words, he made a profit, albeit a posthumous one. Most great collections turn out to be profitable collections as well—and for good reason. They are assembled by fastidious, knowledgeable collectors who are blessed with patience, discernment and (usually) wealth. People so singularly gifted will invariably put together a collection that will be desired by other collectors when it is dispersed. But the outsider must clearly recognize that such a collection is assembled for love, not for money. Virtually every profitable collection one can name, in any area, was not mounted with an investment end in view. And virtually every collection put together *solely* in the hope of profit has proved unprofitable, usually because the accumulator lacked the intangible elements of knowledge, patience, acquisitiveness and even love that seem to characterize the great collector. Trying to assemble a worthwhile showing of things you're not interested in is like aspiring to be a master chef without having a taste for fine food. It can't be done. Still, for those who feel, lurking somewhere in their vitals, a nascent urge to collect and who wouldn't be averse to the prospect, however remote, of making a little money while they're at it, five separate approaches seem available. A choice among them would be dictated by the collector-investor's personal makeup and by his bankroll. The five approaches, which will be discussed in turn, can be labeled conservative, speculative, expert, synergistic and utilitarian.

The *conservative* approach involves buying acknowledged value in the expectation of continuing appreciation. A contemporary linguistic tragedy is the fall from grace of the word *conservative*. Readers of all political persuasions should note that a conservative investment technique —one that uses the lessons of the past to make reasoned guesses about the future—must never be thought of as benighted, antisocial or unprofitable. In many investments the conservative approach is the most profitable approach. Too often we tend to think that millionaires are conservative because they are rich, without ever considering the equally plausible converse: that they are rich because they are conservative. In the art world the conservative approach would involve buying the ever-diminishing number of "museum pieces" still on the market. These are the finest works of the most important artists throughout history. Currently, major French Impressionists and old masters are most favored. Prices have been rising for generations, and, barring disaster, these increases should continue. In other words, despite the high initial cost, a purchase at current levels is all but certain to show a profit in the future. Rather like betting on a sure thing.

The other collector pursuits all have their museum-piece equivalents. In the rare-book world they're the incunabula (books printed during printing's infancy—the 15th Century), the early editions of the literary giants (Shakespeare's first folios, Dante's first editions) and the earliest American works (*The Bay Psalm Book* or most anything printed in Boston before 1700). In antique furniture the old masters would be the magnificent pre-Revolutionary French pieces. In autographs, the treasured signatures of the historically great: Napoleon, Washington, Lincoln. In silver, the great Georgian coffee and tea services. In stamps, the classic rarities of the 19th Century, often from faraway colonies of the British Empire. In coins, the scarce and lovely gold items, the great pieces of Greek and Roman antiquity, and the rare "common" coins of the U.S.A., such as the 1804 silver dollar. Whoever invests in any of these classic collector treasures can be certain he is not caught up in a passing fad. Old masters such as these bear the imprimatur of generations of collector approval. They are also backed by a long and steady history of price appreciation.

As with conservatively selected stocks or bonds, the old masters of the collector world hold up well in times of stress. In the last few years the inflation that accompanied the Vietnam war turned more and more investors away from paper securities. Many of these newcomers to collecting, unwilling or unable to pay six-figure prices for major French Impressionists (or their equivalent in other areas), settled for second or sometimes third best. The art world witnessed a colossal run-up in the works of "minor Impressionists," of whom the best known are Maurice de Vlaminck and Chaim Soutine. The speculative tidal wave in antique silver surged out of England and swept over both shores of the Atlantic. Even common western-European postage stamps were bid up all out of proportion to their scarcity value. Inevitably bust followed boom. Many items that had doubled, tripled or even quadrupled after 1965 fell back almost as sharply in 1968 and 1969. But the museum pieces in every field held their own or even increased. In the spring of 1970, as the stock market touched a ten-year low, Van Gogh's *Le Cyprès et l'Arbre en Fleurs* fetched an unprecedented $1.3 million, and the penny magenta postage stamp reached its record $280,000. Obviously such old masters aren't cheap. Their gilt-edged investment security is out of reach for all but the wealthy; so the less well-off will have to look elsewhere.

They might want to investigate the *speculative* approach. This technique involves buying relatively inexpensive items in hopes they will become significantly more valuable. Given great timing or great good luck (or both), this can prove enormously profitable. But it's also highly risky and sure to produce many more disasters than successes. And, as we know, only the successes will be publicized. We read about Jasper Johns's *Coat Hanger I*—black-and-white lithographs that sold in 1960 (from an edition of 35) for $75 each and are today worth perhaps $4000 apiece. But we don't hear of the tens of thousands of other prints, equally unarresting, that also sold for $75 in 1960—and are today worth nothing at all. We read how Mickey Mouse watches increased 1250 percent in the last five years (while blue-chip stocks dropped 20 percent), but we don't read about all the other pop/camp garbage that today could not find buyers at any price.

Common seven-cent U.S. airmail stamps, of which almost 100 million were issued ten years ago, now sell for up to $25 a pair. But the vast preponderance of other U.S.

stamps issued at the same time now sell, in quantity, for less than their face value. Anyone who bought 100 copies of each stamp at the post office back then would have nice profits in his airmail but losses in everything else. Moreover, he might well have missed the airmail stamp. It was so common no one bothered to save any. That's why it became scarce.

With a carefully selected subject and enough cash to see a commitment through, the speculative approach offers the intriguing possibility of the collector's affecting the market himself. Cognoscenti of the art-object scene have frequently remarked the breathtaking price increases, in the last decade or so, of ornamental glass paperweights, most of which were produced in the 1840s. *Auction* recently described a "single Clichy convolvulus" (a certain sought-after paperweight type) that sold in 1953 for $216, was resold in 1965 for $1152 and resold again in 1968 for $6120. Such growth is typical for classic paperweights during this period, and much of the increase seems attributable to the robust collecting habits of one man—Arthur Rubloff, the multimillionaire Chicago real-estate developer. Rubloff now owns around 900 classic paperweights (out of a floating supply estimated between 20,000 and 30,000). This is a serious and thoughtfully constructed collection, probably the largest and finest ever assembled. (Even King Farouk, whose name still looms as large as the man himself in the annals of collecting, only had 300 paperweights.) Rubloff, incidentally, would strongly deny anything speculative about his entry into the paperweight world, and he would surely be correct. As is typical, his collection was mounted without thought of profit. In fact, Rubloff views his role in the great paperweight run-up with something close to distaste and insists that his collection will never come onto the market again. Perhaps this is for the best. Rubloff's buying impetus is no longer supporting prices, and they have dropped off somewhat.

Similarly, candid cameraman Allen Funt has sparked a minor revival in the paintings of Sir Lawrence Alma-Tadema—one of those artists, mentioned earlier, who commanded six-figure prices in the 19th Century and subsequently declined to virtually nothing. Alma-Tadema was not only knighted but almost apotheosized during the Victorian era. He produced historical canvases of flawless and soaring mediocrity, works that today evoke the memory of late-show movies and Cecil B. DeMille. Funt, who has the money, is tickled by these paintings (Alma-Tadema called them "opuses") and has managed to pick up perhaps one-tenth of the artist's total output—no mean feat. So Alma-Tademas, which once sold for tens of thousands, now sell for thousands instead of hundreds. But even in 1970 one of the artist's many didactic works, this one engagingly entitled *The Strangling of Galeswinthe at the Orders of Fredegonde*, was knocked down for $96.

While it's rewarding to get in at the ebb point in a new collector wave, the man who speculates in collector's items runs the constant risk of being caught in shifting tides. Andy Warhol's *Campbell Soup Can with Peeling Label*, a battered vegetable-beef version of the pop classics he was selling in the late 1950s for peanuts, fetched $60,000 at auction in 1970—an all-time record auction yield for the work of a living American artist. (Recently broken by Roy Lichtenstein's *Big Painting No. 6*, which realized $75,000.) Surely such canvases speak to the mindless materialism of mid-century America, and presumably they still fire whatever passes for imagination in the Manhattan cocktail-and-communications set. But whether they will prove enduring works of art—or profitable investments—remains to be seen.

In fairness to pop-art fans, the philistines said the same thing to Mrs. Potter Palmer, who during the 1890s was paying outrageous three- and sometimes four-figure sums for the innovative and impressionistic works of a group of youthful Parisian hooligans. The first Impressionists she purchased—four Renoirs, for which she paid a total of $5000—are easily worth millions today, and her entire collection, the nucleus of the dazzling Impressionist showing at the Art Institute of Chicago, represents a fortune almost beyond counting.

Such is the problem that the speculative art buyer—or the speculative buyer of any of the collector investments—must confront. Taste and a good eye are oft-cited prerequisites—but no one knows whose eye is good and whose taste enduring until after the fact. What's exalted in one generation is ridiculed in the next and forgotten by the third, and yesterday's atrocity is tomorrow's masterpiece. In retrospect nothing is easier than saying what should have been bought 20 years ago. It's easy to say, in 1971, that the advent of psychedelia ten years earlier would rekindle an interest in its spiritual ancestor, *art nouveau,* so that the timely purchase of Aubrey Beardsley prints, L. C. Tiffany lampshades and all the other flotsam from this peculiar and fascinating epoch would be richly rewarding. (Tiffany wisteria lamps, available for $100 or so in the 1950s, now command $15,000 to $20,000; Truman Capote, you will be happy to learn, owns *two.*)

It's equally easy to say that the apotheosis of camp—pop and op art—would create demand for its forebears, old comic books and trompe l'oeil paintings, so that a purchase of these, at the proper time, would also prove profitable. And it's just as easy to say that the awakening of black cultural awareness was bound to increase the value of American art and Negro- or slavery-related objects or documents. (A field, incidentally, where prices are a long way from their peak.) These statements are easy to make because they are all made after the fact. But without the advantage of hindsight, who in the world can know? The years of American involvement in Indochina have *not* kindled any new interest in its magnificent Khmer artifacts nor in anything else Indochinese. (A stunning Cambodian head of Buddha dating from the Seventh Century and surely something of a minor masterpiece from the early days of a civilization that was to produce the miracles of Angkor Wat sold for just $175 at Parke-Bernet in 1970). The trend toward much greater sexual freedom has aroused no new longings for the pornographic art and literature of yesteryear. The assassination of President John F. Kennedy sparked no new infatuation (as many history collectors expected) in Lincoln's assassination or Lincolniana—though it did set off a frenzied speculative scramble for Kennedy-related coins, stamps, manuscripts and other mementos, a search that must have culminated, in a way, when a Nashville collector of Kennedyiana purchased the Texas School Book Depository Building at auction for $650,000—because he "just didn't want to see it torn down or turned into something distasteful."

In short, nothing is more fickle than popular taste, and no bet more hazardous than a bet placed on it. Then, too, even if you wager correctly, you may not have the satisfaction of spending your profits. In the middle of the last century, when wealthy American taste makers were paying boxcar figures for the cloying Barbizon canvases you now find over the player piano at plastic Gay Nineties bars, one eccentric collector, James Jackson Jarves, spent a decade in Italy (and $60,000, then a goodly sum) gathering an unbelievably exquisite collection of Italian primitive paintings—madonnas on gold backgrounds and the like—which at that time were universally ignored. Jarves subsequently fell on bad times and found, to his chagrin, that he couldn't sell his collection for one-third its cost. The cultural meccas of Boston and New York rejected his offers outright. Yale University finally took the paintings as collateral on a $20,000 loan. When Jarves defaulted, Yale had to swallow the collection, because no one else wanted it. The paintings—including priceless masterpieces by Gentile da Fabriano, Sassetta and Antonio Pollaiuolo—blushed unseen for 50 years, wasting their sweetness on the dank air of a New Haven warehouse. Thereafter, when their place in art history was acknowledged, Jarves came to be known (posthumously, of course) as a collector of great genius and rare discernment—a man far ahead of his time. Too far ahead for his own good.

The *expert* approach is much less hazardous and can be extremely profitable—if you are an expert. This simply requires an ability to recognize value that has not yet been recognized. Usually a serious collector will be quite knowledgeable in his own field. He certainly should be, for his own protection: The possibility of forgery or other fraud exists wherever collectors are willing to pay high prices for items that can be reproduced cheaply. (A 5000-year-old papyrus in the Stockholm Museum gives detailed instructions for forging gemstones from glass, and as early as the First Century A.D. the poet Phaedrus lamented the flood of phony antiquarian art that was muddying the waters of Augustan Rome. In the late 1960s forgeries cropped up in the relatively innocuous fields of campaign-button collecting, just plain button collecting and liquor-bottle collecting.) If a collector is very serious, or if his specialty is relatively narrow, he can count on knowing more than most dealers. The exigencies of business make dealers carry such a broad spectrum of wares that they can never appreciate the manifold subtleties of this or that item. So the knowledgeable and eagle-eyed collector can sometimes perceive great value where the dealer sees only merchandise. Dealers actually enjoy being "conned" in this fashion. After all, they make a profit on everything they sell. The find will certainly bring the collector back, and the attendant publicity from a major discovery will bring out droves of bargain hunters, most of whom will buy junk at inflated prices.

J. Paul Getty is renowned for his expertise in other areas, but possibly the best investment he ever made was a painting, or, as he describes it, "an unprepossessing canvas . . . in somewhat poor condition," that he purchased for $200 at a London art auction in 1938. It turned out to be Raphael's long-lost *Madonna of Loreto*, worth literally millions today. More recently a suburban Chicago collector of religious prints, attending a rummage sale at a local church, purchased an excessively rare Rembrandt etching—*Jesus Healing the Sick*, worth perhaps $15,000—for a dime. A Pennsylvania woman bought one of the aforementioned T'ang funerary horses at a rural house sale near Wilkes-Barre for $5; she resold it, through Parke-Bernet, for $11,500. And a diligent search through old Philadelphia court records led Alfred Frankenstein, an expert in 19th Century American painting, to two spinster sisters whose home was a minor treasure trove of "lost" paintings and other memorabilia of the great American trompe l'oeil master William Harnett. One of the most important paintings from this find, *Front Face,* a portrait of a Negro child in a soldier suit, realized $67,000 at Parke-Bernet in 1970.

Sometimes the line between expertise and plain dumb luck is very thin. Also at Parke-Bernet, the story is told of a pair of silver-and-crystal candlesticks that sat for decades as an overweight centerpiece on a Long Island dining-room table. No one will know how many hundreds of dinner guests peered around these gray obtrusions to talk to a tablemate. A Manhattan interior decorator finally took a liking to them—after all, they'd make a *stunning* pair of table lamps—and purchased them for a few hundred dollars. Before operating on them, however, he had them appraised at Parke-Bernet, and lucky he did. The set was found to be an exceedingly rare pair of 16th Century Parisian candlesticks, of which only one other pair is known. The find realized $47,000 at auction, highest price paid for a silver item during 1969.

An even more astonishing art discovery involved a hapless New York junk dealer. During the depression, before he became famous, Jackson Pollock, like so many others in every creative endeavor, labored for the Works Progress Administration. Dozens and dozens of Pollock's early realist canvases somehow wound up in a government warehouse in Queens. At the height of World War Two, during an acute shortage of piping insulation, the junk dealer purchased the lot—for 4 cents a pound. He was disappointed to discover that their insulating value was negligible, but he managed to unload them on a Greenwich Village bric-a-brac shop, which in turn retailed them for between $3 and $25. Today these same paintings sell for anywhere between $6000 and $12,000.

The *synergistic* approach is among the least rewarding

financially but highly gratifying in spiritual terms and especially attractive to the interested amateur who has neither a great fortune at his disposal nor a great store of expertise to draw upon. The synergistic approach takes advantage of a quirk of collecting: In many instances, as a collection develops, the whole becomes progressively more valuable than the sum of its parts. Sometimes you don't need many parts. A small yellow envelope bearing a U.S. five-cent stamp from 1847 (the first year the government issued stamps) and socked with a blue oval steamboat cancellation is a lovely collector's item worth $500 or more. A similar envelope from the same correspondence, addressed in the same hand to the same place and bearing the companion ten-cent stamp is even more desirable, worth over $1000. But when the two are gathered together, they comprise a matchless and unique philatelic showpiece. Value? When last auctioned, close to $10,000; perhaps $15,000 today. Similarly, a single Blue Fitzhugh teacup is a quaint curio worth a few dollars. A cup with matching saucer is much more interesting—$50 or so. A matched pair of cups and saucers is quite desirable—$300 at least. And a full service is a pearl beyond price. A Philadelphia dealer actually owns such a set and says only a museum could afford it.

The appeal of this approach to the novice collector-investor is obvious: If you can find one of something, chances are you might someday find another. Magically, both increase in value just by being brought together. Note, however, that the synergistic approach applies only to objects that (for whatever reason) are more desirable grouped than individually. Sixty random Picasso prints are no more valuable en masse than singly. But if each of the 60 is dated a different year between 1911 and 1970, then the owner has a marvelous insight into a great artist's development—as well as an extremely valuable collection, worth many times what its parts would yield separately.

The *utilitarian* approach also provides benefits more spirited than financial, but in addition it offers material comforts of the have-your-cake-and-eat-it-too variety, and it holds a special appeal for relatively youthful newcomers to the collector-investment field. This technique takes advantage of the fact that many pieces of antique furniture (as well as other useful or decorative household items) are just as comfortable and attractive as their latter-day equivalents, no more expensive and decidedly a better investment. Faced with furnishing a new apartment, for instance, a man could easily spend a few thousand dollars on stainless-and-walnut-and-Plexiglas right off the floor at Bloomingdale's. A few years later, when he finally realizes how dreary and tasteless it all is, he'll be lucky to emerge with a decent tax write-off by donating it to the Salvation Army.

The same amount of money would have gone a long way toward purchasing a suite of genuine antiques that, assuming normal wear and tear, would ultimately be resalable at a price very close to its original cost or perhaps even at a profit. Of course, genuine furniture masterpieces are out of the question here. Even given the $100,000 purchase price, no one in his right mind would ever *use* a Philadelphia highboy or a Louis XVI salon chair—least of all in the chaotic and hostile surroundings of a mid-city apartment. But great numbers of antique pieces, in many different styles and eras, sell for prices close to the contemporary equivalent. American furniture from the Federal and Empire periods, for instance, is still available at bargain-basement prices; Federal-period pieces, especially, seem to wear well in a modern decor. At every third antique shop on the eastern seaboard you can buy those comfortable English-country captain's chairs, *circa* 1830 or 1840 (the round-backed type, where back and arms are formed from the same curve), sturdy as the day they were made and glossy with the patina of generations of use, for between $75 and $100. Contemporary reproductions of inferior material, workmanship and design begin at about $80. In London you can still purchase 17th Century coffers, heavy oak chests, usually strapped in leather or metal, the earliest pieces of household furniture that survive, for under $100. Many of these predate the Pilgrims, and all served in the age when everything of value in a typical household could be locked up in one heavy trunk. Besides being starkly beautiful in their own right, these antique pieces work well in any modern surroundings and without desecration can provide first-rate accommodation for tape decks and turntables and similar 20th Century necessities.

The utilitarian approach even works with art, as evidenced by the example of Theodore Pitcairn, an obscure Pennsylvania theologian who vaulted into the headlines in 1968 when he released an item from his long-cherished collection of French Impressionist paintings. The work was Monet's *La Terrasse à Sainte Adresse*. Pitcairn had purchased it for $11,000 in the 1920s and then must have had trouble justifying this eccentricity to his clerical friends. The painting sold at Christie's for $1,411,200, an Impressionist record. After the sale, when eager reporters pressed him to explain his peculiar investment genius, the perplexed reverend thought for a while and finally declared, "I only bought things that I wanted to hang in my house."

Granting the extremity of this example, the technique also applies on a more modest level. The price of a few Keane children and a pink-hatted clown will buy a worthwhile Chagall lithograph or a signed-in-the-plate Picasso print. And out-of-the-way antique shops or even thrift shops will occasionally yield fairly complete settings of Victorian silverware, in ornate patterns that are just now reemerging as popular, for a fraction of the cost of a modern imitation. High Victorian fainting couches and settees—resplendent with hand-carved mahogany cherubim—still can't find homes at $100 each, despite what is supposed to be a renaissance in Victoriana and despite the observable fact that they couldn't be reproduced today at almost any price.

Obviously purchases employing this technique can't be made with a straight investment end in view. Comfort, style and setting must be considered as well. Virtually all low-priced antiques are purchased for use, not for contemplation; so appropriateness, comfort and durability should loom large in the mind of the would-be purchaser, if not for his own satisfaction, then for protection when he sells. The much-heralded Victorian revival, for instance, despite a decade of ballyhoo, has yet to affect the price of Victorian furniture. In years to come the boom in Victoriana might well turn out to be just another journalistic fantasy. In truth, most high Victorian furniture is hideously ugly. The kindest thing to be said about it is that it doesn't wear well in a contemporary setting. Unless you own an unconverted brownstone or are decorating a *fin-de-siècle* brothel, there's almost nothing you can *do* with it. On the other hand, *art nouveau* furnishings—Tiffany floor lamps and vases, for instance, work well in modern surroundings and are already priced accordingly.

If you succeed in finding, say, a set of dining-room chairs—no matter what the style or period—that fit comfortably in modern surroundings and that have the added virtue of being well-wrought antiques, then you can be certain they will be equally appealing and serviceable to others if ever you sell them. If you buy or sell through a dealer, chances are you won't make a profit, and if you do, it will surely be small. (The overhead involved in running an antique dealership is staggering.) But in the interim you will have enjoyed years of use at little cost. Not even the best contemporary furniture—at least for the foreseeable future—can make that statement.

Whichever technique the novice chooses, he'll soon find there are only two major sources of material: dealers and auction houses. As a general rule the newcomer should start out with a dealer, avoiding the auction market until he has attained a bit of expertise. Some dealers are obviously better than others, but instinct and spadework will soon locate one who's *simpatico*. Most all dealers know their field; if they didn't, they wouldn't last in it. Often they have turned to dealership after being collectors themselves. Either their collection or their love of it grew so great as to demand their total energies. Such men will discuss their field knowledgeably and endlessly, delighting in leading the newcomer through its nuances. (Of course, they're developing a good customer in the process.)

Additionally, dealers have their reputations to guard. Collectors are notoriously cliquey. One collector's goodwill can mean three or four new customers. Toward this end, many dealers back their wares unconditionally, forever. Instances abound where dealers have taken back items, even after decades, when they have been found to be other than what they were sold as. Dealers also extend credit—usually interest-free—to favored customers. For anyone more investor than collector, this can be crucially important. Even the expert collector will rarely dispense with dealers' services. First, such a collector would probably number dealers among his closest friends. Then, too, a successful dealer has lines out the world over and good connections with fellow dealers. Once he knows a collector's interests, he'll be able to unearth material that no collector, no matter how dedicated, could hope to locate on his own.

Such services don't come cheap. Especially if the dealer's goods are bulky—furniture or paintings, for example—he will need a costly showroom, usually in a posh neighborhood. Just to break even he's got to mark up his goods considerably. Not a rare-object dealer in the country has a markup per item of less than 50 percent. For slow-moving items, 100 percent—or more—would be typical. Dealers will usually repurchase things they've sold, but unless considerable time has passed or the item has proved extraordinarily popular, the collector shouldn't expect to recoup his original price or anywhere near it.

The desire to avoid the dealer markup attracts collectors to the auction market. Auctions, after all, are where dealers get many of their wares. The collector who buys at auction can expect to save perhaps 50 percent off dealer prices. However, buying at auction is fraught with perils. The need for expertise is great and immediate, since goods cannot be returned unless instantly proved counterfeit. Also, the prospective buyer at auction is never certain he's bidding against real competition. This doesn't faze the collector, but it should the investor. Sometimes an agent of the owner will attempt to bid the price up; other times the auctioneer will be pulling bids off the wall, in an attempt to meet an undisclosed minimum price (called a *reserve*) below which the owner will not sell.

An additional difficulty, and one that is generally not appreciated even by million-dollar art investors, is that speaking strictly from an investment standpoint, the auction market is a poor place to buy blue-ribbon material. Assume a first-class and undeniably authentic Rembrandt painting were to be discovered and offered at auction. The attendant publicity would reach collectors the world over. Every serious potential buyer would be represented at the sale. Bidding would be spirited and high. And the ultimate winner would be forced to pay more than any other informed buyer thinks the painting is worth. That's how auctions work. If the successful bidder is a collector or a museum director, fine—he has his Rembrandt and doesn't care what he paid. But if he is an investor, he finds himself in a difficult position. The people he outbid are the very ones he could reasonably hope to sell to later on—and he's already paid more than they are willing to.

This is why so many big-time art purchases are private transactions, where price is never a matter of record. Auctions are wonderful places to buy items whose value has not been appreciated by others. But strictly from a profit-and-loss point of view, they are not the best way to invest in museum-class pieces, about which everything is already known.

But if all you're interested in is profit, you shouldn't be dabbling in collector's items at all. As money machines, the stock or commodities markets are much more attractive. After all, there are only 50-odd commodities and 1500-odd major stocks. But the universe of rare books, autographs, paintings, prints, antiques and God knows what else contains millions or even billions of collectable items—and no two of them are exactly alike. Only if you are willing to forgo a chunk of the profits (and the losses) that you might run up in the more traditional investment media, and only if you have a genuine desire to collect, should you make the plunge.

However you buy and whatever you buy, you'll be better off both monetarily and spiritually if you know what you're doing. In the collector-investment world perhaps more than anywhere else, knowledge pays rich dividends. No matter what you elect to collect, you'll find, if you look long enough, books, magazines, monographs and other collectors—all good sources of advice. But such advice is just words. Words can be helpful, but not as helpful as an intimacy with the objects themselves, an intimacy that can come only by finding, buying, holding and even loving them. In other words, by collecting them. You'll probably make false starts and surely make bad buys. Maybe good buys, too. But if you select a compatible subject and keep at it, you'll eventually find that you're learning things, that you're enjoying yourself—and perhaps even that you're making some money.

V
The Commodities Market

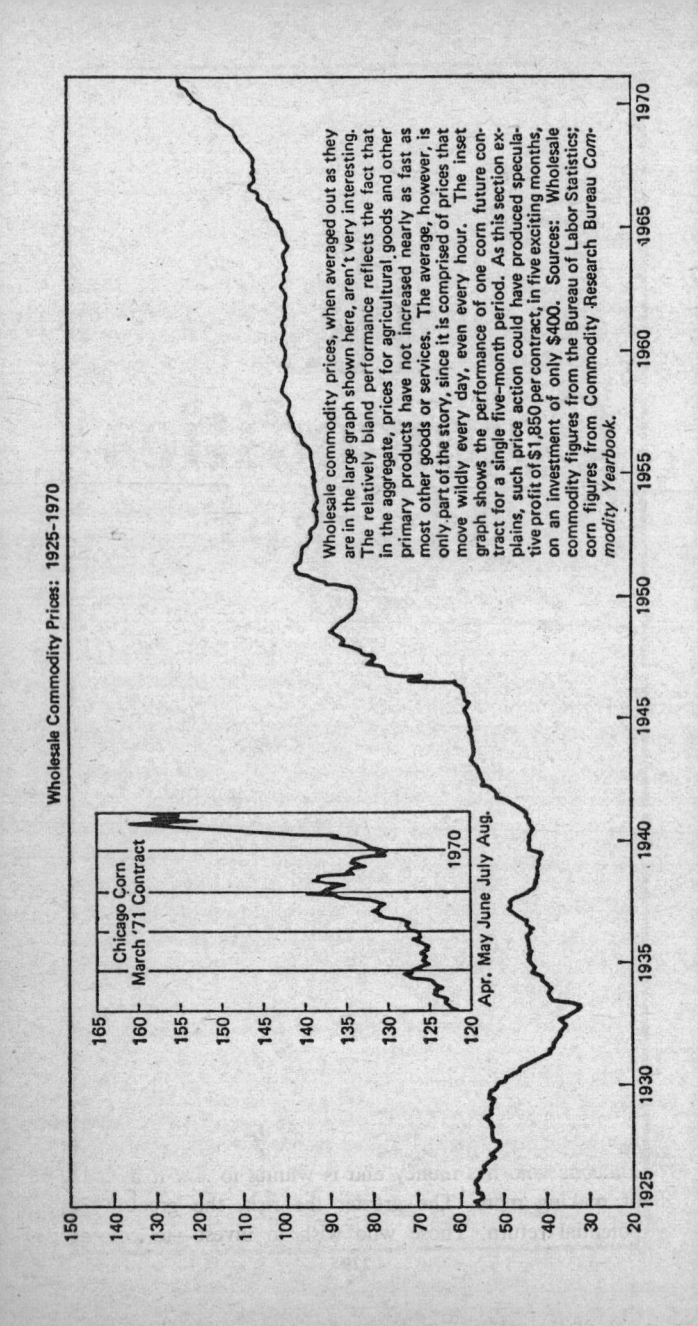

Wholesale Commodity Prices: 1925-1970

Wholesale commodity prices, when averaged out as they are in the large graph shown here, aren't very interesting. The relatively bland performance reflects the fact that in the aggregate, prices for agricultural goods and other primary products have not increased nearly as fast as most other goods or services. The average, however, is only part of the story, since it is comprised of prices that move wildly every day, even every hour. The inset graph shows the performance of one corn future contract for a single five-month period. As this section explains, such price action could have produced speculative profit of $1,850 per contract, in five exciting months, on an investment of only $400. Sources: Wholesale commodity figures from the Bureau of Labor Statistics; corn figures from Commodity Research Bureau *Commodity Yearbook*.

19. PORK BELLIES VERSUS AT&T

Not too many years ago one of the most successful amateur commodity traders in the country, a former psychiatrist, made his speculative debut in spectacular fashion. He gave his broker $5000 with detailed written instructions to buy wheat when the price reached a certain level and to use the profits to buy more at higher levels. Then—to avoid the temptation of changing his mind—he left for Trinidad for five months. When he returned, he had a profit of over $200,000 waiting for him. Perhaps he was psychic—or just lucky. But he did prove—at least in this instance—that novices *can* make a killing in the commodities market.

To the outsider—like our psychiatrist before his happy initiation—no speculative arena in the world appears as formidable as the commodities market. Those small-faced columns of type in the financial pages of the newspaper—replete with months, foodstuffs and indecipherable figures—provoke outright apprehension in even the most intrepid stock-market plunger. This scene, the uninitiated too often conclude, is for big-timers only.

Such an attitude is both unfortunate and mistaken. Those who make a living in commodities—from brokers on up to the governors of the big exchanges—are doing everything they can to dispel it. But myths die hard, and the myth of the big-time grain operator—privy to inside information, ruthlessly crushing small speculators as he makes millions in a few days by buying and selling carloads of a product he'll never see—is as persistent as it is false.

In fact, the commodities market is no more hostile to the small speculator—one cannot in conscience use the word *investor*—than is the stock market. A speculator is someone who has money and is willing to risk it in hope of making more. The greater the risk, the greater the potential return. Those who wish to invest—to commit money at smaller risk in hope of realizing proportionately small profits—probably belong in stocks or mutual funds. But those who wish to speculate—who have the money to risk, the brains to commit this money intelligently and the stamina to see their commitment out—ought to look into commodities.

The notion that commodities trading is exclusively the purview of wizened old veterans and horny-handed farm tycoons is especially unfortunate in that it tends to discourage young men from taking a plunge. Commodities trading is uniquely suited for the relatively young. An unattached young man is far more likely to have $1000 or so to venture in a situation where the potential gain (one-month profits of 100–1000 percent are not unheard of) justifies the risk. He has probably not yet reached that happy plateau from which he must seek the tax shelter of long-term capital gains. (Commodities profits—and losses—usually run up in less than six months. You just add them to your salary and pay regular income taxes on the lot.) And he is far more likely to have the time required to take an intelligent position in commodities and to have the independence and flexibility to see his position through—or to retreat discreetly when the heat is on.

The buying and selling of goods to be delivered in the future—which is what commodity trading is all about—may be as old as commerce itself. The first authenticated instance occurred in 17th Century Japan (where landowners sold receipts for unharvested rice crops), though there is reason to believe that Assyrian wheat growers set up similar deals 3000 years earlier. Regardless of the crop or the era, the basic idea is that prices fluctuate. Prices of agricultural goods—harvested one or two months a year but needed all year round—fluctuate wildly. Before the advent of organized futures trading, grain would sell for almost nothing when it was plentiful (usually right after harvest), then gyrate madly, according to the vagaries of weather, shipping, demand and whatnot. This pleased neither the growers (who often felt they weren't getting a fair price for their crops) nor the processors (who usually had to bid higher and higher for diminishing supplies of grain as the season wore on and faced the risk of colossal inventory losses if prices plummeted). To escape this dilemma, growers began selling contracts for future delivery of goods at current prices. Such future-delivery contracts protected the farmer from losses that might occur if his produce were in oversupply (having already sold the goods, he didn't care what happened to prices after that) and protected the processor from losses he might incur if prices were to increase (having already purchased, he didn't care, either). In time, futures contracts became standardized and negotiable, and speculators leaped eagerly into the middle. If they thought the price of grain was going up, they would buy contracts to receive it, in hope of subsequently reselling the contracts at a profit. If they thought the price was going down, they would contract to deliver grain at current prices, in hope of fulfilling the contract later on at a cheaper rate.

The commodities markets have become more formalized over the years, but the essentials haven't changed. Today anyone with a reasonable credit rating and a modicum of loot (as little as $300 is required on some commodity contracts) can take a plunge. The odds are stacked against winning (three out of four trades lose money, according to the Commodity Exchange Authority), but if you follow a few basic rules, you can be reasonably assured of emerging relatively unscathed—and perhaps even wealthy.

Trading in commodities is no more difficult than trading in stocks. You simply call your broker and tell him what you want done. Obviously you can't contract to receive a freight car full of frozen pork bellies the way you might buy a few shares of Xerox and then sit back and wait for them to appreciate. Sooner or later, depending on how distant your contract, you would face delivery of the goods. At some point this nightmare bedevils all novice commodity traders, but in fact it's not worth lost sleep. Fewer than one percent of all trades involve people who actually have the goods or are willing to take them. The rest are speculators like yourself. Even in the highly unlikely event that you find yourself still holding a contract after the date on which you may receive notice of delivery, there are many ways to extricate yourself.

Since you can't hold commodities for the long pull, they are not—in the classical sense of the word—an investment. They are a speculation—and an exciting one. In many ways commodities better lend themselves to intelligent speculation than do stocks. Above all, commodities provide action—the sort of mercurial price movement that dilates the speculative veins and lets the adrenaline gush through unobstructed. Most novice commodity players (and a good many pros) are former stock watchers who got bored waiting weeks or even months for their investments to *do* something. A decently followed commodity can compress a year's stock-market action into one glorious afternoon. As a successful young silver trader puts it: "I figure I can make money in any market so long as prices are fluctuating. The more the fluctuation, the better my chances. For me commodities are ideal."

Moreover, the commodities market is simpler than the stock market. Since there aren't nearly as many commodities as there are stocks (active futures trading is confined to fewer than 25 basic products), in selecting your trade you do not have to sift through such a wealth of data. A stock trader, for instance, might be reasonably certain of the general direction of the Dow-Jones industrial stock average, but unless he buys all 30 stocks that comprise that average figure, he can't cash in on his knowledge. No matter how good his awareness of the general trend in stocks, he still finds himself frustrated by crosscurrents in individual stocks among the 1500-plus now traded on the New York Stock Exchange alone. The individual stock represents such a small fraction of the market that it can easily move against the trend—either through sheer perverseness or through back-room manipulation.

In commodities each stock is a market in itself. Once you understand wheat, you don't have to go on to understand an individual stock; you already do. Since there are only two dozen commodities of any real significance, it's at least possible (though not recommended) to keep an eye on all of them at once. While specialized, the markets in individual commodities are hardly small. One day's transactions in wheat or corn alone will often exceed, in dollar volume, a whole day's trading—in all stocks—on the New York Stock Exchange. As an example, on one hectic day in late 1970, 193 million bushels of corn—worth close to $300 million—changed hands. The total value of New York Stock Exchange trades that day was $200 million.

Given such volume, it's understandable that commodity orders can be executed much more rapidly and in much larger numbers than stock orders, which means you can buy and sell relatively large quantities without adversely affecting the price structure. And since all commodity prices are established, in the various exchanges, at open *outcry* (analogous to a public auction), there's less likelihood of getting an order filled at an unfavorable price—as happens all too often in the stock market, where prices are established not at auction but through specialists who supposedly moderate price swings, but who have more than once been accused of doing just the opposite.

In commodities the margin—that percentage of the purchase price you must put up to make a purchase—is breathtakingly low, as little as 5 percent, compared with 65 percent currently for stocks. This means you get tremendous leverage: At a 5-percent margin rate you can buy $10,000 worth of grain for $500. If the price goes up just 10 percent (as it often does in a matter of weeks), you make $1000—a 200-percent return. Of course, you can lose that much just as quickly.

If margins are low, commissions are even lower. Stock-market commissions, as we have seen, are extracted from both sides of the transaction. You pay one commission to get in and another to get out. This is because many people buy stocks and hold them forever. You can't do that in commodities; so one commission pays for both sides of the transaction. The lordly sum of $45, for instance, will get you in and subsequently out of a 10,000-ounce silver contract whose cash value usually exceeds $15,000. Your margin requirement would be $1000. A comparable stock transaction, buying and subsequently selling 300 shares of a $50 stock, would require a margin of $9750 and run up commissions well over $400. The commodity speculator, in other words, has a 10-to-1 advantage over the stock speculator, both in terms of the commissions he pays and the leverage he enjoys.

Considering all this leverage, it's ironic that commodities are actually a *safer* investment than stocks in several important respects. First, the bookkeeping aspects of commodities trading are highly automated. There are no certificates to keep track of, no contracts to sign, in fact, hardly any paper work to speak of. The chance of broker back-room foul-up is minimal. More important, the commodity speculator is well protected if his brokerage house suddenly collapses. This was always thought to be a remote possibility—until mid-1970, when half a dozen brokerage firms went bankrupt and thousands of investors found that stocks the houses were holding for them—certificates the investors had always assumed were inviolably theirs— were actually tied up in the firms' liquidation.

As these words are written, almost a year later, the mess still hasn't been cleaned up. Yet, as far as can be known, not a single commodity speculator lost so much as a cent through brokerage failure, the reason being that the Commodity Exchange Authority, which regulates about three-fourths of all commodities trading, is a much sterner overseer than its stock-market sister, the Securities and Exchange Commission. The SEC has long pushed the stock market toward a policy of "self-regulation"—a bureaucratic euphemism for no regulation whatever. The CEA is less naïve. Among other things it insists that money in regulated commodity accounts be rigidly segregated from the broker's house funds. If the firm comes tumbling down, commodity speculators aren't affected. Had the SEC seen fit to enforce a similar policy, many shell-shocked stock speculators would be a lot fatter today.

Perhaps not surprisingly, given these many virtues, the volume of commodity trading has increased more than fourfold since the late 1950s. In the U.S. today, futures trading actually takes place in more than 50 commodities, but only about half of these are of any real interest to the speculator. They divide into four basic categories. *Grains* include barley, corn, flaxseed, oats, rye, wheat and—even though they're not a grain—soybeans and soybean by-products. Most grain trades take place in Chicago, on the mammoth Chicago Board of Trade, where almost 60 percent of all commodity transactions occur. You can also buy various grains in Minneapolis, Kansas City and Winnipeg. *Animal products* include live cattle and hogs, iced broilers (whence comes the Kentucky Colonel's fried chicken), fresh eggs and frozen pork bellies (from which bacon is sliced). Except for the broilers, all these are sold on the Chicago Mercantile Exchange, feisty and volatile competitor of the Board of Trade. Through jazzy advertising, among other things, the "Merc" has recently transformed itself into an important factor in the commodities business, accounting in 1970 for one-third of all transactions. *Metals* include copper, platinum and silver, sold on various smaller exchanges in New York, though silver is now also traded in Chicago. The rest, mostly plant products, includes cocoa, cotton, frozen concentrated orange juice, lumber, potatoes, plywood and sugar. (For technical information on the speculative aspects of all these commodities, consult the chart on pages 236–37.)

Prices are generally recorded in cents per unit—bushel, pound, ounce or whatever lowest selling unit the commodity best suggests. A newspaper price of "173½" for Chicago December wheat, for example, means that wheat for delivery in Chicago next December is now selling at $1.73½ a bushel; "167.50" for July silver means that silver deliverable next July in New York is selling at 167.5 cents per troy ounce—$1.675, if you will. A price of "27.01" for March 1973 cocoa means that cocoa beans for delivery in New York during that month are now selling at 27.01 cents a pound. Financial papers usually

THE MOST ACTIVE COMMODITIES (contracts, commissions and prices)

COMMODITY	NAME OF EXCHANGE / TRADING HOURS (E.S.T.) MONDAY THROUGH FRIDAY	SIZE OF SINGLE CONTRACT	MARGIN RATE — amount you must put up initially to secure a single contract	MARGIN RATE — if your margin shrinks to this, you must make up the loss	COMMISSION minimum brok'r'ge for both purchase and sale of contract, deducted after you're out	MINIMUM FLUCTUATION smallest increment of price change — PER UNIT	MINIMUM FLUCTUATION — PER CONTRACT	MAXIMUM DAILY MOVE maximum permissible price move above or below previous day's closing; ordinarily, this is the most you can make or lose in a single day — PER UNIT	MAXIMUM DAILY MOVE — PER CONTRACT
BROILERS (ICED)	Chicago Board of Trade 10:15 A.M.-2:05 P.M.	25,000 lbs.	$300	$200	$25	.025¢	$6.25	2¢ per lb.	$500
LIVE CATTLE	Chicago Mercantile Exchange 10:05 A.M.-1:40 P.M.	40,000 lbs.	$600	$400	$36	.025¢	$10	1¢ per lb.	$400
COCOA	New York Cocoa Exchange 10 A.M.-3 P.M.	30,000 lbs.	$1000	$700	$50 + $70	.01¢	$3	1¢ per lb.	$300
COPPER	Commodity Exchange Inc. (N.Y.) 9:45 A.M.-2:10 P.M.	50,000 lbs.	$1500-$2000	$1125-$1500	$50 + $1.50 exchange fee	.05¢	$25	2¢ per lb.	$1000
COTTON (#2)	New York Cotton Exchange 10:30 A.M.-3:30 P.M.	100 bales (50,000 lbs.)	$500-$750	$250-$500	$45-$55	.01¢	$5	2¢ per lb.	$1000
EGGS (FRESH)	Chicago Mercantile Exchange 10:15 A.M.-1:45 P.M.	600 cases (18,000 dozen)	$500	$300	$36	.05¢ per dozen	$9	2¢ per dozen	$360
CHICAGO GRAINS: WHEAT, CORN, OATS, RYE, SOYBEANS	Chicago Board of Trade 10:30 A.M.-2:15 P.M.	5000 bushels	corn: $400 oats: $250 soybeans: $600 rye: $500 wheat: $350	corn: $250 oats: $150 soybeans: $500 rye: $300 wheat: $400	oats: $18 wheat, corn and rye: $22 soybeans: $24	.125¢	$6.25	rye, soybeans and wheat: 10¢ per bushel	rye, soybeans and wheat: $500 corn: $400 oats: $300
MINNEAPOLIS WHEAT	Minneapolis Grain Exchange 10:30 A.M.-2:15 P.M.	5000 bushels			$22 for all grains except oats ($18)	.125¢	$6.25	10¢ per bushel	$500
KANSAS CITY WHEAT	Kansas City Board of Trade 10:30 A.M.-2:15 P.M.	5000 Bushels			$22	.125¢	$6.25	8¢ per bushel	$400
								6¢ per bushel	$300
WINNIPEG GRAINS: BARLEY, FLAX, RYE	Winnipeg Grain Exchange 10:30 A.M.-2:15 P.M. (All prices in Canadian currency)	5000 bushels flax: 1000 bushels	barley: $350 flax: $200 rye: $500	barley: $200 flax: $100 rye: $250	barley and rye: $20 flax: $5	.125¢	barley and rye: $6.25 flax: $1.25	rye and barley: 10¢ per bushel flax: 15¢ per bushel	rye and barley: $500 flax: $150
HOGS (LIVE)	Chicago Mercantile Exchange 10:20 A.M.-1:50 P.M.	30,000 lbs.	$400	$300	$30	.025¢	$7.50	1 1/2¢ per lb.	$450
LUMBER (2 x 4s)	Chicago Mercantile Exchange 10:45 A.M.-2:15 P.M.	40,000 ft.	$200	$100	$30	.025¢	$10	.075¢ per ft.	$300

THE MOST ACTIVE COMMODITIES (contracts, commissions and prices)

COMMODITY	NAME OF EXCHANGE TRADING HOURS (e.s.t.) MONDAY THROUGH FRIDAY	SIZE OF SINGLE CONTRACT	MARGIN RATE — amount you must put up initially to secure a single contract	MARGIN RATE — if your margin shrinks to this, you must make up the loss	COMMISSION minimum brokerage for both purchase and sale of contract, deducted after you're out	MINIMUM FLUCTUATION smallest increment of price change — PER UNIT	MINIMUM FLUCTUATION — PER CONTRACT	MAXIMUM DAILY MOVE maximum permissible price move above or below previous day's closing—ordinarily, this is the most you can make or lose in a single day — PER UNIT	MAXIMUM DAILY MOVE — PER CONTRACT
ORANGE JUICE (FROZEN CONCENTRATED)	New York Cotton Exchange 10:15 A.M.-2:45 P.M.	15,000 lbs.	$600	$450	$45	.05¢	$7.50	3¢ per lb.	$450
PLATINUM	New York Mercantile Exchange 9:45 A.M.-1:00 P.M.	50 ounces	$600	$420	$45 + $2 clearing fee	10¢	$5	$10 per oz.	$500
PLYWOOD	Chicago Board of Trade 11:00 A.M.-2:00 P.M.	carload (69,120 sq. ft.)	$500	$300	$30	.01¢	$6.91	7¢ per sq. ft.	$484
PORK BELLIES (FROZEN)	Chicago Mercantile Exchange 10:30 A.M.-2:00 P.M.	36,000 lbs.	$900	$600	$36	.0025¢	$9	1 1/2¢ per lb.	$540
POTATOES — IDAHO	Chicago Mercantile Exchange 10:00 A.M.-1:50 P.M.	50,000 lbs.	$300	$200	$25	.01¢	$5	.35¢ per lb.	$175
POTATOES — MAINE	New York Mercantile Exchange 10:00 A.M.-2:00 P.M.		$200-$300	$140-$210					
SILVER — CHICAGO	Chicago Board of Trade 10 A.M.-2:25 P.M.	5,000 oz.	$750	$500	$30	.1¢	$5	10¢ per oz.	$500
SILVER — NEW YORK	Commodity Exchange, Inc. (N.Y.) 10 A.M.-2:15 P.M.	10,000 oz.	$1500	$1125	$45	.1¢	$10		$1000
SOYBEAN MEAL	Chicago Board of Trade 10:30 A.M.-2:15 P.M.	100 tons	$400	$250	$30	5¢ per ton	$5	$5 per ton	$500
CRUDE SOYBEAN OIL	Chicago Board of Trade 10:30 A.M.-2:15 P.M.	60,000 lbs.	$400	$250	$30	.01¢	$6	1¢ per lb.	$600
SUGAR #11 (RAW) WORLD MARKET	New York Coffee & Sugar Exchange 10 A.M.-3 P.M.	50 long tons (112,000 lbs.)	$400	$200	$15-$30	.01¢	$11.20	1/2¢ per lb.	$560

Maximum permissible daily price moves usually change during final month of contract. Margin rates are typical, but can vary among brokerage houses. Most houses offer special rates for "straddles" and one-day trades. Information was believed accurate at presstime, but may change. See your broker.

record the opening price, the high for the day, the low for the day, the closing price and the change the closing price represents over the previous day's close. Looking at the newspaper listings, you will see that futures contracts are not sold for every month. Usually there are six contract months in a year, sometimes fewer or more, depending on harvest patterns and producer needs. From time to time the exchanges will add a new contract month or eliminate one in which trading is no longer active.

The exchanges themselves are simply places where buyers' and sellers' representatives gather to conduct their business. Most exchanges have both the allure and the acoustics of a high-school gymnasium. Trades are accomplished through those traditional bulwarks of the free market: hand waving, shouting and jumping up and down. These activities are wisely confined to small arenas comprised of concentric octagonal rings. Because of their kinship to the holes in the ground in which commodities were first traded, the arenas are still called *pits*.

20. TRADING TECHNIQUES

Selecting your commitment—and doing the study required to make it a good one—is, of course, the most difficult part of the game. Decidedly the easiest way to learn about a commodity is to take a position in it. It is astonishing how interested you will become in Chicago July wheat once you have contracted to receive 20,000 bushels of it. The weather in Kansas, ice floes in the St. Lawrence, the Food for Peace program, bumper crops in Australia, drought in India, turmoil in China—all these take on an intimately personal relevance when hard cash is at stake. While this is the easiest way to learn about commodities, it is also the costliest. In commodities, as in stocks or anything else, investigation should precede investment.

Ideally, the novice who plans to go into commodities should spend weeks—even months—getting the feel of the action before he makes his first trade. If he has some prior experience in stocks, he already knows the value of the *Wall Street Journal*—which is certainly the finest financial newspaper published in the U.S. today and whose front page alone often contains more significant news than can be found in most big-city dailies. While the *Journal* will provide a broad and easily digestible picture of world events and their relation to business and the marketplace, its commodity coverage is regrettably sketchy. For this reason virtually all serious commodity traders also read the *Journal of Commerce*, a daily newspaper published at 99 Wall Street. Half of the *JC* is devoted to shipping ads of little consequence to anyone except exporters and smugglers, but the rest is made up of commodity news and penetrating economic reportage.

A wealth of commodity "advisory services"—literally hundreds of them—publish weekly newsletters telling you how you can double or triple your money in a dazzlingly short time. The old counter "If they're so smart, why aren't they rich?" might apply here, except that in commodities there's a legitimate answer. So much of successful commodity trading depends on self-discipline that it's quite reasonable to encounter veteran traders who, like Alice, dispense very good advice—but can't follow it themselves. Doubtless some of these have fallen into the advisory game. In the aggregate, however, the services make many more losing recommendations than winning ones, which makes them no better than individual speculators, who do likewise. A good service will at least provide information you can't secure elsewhere, and this alone, recommendations aside, might be worth the price of admission—which is rather steep, often running up to $150 a year. Most services offer a free sample newsletter or a month's subscription for a few dollars; so little is lost in trying them. There are so many, viewing the commodities market from such varying angles, that perhaps you'll find one that works for you.

Once you've familiarized yourself with the functioning of the market, you can begin trying to outguess it. As in the stock market, there are two basic methods of determining how commodity prices will move: fundamental analysis and technical analysis. The two are certainly not mutually exclusive, but in commodities the most rabid proponents of each tend to divide, for reasons unknown, into hostile camps. (A much more detailed examination of both techniques is included in chapter 2.)

In commodities fundamental analysis is very straightforward. Its assumption is that once you understand all the supply-and-demand factors at work—the fundamentals—you will know which way the price of a commodity will move. Relying mainly on the reams of data emanating daily from such sources as the Department of Agriculture, fundamentalists compute the potential supply for the year (adding imports, exports and leftovers from previous years) and weigh this figure against what they think the demand will be. Then, bearing in mind seasonal price patterns that tend to repeat themselves in most agricultural commodities and even in some nonagricultural ones, they compare the current price with prices in previous similar years. All this supposedly tells what the current price will do—and often enough it does. Government price supports—and government-owned surpluses—muddy the waters somewhat in corn, cotton, oats, rye, soybeans and wheat (to name a few), but less and less so as world shortages mount and farm surpluses disappear. Except in cotton, in fact, there are no more surpluses to speak of.

Since they have their eyes on the facts, fundamental traders can sometimes profit from special situations. Anyone who read the newspapers in early 1967—or who examined the coins in his pocket—could have sensed that the Treasury was running out of silver. Ultimately the government would have to stop selling it to all comers at $1.29 an ounce. This finally happened on May 18—and in the next ten days or so silver rose more than 30 cents an ounce. A speculator farsighted enough to buy one 10,000-ounce silver contract just prior to May 18 would have seen a $700 investment grow to more than $3500 in one exciting fortnight.

In commodities, as in stocks, the great advantage of trading on the basis of the fundamentals is that the investor need not watch day-to-day price movements. Fundamental analysis unearths long-range price trends. If in your heart you know you're right, you can just wait it out. This was precisely the course followed by our psychiatrist friend who parlayed $5000 into $200,000 while basking in Trinidad. He had deliberately repaired to a village lacking telephones and newspapers. "I couldn't have sweated it out if I had to watch the prices every day," he says. "I would have sold out too soon or perhaps overpyramided and been wiped out on a minor setback." The fact that wheat moved up almost a dollar a bushel in his absence didn't hurt, either, and testifies to his sound assessment of the fundamentals. Of course, had he been wrong, he would have lost most of his $5000.

An even more dramatic situation involved Ed Wilson, a Chicagoan who makes his living speculating in commodities. Wilson graduated from Harvard in 1950, bought a seat on the Chicago Board of Trade in 1952 (seat owners pay very low commissions) and has been knocking down a six-figure income with some regularity ever since. According to a *Wall Street Journal* account, Wilson took off for Europe in the summer of 1968—leaving his name on contracts to deliver one million bushels of wheat. "People thought I was crazy to go away with that big a position," Wilson says, "but I was certain that there was such a glut on the world wheat market that the price had to head down."

However, on shipboard he got cold feet and tried frantically—and unsuccessfully—to reach Chicago by ship-to-shore phone. When the ship finally docked in England, Wilson scrambled off to a telephone—only to learn that his fundamental analysis had been correct. He ultimately covered his contract obligation with a 25-cents-per-bushel profit—$250,000.

Like their stock-market counterparts, technical analysts in commodities avoid the fundamentals wherever possible. They reason that since *all* factors affecting the market are reflected in the market's price movement, the best way to locate the trend is to study the price movement itself, through charts. The most popular is eloquently called a *vertical line chart* (opposite). On the chartist's graph paper, price is read from the horizontal lines (usually in eighths of a cent), and each vertical line represents a trading day. Every evening the chartist draws a line between the day's highest and lowest prices and then, for good measure, adds a dash to indicate the closing price. If the chartist reads his drawings correctly, so the theory goes, the market, reflecting all the fundamentals, will itself tell him what it is going to do.

This is a beautiful theory, because it obviates the depressing prospect of having to read magazines such as *Feedstuffs* and *Hampshire Herdsman*. The true technical analyst does not want his mind violated by a single fundamental. He reasons that any news he might hear would prejudice his reading of the charts, which already reflect the news.

CHICAGO CORN
September 1967 contract

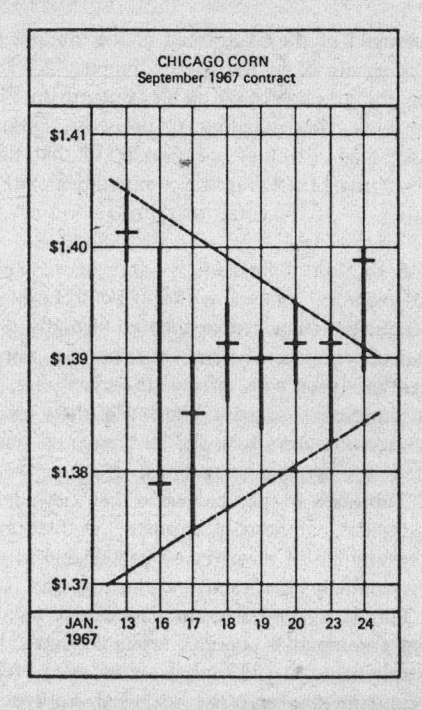

Chart trading seems to work especially well in commodities, perhaps because price movements are so volatile that they telegraph lots of signals to the man who is listening. Consider the triangle in the chart shown. This is a rather common formation, analagous to the stock-market formation illustrated on page 32. In the corn instance shown here, the progressively narrowing price range indicates that all potential buyers and sellers have gradually been cleaned out of the triangle area. When the price *does* move beyond the bounds of the triangle, it can be expected to break sharply above or below the base lines—since there are presumably no buyers and sellers left inside. Chart traders look for such formations (there are dozens of different types, of relative degrees of certitude), and when the price breaks out, they will buy or sell, depending on their assessment of the basic trend of the market. In fact, after breaking out of its triangle on January 24, the corn plotted on the graph scooted all the way up to $1.42. If you still think chart trading is properly classed with necromancy and astrology, bear in mind that there are thousands of chart traders in the commodities market each day; so they often force the market to conform to their charts.

One of the most interesting—and least explored—aspects of technical analysis is that chart techniques seem to work equally well when applied to virtually *any* non-mathematical sequence of numbers. You can plot flips of a coin, red and black wins in roulette—even pure, random numbers. In each case your chart will show marketlike action: congestion areas followed by breakouts, line trends punctuated by "typical" reactions, even an occasional "panic." This leads to the conclusion that the judgment of the marketplace, supposedly a precise evaluation of the considered opinion of a universe of intelligent buyers and sellers, is actually governed by the vagaries of sheer chance. This is a very pleasant and democratic way of looking at commodities. Besides explaining what is otherwise unexplainable, it gives everyone an even break.

The fundamental and the technical approaches are strikingly different. The results one can expect to obtain from each are just as dissimilar. Generally the fundamental trader will catch larger price moves, because he will hit them closer to the extremes and ride them further. Chester Keltner, a fine fundamental grain trader who lives in Kansas City (and publishes an advisory letter there), once took a profit of 85¾ cents a bushel in a single position in Chicago May wheat—about a $4300 profit on each contract (then selling at $500). He himself admits he never could have made such a profit had he been technically inclined, because the charts would have told him to sell prematurely.

The drawback is that the fundamentalist must be able to stand large losses. Because he doesn't follow the daily market trend, he may make his move too early. And no matter how sound his assessment, he may have to sweat through disastrously unfavorable action—losing literally thousands in the process—before the market finally vindicates him. Unless he has real confidence in his plan—and the cash to back it up—the market may do him in.

If he plans his trades correctly, the technician never faces the prospect of huge losses. When he decides the market is going to move, he gets in. If he's right, well and good. If the market goes against him, he gets out immediately, at a small loss. The big danger he faces is not in many small losses (which one reasonable profit will more than cover) but in taking his profits too quickly. Attuned to every market move, the technician tends to see each minor setback—which wouldn't perturb the implacable fundamentalist—as heralding a larger sell-off.

Working for the technician, however, is his utter disregard for value. Thomas Lodge's maxim ("Buy cheap and sell dear") is anathema to the chartist. Since he follows the price trend, he much prefers to buy dear and sell dearer or sell cheap and buy back cheaper. A successful chart trader—in the course of a few weeks—might buy soybeans at $2.16 a bushel, sell them on a minor reversal at $2.19, buy in again at $2.22, sell out when the market hesitates at $2.26, then buy back again at $2.30 and ride it up to $2.34. This sort of jockeying strikes terror in the soul of the fundamentalist—who usually finds it difficult, once he has sold out of a position, to buy back into it at a higher price—but as long as the technician's method works, and it oftentimes does, his fundamental cousin can't criticize too loudly.

A very reasonable commodity-trading method would be to combine the best aspects of both techniques. This would involve using the fundamentals to locate potential long-range price moves and then using charts to limit losses by determining the precise time and place to make the trade. Unfortunately the two techniques appeal to such different personalities that the investor would have to approach schizophrenia to master them simultaneously.

Somewhere in the nether world between the fundamental and technical approaches lie the mechanical trading rules. These attempt, by precise mathematical means, to provide infallible guides to profitable trading. Most of them have no merit at all, but some, especially those that try to take advantage of price trend, are worth considering. Most trend rules try to formulize what the chartist does instinctively. The rules determine which way prices are going and point out places to buy and sell. Most of these are too complicated to consider here, but if you are seriously interested in them, you should refer to Keltner's *How to Make Money in Commodities,* which treats several of them extensively—including one that would have produced profits in nine out of ten years (1950–59) in soybeans, for a total net gain of $21,354 on a $1000 margin account. Keltner wisely points out that such rules can also rack up a distressingly large number of small losses. What proved a golden rule in soybeans, for instance, once produced 13 consecutive losses in wheat—in less than three months. During this debilitating setback, most traders would probably have thrown the rule out the window and perhaps jumped out after it—no doubt just when a hefty profit was imminent. Trading mechanically takes money, but it also takes stamina, reserves of which are often thinner than one's billfold.

The one man most intimately associated with mechanical trading rules is Richard D. Donchian, a commodity analyst who was formerly the head of commodity research for the brokerage house of Hayden, Stone. Unfortunately this was one of the firms that almost disappeared during the 1969–70 stock-market collapse, surely no fault of Donchian's, whose weekly reports are without peer. Many of Donchian's rules are based on what are called *moving averages,* and the results are impressive. Donchian's "20 and 5-day moving average method," applied across the board since the beginning of 1961, with positions limited to one contract per commodity and no profits reinvested, showed profits up through 1969 of $46,741 on an average investment of less than $15,000. This technique, unfortunately, involved speculators in a great number of transactions each year, satisfying the cravings of the action-hungry but running up a fortune in commissions. The rule left the speculator vulnerable to what in the trade is known as *whipsawing*—being forced in and out of a commodity, each time at a loss, by progressively widening price swings. But it proved profitable in seven of the nine years tested.

Another of Donchian's techniques—a childishly simple device called the "four-week rule"—was recently discovered to rank premier among a dozen widely followed mechanical techniques. This rule is simplicity personified: (1) Buy whenever the price exceeds the high of the four preceding calendar weeks. (2) Sell whenever the price goes below the low of the four previous weeks. (3) Get out on the last day of the month before the contract expires.

The superiority of the four-week rule was determined by a massive computer study of the overall effectiveness of all the most popular mechanical trading techniques. Over the six-year period surveyed (1963–68), the best commodities to trade with this rule turned out to be copper, sugar, soybean oil, wheat and pork bellies, in that order. Incredibly, counting commission costs, the four-week rule produced profits in these five commodities averaging 265 percent a year. In other words, using this rule in these five commodities, the speculator—at least during the period of the study—would have almost tripled his money *every year*. A $1000 initial investment would have grown to close to $350,000 in six years. Interestingly, the rule produced substantially more losing trades than winning ones, even though the winners obviously made a good bit more than the losers lost. The computer study, which includes the rules, as well as the test results, for 12 popular mechanical trading devices, is part of a continuing project of Dunn and Hargitt's Financial Services, Box 101, Lafayette, Indiana 47902—worth an inquiry if you're so inclined.

There are also trading rules—if rules they can be called—that are fundamentally oriented in that they try to capitalize on seasonal price swings. A well-known story tells how a successful grain trader's "secret" was found, after his death, among his effects. The secret (according to Gerald Gold's *Modern Commodities Futures Trading*) was simply a scrap of paper on which was written:

	Buy	Sell
WHEAT		January 10
	February 22	
		May 20
	July 1	
		September 10
	November 28	
CORN	March 1	
		May 20
	June 25	
		August 10

This "system" is now known as "the voice from the tomb," and according to Gold, some traders still regard the dates as important signposts—perhaps with good reason, since year in and year out this cryptic tip seems to generate more profits than losses.

21. CONTROLLING YOUR BROKER

All of the caveats about stockbrokers apply to commodity brokers as well, only more so. Unhappily, any stockbroker is legally qualified to handle commodity transactions (and thus dispense commodity advice) despite the fact that not one stockbroker in a hundred would recognize a frozen pork belly if he ran one down on the expressway. Many stockbrokers turned reluctantly toward commodities in 1969 and 1970 solely as a means of surviving the long, bad stock market. But a speculator who chooses to specialize in commodities will want to find a stockbroker who does likewise, and here the pickings aren't easy. It's a sad but certain fact that all too many commodity brokers are themselves washed-out commodity traders. Having run through their personal fortunes, they find themselves reduced to running through the fortunes of others. Their presence underscores the element of compulsion—even addiction—still associated with the seamier side of commodity trading. Frank Norris had noticed this as far back as 1903, when he published *The Pit,* a novel whose quaint Victorianism clashes charmingly with its exploration of the gritty mechanics of a wheat corner. Even in Norris's time, unstable elements among the relatively well-to-do were drawn to commodities with the same insistence that their cousins among the relatively poor are drawn to the horses. It may take years for a facile incompetent to run through a fortune in commodities. But having done so, and presumably having learned something (though manifestly not enough) in the process, he has little recourse but to become a broker. Perhaps he will become a good one—though there is small evidence that his inability to handle his own money qualifies him in handling that of others. A good broker, one who can consistently take money out of the pit, will not long remain a broker. Why should he? Why should he sit in a boardroom day after day staring at figures and answering hate calls from disappointed customers when he could instead be making money for his personal account?

Many of the successful young men in commodities—brokers or otherwise—view with suspicion anyone who has been in the game more than 15 or 20 years. Commodity trading up through the early 1950s was more a carnival than a profession. The fabled exploits of many of the biggest plungers of that era often unfolded in the razor-thin no-man's-land that separates capitalist derring-do from outright fraud. These operators have now gone to their rewards—in jail or in Brazil—and their acolytes who are still active are, naturally, a trifle suspect. As recently as 1968 an American speculator named Paul Lazarus was found guilty, by a New York court, of conspiring to blow up a vital railway bridge in Zambia in hopes of increasing the price of copper. And in early 1971 government agents on two continents were trying to puzzle out how officials of the Basel (Switzerland) branch of the United California Bank managed to drop about $32 million in unauthorized (and surely uninspired) transactions in cocoa.

No matter how sound your broker's market advice, you should not take it as gospel. The myth that since a man spends ten hours a day in the boardroom living and breathing commodities, he obviously must know more than you do simply doesn't hold up. In fact, the boardroom is the very worst place from which to assess the market, as any good broker will tell you. Rumors flourish in the boardroom the way sores fester in the tropics. Those who watch the market most closely—the brokers and the market analysts—usually succumb to the all too human impulse of overemphasizing the news that supports what's currently happening. When the market is rising, tape watchers subconsciously play up the good news and discount the bad. This is a cumulative process, building up in increments of ever-rosier optimism as prices continue to climb. It causes brokers and analysts to be most bullish when the market is about to turn down and most bearish when it is about to turn up. Be suspicious of all advice,

Controlling Your Broker

but be especially suspicious of advice from brokers.

As you familiarize yourself with the market, you will become less dependent on your broker even for hard information, but you will rely on him more and more to execute your orders precisely. The mechanics of trading are relatively simple, but occasionally confusion, laziness or ignorance—on the part of either broker or trader—can compound with disastrous results.

One area of confusion centers on the margin requirement. This is perhaps the least understood aspect of commodity trading. It is often rather tenuously compared with the stock-market margin, but the two are so dissimilar that there is no parallel. In stocks the margin is the percentage of the cash value of a security that an investor must bring to a transaction. When the margin is 65 percent, as it is now, you can buy $1000 worth of a stock for $650. Your broker lends you the rest—at interest, of course—keeping the purchased shares as collateral.

In commodities your broker lends you nothing; so you pay no interest. The "margin" in commodities is similar to the earnest money you would put down in a real-estate deal. It binds a contract for goods to be received in the future. As in real estate, full payment is not expected until you actually take possession—decidedly an unlikely event in commodities. While the value of your contract fluctuates, your earnest money must remain constant.

Say you buy 5000 bushels of Chicago December wheat at $1.85 a bushel. The minimum customer margin requirement for wheat, set by the various exchanges, usually with the blessing of the Commodity Exchange Authority, is now 10 cents a bushel. Perhaps—if you are a new customer of indeterminate means—your broker will require a few cents more, to give his company breathing space. At 10 cents a bushel, you must put up $500 to bind your 5000-bushel contract. You are agreeing to receive a freight-car load of wheat—at $1.85 a bushel— sometime next December. You put up money to show your good faith—and your solvency, should wheat decline and you find yourself committed to buy at a price above the market. If the price does go down, say, 5 cents a bushel, you have lost $250. Your earnest money is no longer adequate, and you will receive a *margin call* for more. In practice you have a few days' grace, but unless wheat rallies quickly, the margin call means you have to cough up $250 or be sold out.

It's usually unwise to meet a margin call, but say you do and then the wheat rallies. When it gets back to $1.85, your contract is worth $250 more than is needed to secure it, and you may withdraw that much. Thereafter, if the wheat goes up another 10 cents a bushel, your contract would then be worth $500 more than is needed, and you could withdraw that, too. In fact, you can keep withdrawing profits as long as you make them.

Short selling is another market enigma, perhaps once again because of confusion that washes over from the stock market. To make a short sale in commodities, you simply contract not to receive the goods but to *deliver* them at some future date. You do this in expectation that prices will fall, enabling you to meet your obligation at a lower price sometime before you're expected to deliver.

Most Americans view short selling in stocks as somehow tainted. "How can you sell something you don't have?" they ask, ignoring the fact that magazines do it whenever they sell a subscription. Perhaps a slightly more sophisticated objection is that it's either un-American or immoral to profit when the value of American industry (which is presumably reflected in its shares) deteriorates. As noted in the section on stocks, the Internal Revenue Service and the Securities and Exchange Commission implicitly recognize the immorality of short selling in stocks and refuse to grant short sellers the tax shelter of long-term capital gains. Short sellers of stocks are also required to pay any dividends that may be declared on the shares they are short, and the SEC insists that short sales be made

Controlling Your Broker

only on upticks—which means you can't sell a stock short until it is rising.

Short sales in commodities may be made at any time. There are no tax penalties and no dividends to pay. In fact, morality in commodities favors the shorts. They, after all, are hoping prices will go down. They want cheap grain—so cheap that everyone can eat. It's the longs—the buyers—who are on the side of starvation. The shorts want superabundance, grain in such excessive quantities as to stuff every starving Indian. It's interesting that the dreams of the one-world liberal and the short-selling commodity speculator should so nicely coincide. Moreover, in commodities there is only a small logical leap between the long and the short side. There seems little substantive difference, for instance, between buying something you don't want and will never receive and selling something you don't own and will never deliver.

But despite the overwhelming case—moral and otherwise—to be made for the short sale of commodities, the speculative public is invariably biased toward the long side. That is, they prefer to be buyers. This is unfortunate, at least for the speculative public. Perhaps it explains why so many small investors regularly lose such large sums in commodities. Bear in mind that for every contract purchased, someone else has to sell one. Futures contracts always involve two parties. For every long in the market, there is a short. While stock prices favor a long position by tending to rise in the long run—due to inflation, increased productivity or progress generally—commodity prices do not. Improved agricultural productivity generally means *lower* commodity prices, so much so that the long-range trend in commodity prices is sideways—or even down. The Commodity Research Bureau price index of 25 commodity futures—based on a 1947–49 average of 100—recently stood at 87. It hasn't been over 100 in almost 20 years. During the same period, the value of an average share on the New York Stock Exchange had risen from $9 to $55 or so.

While there is no long-range bias toward a long position in commodities, this information hasn't penetrated the speculative public, who are inveterate longs. Since the public *is* biased toward the long side, and since the public is usually wrong, then a short position—all other things being equal—is more likely to show a profit. Even if it doesn't, you at least have rectitude on your side.

Once you've located a broker, opened an account and deposited the necessary margin, you'll find that placing an order is relatively simple. (Often, in fact, the difficulty is in *refraining* from placing an order.) You simply call your broker and tell him what you want done. The simplest of instructions is a *market order:* You tell your broker to buy or sell at whatever price prevails. There are also all sorts of limited orders, the best known being the *stop-loss* order, often called a stop. As in the stock market, this is an order to buy or sell at the prevailing market price only after the market touches a certain level.

Stops are especially useful to technically oriented traders who, after studying their charts, might decide that oats will run away as soon as they break out of their current price range. Rather than checking the price of oats every few minutes for days or even weeks, the chart trader would decide precisely to what level oats would have to rise to indicate a breakout and then instruct his broker to enter a *stop-buy* order at that level. When oats finally touch the designated price, the trader's limited order becomes a market order, to be filled immediately at the best price available.

Stops can also be used to protect profits. Say you purchased 5000 bushels of soybeans at 282 ($2.82 a bushel) and the price has risen to 305. You have a profit of 23 cents per bushel—$1150. Not bad. You suspect soybeans may continue to rise, and if they do, you want to ride with them. However, they have run up rather sharply and may turn around with equal exuberance, in which case you would want to get out in a hurry. Here you would decide to enter a *stop-sell* order two or three cents below the current market price—say, at 303. If the

Controlling Your Broker

beans did begin to collapse, you would be sold out automatically, and most of your profit would be preserved. If the beans kept rising, your profits would rise with them, and you could advance your stop periodically, always trailing the market by two or three cents. When the beans finally did turn around—and they always do—the market would sell you out automatically, at a cozy profit, indeed.

There are many varieties of limited orders. MIT orders are the same as those used in the stock market. The acronym stands for "market if touched," and the order is more or less the opposite of a stop, requesting to sell at the market if it runs *up* to such-and-such a price or to buy at the market if it runs *down*. MIT orders are especially helpful to fundamentalists seeking to get in or out at a good price. Another common limited order goes by the suggestive acronym *FOK* (fill or kill), also called a *quickie*. The trader sets his own price; if the order can't be filled immediately at that price, it is canceled.

22. TAX MAGIC: SPREADS AND STRADDLES

Besides normal buying and selling transactions, there's almost an unlimited number of arbitrage possibilities. Arbitrage, as noted in chapter 5, describes the simultaneous purchase and sale of two different but related items. In commodities an arbitrage transaction is called a spread or a straddle. The two terms are generally interchangeable, but old-timers like to use *spread* when they're talking about grains and *straddle* when referring to anything else. For reasons that will be explained below, the cost is much less than a comparable transaction in stocks. In fact, it's actually cheaper to set up a commodity spread than a normal one-way transaction. And since commodities are interconnected by a vast variety of subtle relationships, only your imagination, your bankroll and the Commodity Exchange Authority limit your horizons. The purpose of a spread transaction is to take advantage of price disparities that grow up between related commodities. The assumption is that sooner or later a more normal relationship will prevail.

The most straightforward of spreads involves the same commodity in different months. A glance at the newspaper statistics will reveal that in most commodities the more distant months become progressively more expensive. This is quite reasonable, because the distant futures represent the price at which you can buy, today, goods to be received some months hence. Until delivery, storage costs are borne by the seller. Thus, in a hypothetically normal market, the distant futures should increase in value over the current cash price (usually called the *spot* price) by a sum precisely equal to the carrying charges—the cost of storage, insurance, periodic inspection and whatnot. The monthly carrying charges for each commodity have been carefully computed (it's currently 2¾ cents a bushel for wheat, for instance, and 19/100 of a cent per pound for cocoa), and this computation should be reflected in the distant-future price.

Usually, however, extraneous factors—impending shortages or surpluses, a new government crop-loan program or a whole galaxy of others—send the hypothetical normal market into disarray. Spreads are set up to capitalize on such disarray. Speculators buy one month and sell another, betting that the spread between the two will widen or diminish.

One of the most interesting spreads occurs on those rare occasions when there actually is a "normal" market. When July wheat is selling at a premium of 11 cents a bushel over March, the July price fully reflects the carrying charges—four months at 2¾ cents a month. In such a case there is *literally no risk* in setting up a spread that sells the distant month and buys the near month. This is because the mechanics of the marketplace will prevent the distant month from ever selling at more than 11 cents over the near month. If this were to happen, owners of grain elevators—or anyone else, for that matter—could make a profit simply by buying March grain and simultaneously selling July. They could receive the March grain, hold it for four months, make delivery against their July contract and still show a profit.

Such a tidy situation doesn't usually present itself, but as the premium for distant months approaches the carrying charges, spreads that *sell the charges* (that is, sell the distant month and buy the near month) become progressively more attractive. If you look hard enough, it's not unlikely that you'll discover a spread where the risk is only 1 or 2 cents a bushel—and where the potential profits are limitless. The threat of an immediate shortage could send the near month (which you purchased) into orbit, while the distant month (which you sold) might remain constant or —if it reflects next season's crop—might even plummet, reflecting possible surpluses caused by farmers reacting overenthusiastically to current high prices.

There are many other types of spreads. You can take advantage of price differentials between different markets (buying Chicago July wheat and selling Kansas City July wheat, for instance), between related commodities (buying December oats and selling December corn—since the two are virtually interchangeable as livestock feed), between a commodity and one of its by-products (selling September soybeans and buying September soybean oil), or even capitalizing on such an apparently tenuous relationship as that which ties the price of hogs to the price of corn—on the theory that if corn becomes inexpensive relative to hog prices, farmers will tend to indulge their pigs, rather than slaughter them, until a more favorable relationship prevails.

While the possibilities for spreading are many, they all share the basic characteristic of limiting risk. Having sold March soybeans and bought November, the speculator doesn't care whether the beans go up or down—as long as the gap between his buying price and his selling price narrows. On January 3, 1967, for instance, you could have sold 5000 bushels of March soybeans at 293 and simultaneously purchased 5000 bushels of November beans at 280½. (This, incidentally, was an *inverted* market. The distant futures were cheaper than the near ones—reflecting scarcity in the actual supply on hand and fears of abundance in the next crop.) Seven weeks later, on February 14, you could have canceled the spread, buying 5000 March beans at 285½ and selling 5000 November at 276. You would have lost 4½ cents a bushel on the November transaction but made 7½ cents on the March—for a net gain of 3 cents a bushel, or $150, less commissions of $24. This may not seem a great deal, but it's still over 25 percent, in less than two months, on a $600 margin—and made at a time when the cash price of soybeans dropped more than 10 cents a bushel. Had you simply taken a long position in soybeans on January 3, you would have lost—assuming you stayed around to endure it—over $500.

Because spreads limit risk, margins and commissions are proportionately less. Commissions on a spread are usually much less than the commission on a single transaction. In fact, at least one national brokerage house requires no margin whatever on spreads. You can actually spread a

Tax Magic: Spreads and Straddles

million bushels of soybeans—simultaneously contracting to receive and to deliver goods worth in the aggregate well over $5 million—for the niggardly sum of $4400, representing only the commissions on the transaction. And you don't pay the commissions until after you've got out of the spread. Applying capitalist initiative of this sort to our soybean example, the profit, subtracting commissions, would have been $25,600—in two months, on an investment of literally nothing. While such a transaction is theoretically possible, no sane broker would have let you—or his firm—into it. Yet it's something to consider, at least in a truncated version, after you have established your credit and built up a trading account.

Besides its widows-and-orphans investment advantages, spreading can also be used to beat Uncle Sam—legally, of course—by pushing short-term profits forward from one year to the next or even, *mirabile dictu,* by transforming short-term profits into long-term gains. The tax advantages of long-term capital gains are discussed in detail in chapter 4, but the message, essentially, is this: Half of all long-term gains, up to $50,000 a year, escape tax-free.

Let us first consider the advantages of pushing short-term profits from one year into the next. Assume that late in a given year you find yourself with a $20,000 short-term capital gain. Such things *do* happen, especially in the commodities market. The gain could have occurred somewhere else, of course. As any investor who has ever filled out a tax form knows well, short-term gains, no matter what their source, are matched against short-term losses, no matter what their source, and taxes are required only on the difference. In this example you are a high-salaried bachelor in the 50-percent bracket. This means you stand to owe $10,000 in taxes on your short-term gain. But there's hope. If you can somehow create a $20,000 short-term loss, then this will balance your $20,000 gain, and the result will be zero tax liability. The commodities market is the perfect place—indeed, just about the only place—where this can be done consistently.

You decide to set up a silver straddle. In fact, you will

engage yourself in a 20-contract silver straddle, simultaneously buying and selling contiguous contract months, both of them in the next calendar year. If today's date is December 5, 1971, you might sell short 20 March 1972 contracts and at the same time buy 20 May 1972 contracts. Once you have set up your straddle, a 10-cent move in the price of silver, whether up or down, will give you a $20,000 loss on one side of the straddle and a $20,000 gain on the other. For the moment you're more interested in the loss, because it will eliminate the $20,000 gain that has plagued you all year.

You'll soon discover that silver doesn't take much time to move 10 cents. A week or two usually suffices; sometimes a day will do. And in your case the direction of the move doesn't matter. Assume that by December 20 the price of silver has risen 10 cents. This means your short March contracts have a $20,000 loss. You close out this position happily, creating a $20,000 short-term tax loss, and eliminate your tax liability for 1971. The other side of your straddle, your 20 long May contracts, shows a $20,000 profit. This you lock up by *selling* 20 July contracts. Your $20,000 profit is now solidly hedged, protected whether silver goes up or down, because gains on either side will invariably be offset by losses on the other. In effect, you have pushed your $20,000 short-term profit into the next year, giving you 12 more months to worry about it and, more important, giving you $10,000 additional that otherwise would have disappeared in taxes.

After the new year you liquidate both ends of the deal—*lifting* the straddle, as it's called. Now, from your profits in May silver you have a $20,000 short-term capital gain for 1972, but who knows what 1972 will bring? If you have a bad year, the gain—for tax purposes—will be useful in offsetting your losses. If you have a good year, well, you can pull the same stunt next December and the December after that and, in fact, forever. There are only two drawbacks: the commission costs on the straddles themselves and the prospect of getting *bad fills*—that is, that your simultaneous buy and sell orders won't be executed simul-

Tax Magic: Spreads and Straddles

taneously. The cost of setting up a *tax straddle,* which is what such high-rolling transactions are actually called, can sometimes run as much as 15 percent of the sum you're worried about. But if it's done competently, it can be as little as 5 percent.

Stunts like this occupy that television-gray underworld that separates legal from illegal. Using tax straddles to postpone short-term taxes does not violate the letter of the law, though it may in fact violate the law's intent. Still, people who use such devices ought to realize that they are responding intelligently to one of the peculiar inequities of the revenue code. Taxes on short-term capital gains, if you have them, are payable in full each year. But short-term capital losses are not deductible in full. To the extent that they exceed gains, they are deductible at a rate of only $1000 a year. Short-term winners, in other words, must cough up taxes forthwith, while short-term losers can't deduct in the same fashion.

This unbalanced treatment (amounting to discrimination against losing speculators) makes it highly desirable for those with short-term gains to defer the appropriate taxes as long as possible, on the reasonable assumption that sooner or later a genuine loss will crop up to eliminate the liability. In the example just discussed, had our speculator just stood idle and eaten his $20,000 gain, he would have been forced to cough up $10,000 in taxes on it. And if the following year he were to sustain $20,000 in short-term losses, only $1000 of them would be deductible. Had he used the tax-straddle device to defer his earlier $20,000 gain, then his loss would have offset it, and once again he would emerge $10,000 richer.

If all these machinations sound venal, well, they are. But they are also legal, and they are constantly employed by people who already have a great deal of money and only want more. Until they are made illegal, there is no reason on God's earth why small investors shouldn't know about them as well, so as to make use of them if occasion permits.

Anyone with sufficient motive to digest the last few

pages closely might have perceived an even more remarkable tax dodge. Our speculator, recall, pushed forward a $20,000 short-term gain by simultaneously buying and selling, on December 5, a bunch of March and May silver contracts. But think what might have happened had he straddled not March and May but July and September. A few weeks after December 5, when the silver had gone up 10 cents, he would have closed out his short July contract for a short-term loss of $20,000. Once again this wipes out his tax liability. But now he secures his September profits by shorting a similar quantity of November silver. Having done so, he only need wait six or seven months and then lift his straddle for a virtually certain $20,000 profit—the very crucial distinction being that his profit is taxable as a *long-term capital gain*. This speculator, in other words, has done what is generally thought to be impossible—he has transformed a short-term gain into a long-term one and saved himself half the taxes, in this case $5000.

This example is really just the tip of the iceberg. No one who plays commodities seriously should ever pay so much as a penny in short-term taxes. Given a well-used commodity-trading account, a sizable amount of short-term profits (no matter what their source), a knowledge of straddling and a modicum of imagination, the intelligent speculator ought to be able to make the revenue code whistle *Welfare Cadillac*.

23. THE PSYCHOLOGY OF SUCCESSFUL COMMODITY SPECULATION

More people want to beat the market than beat Uncle Sam. And while there are many "systems" that supposedly permit one to win consistently in commodities—ranging from the engaging simplicity of "the voice from the tomb" on up to the most esoteric of technical methods—it should be apparent that none of them work for long. No matter how good the system, when too many people start using it, the mechanics of the marketplace will crush them.

Systems don't work, but principles do. All successful commodity traders follow a few basic principles. Applying them is more a matter of self-mastery than of market sophistication. There are many wealthy commodity traders today who don't know a kernel of wheat from a flagon of mercury but who profit year after year because they have the psychological attitude that separates the winners from the losers.

To win consistently you must admit that you will make mistakes—not just a blunder here and there but mistake after mistake after mistake. It is difficult to admit that you are wrong. To admit it with hard cash on the line is even more difficult. To take a $500 loss when there's always the prospect that the market will reverse tomorrow and give it all back to you requires monkish implacability. But it is essential.

To win consistently you must enter the market with a plan. Whether it's based on fundamental analysis, charts, an old trader's system or whatever is not particularly relevant, so long as you have a plan. Once you have a plan, you should enter the market only when it promises to give back more than you risk. Good poker players do this instinctively, weighing the odds between the pot and their bet, their cards and the draw. When the odds favor them, they get in. Commodity trading is a colossal poker game.

Many people will ante into the pot, and a very few will rake in the chips. As in poker, if you consistently play the odds and if you can afford to stay in long enough, you're bound to win.

Of course, as in poker, you should never risk money you cannot afford to lose, and even within this stricture, in commodities it is seldom wise to commit all your money to one trade. Even the best of trades may not work out, and if you pyramid your profits, you may find yourself risking ever-greater sums in ever-more-ambitious campaigns. The losses you do take will be whoppers—at the expense of hard-earned gains. If you just plow 10–30 percent of your profits back into your trading account, in the long run you'll have the satisfaction of having enjoyed your winnings.

If you're a winner, when the market runs against you you'll admit your plan was wrong and get out. If you decide to buy wheat at $1.65 a bushel in expectation of its going up to $1.80, you shouldn't stay around if wheat drops below $1.62½. Your plan was wrong and must be abandoned—at a small loss. Many of the most successful traders take losses on 60 percent—sometimes even 75 percent—of their trades. But when they buy wheat at $1.65 and it does run up to $1.80, they have recouped enough to cover a dozen one-cent mistakes and still give them a profit.

The attitude of the losing speculator is precisely the opposite. In fairness to losers, this is understandable. It is normal—though mistaken—to let your losses run and take your profits quickly. "You never lose taking a profit" is another hoary maxim that has been fleecing small speculators since the South Sea Bubble. Of course, you *do* lose taking a profit if you take it prematurely and if one tiny profit has to cover a sizable string of losses—which is almost inevitable in commodities. It's possible—though decidedly unprofitable—for the small investor in stocks to sit on ever-mounting losses through an entire bear market. After all, they're only "paper losses" until they're taken, and the stock is bound to come back someday. But paper losses in commodities have the distressing habit of turning very quickly into real losses. Your $500 margin on a soybean contract, for instance, will dwindle to nothing in a 10-cent move. Anyone who was misguided enough to buy a July 1967 soybean contract at $3.44½ early in 1966 and then compound his delusion by holding on to it down to $2.83 (February 15, 1967) would not only have lost $600, he would have had to ante up that sum five more times just to meet margin calls.

Successful traders never try to call the tops and the bottoms of a price move. They trade with the trend. When prices are going up, they're buying. When prices are going down, they're selling. The loser's attitude—while once again understandable—is once again the opposite. He tends to buy because things look "cheap"—that is, lower than they were last week. The professional knows that if prices are lower than they were last week, chances are they'll be lower yet next week. That's how markets work. If soybeans, after a long move downward, finally do turn around and rally 10 cents a bushel, the loser will be reluctant to get in, because he missed the bottom and he sees the beans as "expensive"—which indeed they are in relation to last week's prices. The pro doesn't think in terms of cheap or dear. He sees that the beans are rising, figures they'll continue to rise—and buys. If he's right, he'll make a nice profit. As the beans continue to move up, he may use his profits to add a few more contracts, at ever-higher prices. He will take care, however, to pyramid *down* rather than up. That is, if he originally purchased four soybean contracts, he may use his profits to add three more, then an additional two—and top it off with one more. This way, should the market reverse, he still emerges a winner.

The loser's impulse is to use *all* his profits to add another contract. Then, if the market is still with him, he'll use all the profits from the two to add two more and so on. Of course, when the market finally turns around—as it always does—he will be wiped out. Usually, just when the losers are jumping back in, finally persuaded that the beans will rise forever, the pro is the one who is selling them.

Prices may still continue to rise, in an orgy of public speculation, but the pro never bemoans the fact that he didn't get out at the top. The loser, groping for the peak, inevitably finds the chasm beyond.

Perhaps because so many losers take such a beating, the commodity exchanges—and most of those who deal in or write about commodities—have erected an elaborate public-relations edifice to justify their own existence. The terms *hedging* and *transfer of risk* recur repeatedly in their outbursts. The theory is that commodity speculation is necessary to permit producers to hedge the risk they run by holding startling quantities of goods whose prices fluctuate. For $20,000, for instance, you could conceivably go into the grain-storage business by building a million-bushel elevator. But once it's full of wheat, a 2-cent decline—hardly an hour's move on a typical day—would cost you the price of your elevator. On a 10-cent decline (the maximum daily limit) you'd be out your elevator and the price of four more to boot.

The futures market, so the theory goes, exists so that persons in such a predicament can hedge their inventories. Once they buy a million bushels of wheat for storage, they can go into the futures market and *sell* a million bushels—at today's prices—for delivery some months off. If wheat declines, they will still have received today's price, and when delivery time comes, they can simply deliver, without a loss. Of course, if wheat goes up, they will still have to deliver—and forgo a profit. But presumably this won't bother them, because they are in the grain-storage business, not the speculating business. Hedging, in other words, is a way to insulate an inventory from price swings—in either direction. Speculators, as the slick brochures from the exchanges readily point out, are willing to assume risks that the grain trade can't afford. Good-hearted humanists that they are, the speculators stake their hard-earned money to provide an active and well-lubricated market for all this hedging.

This is a fine theory, with much merit to support it. But fewer than one percent of all futures contracts are actually settled by delivery. Even granting that many hedges are lifted without delivery, this still means that for every hedging transaction there are six or a dozen speculative trades. Hedging could disappear altogether and you'd hardly know it by looking at the daily volume statistics. Worse, the *hedgers* are speculating. Holbrook Working, a market mathematician who produced several landmark studies, was quoted in *Fortune* a few years ago as having reached the conclusion that hedging is "undertaken most commonly in the expectation of a favorable change in the relation between spot [cash] and futures prices." That means the hope of a profit.

Despite the fact that since 1884 over 400 bills have been introduced in Congress to prohibit or further limit futures trading, the pit's pious efforts at self-justification seem largely unnecessary. Racetracks survive without belaboring the public with their contributions to the improvement of thoroughbred horseflesh. Racetracks flourish because people are self-interested and enjoy the possibility—no matter how remote—of turning a small sum into a fortune. While there are several quite valid justifications for commodity-futures trading—for instance, besides helping hedgers, it provides small farmers with widely published figures that enable them to get a fair price for their crops—this one is sufficient. Public participation in the commodities market would be greatly increased if those involved in the market would stop drumbeating its undeniable economic usefulness and describe it in terms speculators could understand: as a giant government-sanctioned lottery where the losses can be staggering and the rewards immense.

VI
Conclusion: Success Is a State of Mind

24. CONCLUSION

Ever since the Puritans settled in New England, Americans have assumed that material success is a reward reserved for the very few who somehow combine intelligence, experience and diligence. How this assumption came to popular acceptance is not the subject of this book. Readers who are interested should refer to the works of the late Perry Miller. The operative fact is that more than three centuries after the Puritans, this myth has proved so persistent that it still works even in converse: Anyone who has made millions is deemed not only a hard worker but intelligent and learned as well. The opinions of such men are sought out on talk shows. Their personal idiosyncrasies provide fodder for society columnists. The story of their success is found worthy of ghostwritten autobiography. Their marital peccadilloes show up in the "People" section of *Time*. And their work habits comprise case studies for generations of MBA students.

But the fact is that most of the people who have amassed great speculative wealth in contemporary America—those who have created fortunes rather than inheriting them—are not, as a rule, terribly intelligent, terribly well educated or even terribly hard workers. There are exceptions, of course. But not many. And most of these are intelligent enough to admit that brains, knowledge and diligence had precious little to do with their speculative success.

In the course of researching and writing this book it has been my privilege, if privilege it should be called, to become acquainted with at least 20 youthful millionaires. (*Youthful* for these purposes means under 40, and *millionaire* refers to anyone who, if tomorrow he sold all he owned, would realize in excess of $999,999.99.) Virtually all these people (one of whom, incidentally, is a woman) owe their fortunes, to a greater or lesser extent, to successful speculation in the markets this book has described. Some have gambled in the markets and used their winnings to set up a lucrative business. Others have set up a lucrative business and then taken it to the markets to multiply their wealth. Most have done both. When you get up to the million-dollar level, market success and business success are virtually interchangeable. One talent enforces the other, like a beehive in an apple orchard.

But none of these people are the sort who graduated first in their high-school class, who made Eagle Scout or who ran the college newspaper. None won Rhodes scholarships or got their Ph.D.'s at 23. None of them are folks whose conversation one would seek out or whose insights one would cherish. In fact, anyone who actually possesses the virtues that society somehow imputes to these people—intelligence, learning and indefatigability—would find them an exceedingly dull group. Yet they have made millions in the markets.

What do they have in common? Well, besides wealth, they share one of the running themes of this book: psychological self-mastery. These are all men who know who they are, where they have been, where they are going and how they intend to get there. They have an instinctive appreciation of the dual nature of knowledge. Recall that Dr. Johnson declared there are two distinct types of knowledge: the things you know and the things you don't know but can find out. Knowing what you don't know seems the barrier here. Once a speculator appreciates his own gaps, he can always find ways to fill them. Why, for instance, should you spend six years of your life learning about pollution engineering when for $100 a day you can buy the services of someone who already knows it all?

Above all, successful speculation requires not knowledge, nor training nor some unique insight into human affairs, but simple self-awareness. You must know your strengths, appreciate your weaknesses and mercilessly throttle the temptation to lie to yourself. This is not as easy as it sounds. The typical small investor, especially after he has enjoyed a few successes, tends to exaggerate his strengths and underestimate his weaknesses. In the world of speculation perhaps more than anywhere else, the penalties for inaccurate self-appraisal are high. Self-delu-

Conclusion

sion has the habit of turning very quickly into self-destruction.

Throughout this book I have tried to present useful insights into the mechanics of the marketplace and equally useful insights into the psychology of successful speculation. The mechanics are easy to state and easy to grasp. The psychological elements are not. Many of them, unfortunately, run counter to a normal appreciation of reality. The instinct to hold a losing investment, for instance, "until it gives me my money back" is perfectly reasonable—but disastrously mistaken. It ties up the speculator's limited capital in bad investments when he should be pouring all he has into good ones.

The instinct to buy more of something because it's now cheaper than it was when you first bought it is equally alluring—and equally demented. So, too, with the desire to sell out of an investment the moment it shows a small profit. This is an appealing alternative—except that it will never produce more than small profits, which will hardly offset losses elsewhere. Principles like this are easy to write down. I have tried to enumerate as many as I know, especially in chapters 6 and 23. But putting such principles into use is a task of a higher order.

Simply stated, the psychological self-mastery that seems requisite to market success cannot be derived from a book. The requirements are different for each individual case. Even if all cases could be illuminated—and surely they couldn't—the result would still be dubious, because self-mastery is something you can't learn from others. You either have it or you don't—and until you bet, you can't tell. If after two or three years of systematic investing you find yourself making money with some consistency, you can safely assume that you have it. If you emerge an equally consistent loser, you should probably assume that you don't, and you should quit before you lose even more.

This writer's personal opinion is that most speculators don't enter the markets to make money. They speculate in order to prove something to themselves. Sometimes the goal of making money can be peripheral or even antagonistic to such a task. Consider, as an example, the staggering number of well-heeled doctors who manage to lose boxcar sums year after year, in good markets and in bad, through inept speculation. These men aren't stupid, nor are they as naïve about money matters as many people think they are. Isn't it at least possible that somewhere in the unexplored depths of their psyches they are trying to punish themselves —perhaps for tax-evasion or exorbitant fees? This is a wild example, but chances are your stockbroker can provide others to prove the point.

If it's money you want, well, the money is there to be taken—provided that you actually take it, permanently and irrevocably. The measure of a truly successful speculator is not the size of his brokerage account but what it has produced for him over the years. Failure to take money out of the market when it is available is rather a pinnacle of self-delusion. After all, it assumes that continuing success is inevitable. This is an assumption that no one can make. One cannot speculate successfully without admitting the possibility of failure—even disaster—and actually planning for it. Having all your money always in the market is a very poor contingency plan.

Almost 300 years ago Joseph de la Vega, an itinerant Portuguese who has the dubious distinction of being the first articulate observer of markets and speculators, summed up the ephemeral nature of market success in a sentence whose message is as valid today as it was in 1688: "Profits on the exchange are the treasures of goblins: At one time they may be carbuncle stones, then coals, then diamonds, then flintstones, then morning dew, then tears." Then, as now, the choice is between diamonds and tears, with many other stopping points along the way. And then, as now, the speculator's internal makeup determines his reward.

BIBLIOGRAPHY

This is not a bibliography in the conventional sense of the word. Bibliographies are a proper conclusion to Ph.D. theses, where they intend more to impress than to enlighten. I sincerely don't mean to impress a soul when I say that in the course of researching and writing this work I have read hundreds of investment books and thousands of investment-oriented magazines and periodicals. Quite the contrary. I genuinely wish I had never read any of them. They are, almost to the last one, uniformly dreary, poorly written and uninformative. The main message I can bring you from this entire debilitating experience is that the frequency of plagiarism among investment-oriented publications is simply staggering. An interesting fact appears in newspaper A, gets quick embellishment in weekly magazine B, is well on its way toward being history when it appears in monthly magazine C, has been transformed into unquestionable truth by the time it shows in book D, and becomes something students must memorize by the time it is apotheosized in textbooks E, F and G. All this even though it was dead wrong when first set to print.

I would not deign to list such sources even if space permitted. Instead, here's a brief list of references—generally arranged to conform with the five major sections of this book—that readers might want to consult if they are interested in learning more than I have been able to tell them or if they want to keep posted in ongoing events after reading this book. All are works I personally visit with, regularly or irregularly. Where possible, I have tried to point out salient strengths or weaknesses. My bias is decidedly toward printed works that are not only informative but readable. This last criterion is surely why the list is so short.

To begin at a general level, for anyone interested in investing in virtually anything, a daily exposure to the *Wall Street Journal* is imperative. I have praised the *WSJ* sufficiently in the preceding pages. Suffice to say that it is certainly one of the best daily newspapers published anywhere. A mail subscription to the *Journal* costs $34 yearly and will reach almost anyone in the continental U.S. on the morning of its cover date. Beyond this, the magazine *Business Week,* despite its portentious title and its chamber-of-commerce bias, provides interesting, useful and sometimes original insights into all markets. This, too, is worth a subscription, even if it speaks to you—as often it will—only one week in four.

THE STOCK MARKET

Hardly any area of human endeavor has inspired more bad books than the stock market. I have read scores of them and find myself hard pressed to recommend half a dozen. Far and away the best introductory book is Louis Engel's *How to Buy Stocks*. Despite the fact that its author was a high-paid publicity man for the nation's largest brokerage house, this book presents all the basic information in a sensible and clearly written manner that any novice can read and profit from. It's available in a Bantam paperback for under a dollar, but many Merrill Lynch offices will give copies free to potential customers.

Security Analysis, by Benjamin Graham, et al. (McGraw-Hill, $10.95), is the bible for investors inclined toward determining stock values from corporate and economic statistics. This is a long, thorough and very difficult book. Any investor who reads it from cover to cover probably deserves a prosperous future as fair compensation for his efforts. The chart investor's equivalent is *Technical Analysis of Stock Trends,* by Robert Edwards and John Magee ($14 from John Magee, Inc., 360 Worthington Street, Springfield, Massachusetts 01103). This is somewhat easier reading, liberally punctuated with illustrations.

The Battle for Investment Survival, Gerald Loeb's perennial best seller (Simon & Schuster, $6.95), is a breezy and informative work that presents, in no particular order, the author's many insights from half a century as an investment counselor and financial writer. Standard & Poor's *Stock Guide,* a monthly compilation of statistical data on more than 5000 popular stocks, offers a wealth of corporate figures in a compact and accessible format. It's a valuable reference volume for anyone who follows Bernard Baruch's maxim of investigating before he invests. It's $24 a year (12 issues) from Standard & Poor's Corporation, 345 Hudson Street, New York, New York 10014.

Of the staggering number of how-I-got-rich-in-the-market books that appear each year, one recent and little-known work, *Beating the Street*, by Burton Fabricand (David McKay, $5.95), seems a cut above the rest. Dr. Fabricand, who has written on such varied subjects as nuclear physics and parimutuel betting, here presents a reasoned and nonoccult approach to the stock market, based on probability theory and the public anticipation of corporate profits. Readers who don't care to develop a market system of their own might do worse than to try this one.

MUTUAL FUNDS

Ordinary sources of investment information are generally deficient in their coverage of mutual funds. Both the *Wall Street Journal* and the *New York Times* occasionally run perceptive reports about funds. *Barron's* (mentioned on page 23) reports on funds irregularly and four times a year ranks them and discusses what stocks they are buying and selling. *Forbes* (published twice a month at 60 Fifth Avenue, New York, New York 10011—subscription price $9.50 annually) runs a regular column about funds and a complicated rating each August.

An expensive monthly magazine called *Fundscope* ($50 a year from 1800 Avenue of the Stars, Los Angeles, California 90067) publishes more statistics about mutual funds than most investors would ever care to interpret. For anyone interested in making an exhaustive (and exhausting) comparison of the past performance of various funds, this would be a red-check source. Typographically, *Fundscope* has all the allure of a supermarket handout, and it's heavily biased in favor of load funds—in fact, its primary purpose seems to be to arm load-fund salesmen with selling ammunition.

The jazziest, most candid and most interesting of all the

literature about mutual funds is a monthly magazine called *The Institutional Investor*. Its editor is George J. W. Goodman, alias "Adam Smith." Sad to say, circulation is supposedly confined to money managers. Borrow a broker's copy, or send $30 (for 12 issues) to 140 Cedar Street, New York, New York 10026, and see what happens.

Yale Hirsch's *Manual of Mutual Funds*, revised annually, provides performance figures and addresses for nearly all funds, along with 30-odd large-type pages of not too sophisticated general information. It sells for $1.95 and is available at bookstores or from the author-publisher at 527 Madison Avenue, New York, New York 10017.

Norman (*How to Avoid Probate!*) Dacey has authored a $4.95 paperback, *Dacey on Mutual Funds* (Crown), worth reading if only for its factual forays into the dark underbelly of mutual-fund management. Dacey is an antiestablishment iconoclast, intimately familiar with the shortcomings of the mutual-fund industry. Few people will agree with everything he says, but he has been right more often than wrong, and his role in the fund world is comparable to Ralph Nader's in the auto industry.

THE BOND MARKET

The investor in search of useful information about bonds and the bond market is much worse off. There is not a single book, dealing with bonds and nothing else, that I can recommend. Public participation in the bond market is too recent a phenomenon to have spawned a decently written popularization. The *Weekly Bond Buyer*, mentioned on page 157, will provide scads of information for readers who are already familiar with bonds. Those who aren't might as well read *Pravda*. The huge bond firm of Salomon Brothers & Hutzler publishes a brief and readable weekly bond letter and periodically emits colorful and sometimes witty analyses of various facets of the bond world. Unfortunately, distribution of these works is largely limited to the firm's clientele. On a decidedly peripheral subject, Sidney Homer, the Salomon Brothers partner who is generally acknowledged to know as much about bonds as anyone anywhere, has written one of the most remarkable books this writer has ever seen. The title is *A History of Interest Rates* (Rutgers University Press, $10), and the subject matter is just that: a learned tracing of the meanderings of interest rates the world over for the last 4000 years. To be sure, one must be almost morbidly preoccupied with the cost of money to sit down with this opus (600 pages, 81 tables, 73 charts), but for anyone who is, the rewards justify the effort. Considering the subject matter, the book is not only readable but even charming. One leaves it regretting only that Mr. Homer has not seen fit to lend his considerable talents to a less esoteric subject —such as a popular exploration of the contemporary American bond market.

THE COLLECTOR INVESTMENTS

No single publication treats the collector investments per se. As a matter of fact, while collector's items certainly form a logical and well-defined investment area, few authors or journalists have even thought of them as such. Many special-purpose magazines and newspapers treat individual collector areas—stamps, for instance, or antique furniture or prints—from the collector's point of view, but to the extent that they are worth reading, they tend to ignore or disparage the investment aspects of their field. *Auction*, described on page 209, seems moving slowly into this void. It is published by the same organization that produces the *Institutional Investor* and shares many of *II*'s virtues. The only English-language newspaper that covers art-world developments to any serious extent is the *Times* (London). Unfortunately, the cost of an airmail subscription runs to hundreds of dollars a year. The Sunday *Times*, shipped surface, is a reasonable substitute.

Two books deserve mention. *The Economics of Taste*, by Gerald Reitlinger, is a three-volume opus that traces the history and the rationale of art-world price changes— two volumes for paintings and another for art objects— between 1750 and 1970. This is truly an intimidating work: 2000-odd pages crammed with facts, dates, prices and opinions—a treasure trove for anyone interested in the social history of effete snobbery. But one needs a working knowledge of French, plus an intimate familiarity with the arcana of art and antiques, in order to negotiate it. All three volumes were originally published in London but have reappeared on these shores under various colophons. This is the only work I know of that deals directly and unabashedly with the money aspects of art collecting. But it's tough going.

In a much lighter vein, a book called *The Proud Possessors* provides interesting insights into the habits and habitats of big-time U.S. art collectors through the last century. The author, Aline Saarinen, wife of the well-known architect, offers delightful and well-researched explanations of what makes big-time collectors tick. Little here directly speaks to investors, but the book does yield a broad view of the art-collecting world, and those who are interested will find it fun reading.

THE COMMODITIES MARKET

Two things characterize most books about commodity speculation: They are not very well written, and they are frightfully expensive. The best single work I know is Gerald Gold's *Modern Commodities Futures Trading* (Commodity Research Bureau, 87 Beaver Street, New York, New York 10005). It was first published in 1959 and has since undergone at least four revisions. At $10 for 250 pages, it surely can't be called a bargain. Much of its technical data is more useful to brokers or farmers than to speculators. Still, to my knowledge, it is the best there is. Chester Keltner's *How to Make Money in Commodities* (available from Keltner Statistical Service, 1004 Baltimore Avenue, Kansas City, Missouri) contains a wealth of information for speculators interested in fundamental commodity analysis and some interesting observations about mechanical trading rules. The *Journal of Commerce*, mentioned on page 239, is the daily newspaper read by most serious commodity traders, especially those who are fundamentally inclined. Its commodity reportage is deep and sticky—like quicksand—but its daily commodity statistical section is the best available.

INDEX

Abacus Fund 131
Adams Express Company 130
advisory services 24-26
  commodities market 239-40
Alaska: municipal bonds 159-60
Alma-Tadema, Sir Lawrence 183, 214-15
American Board of Trade 155
American DualVest Fund 134, 138-39
American Investors Fund 124
American Stock Exchange 16, 19, 45, 47, 50, 53-54, 62
  See also stock exchanges
antique collecting (as investment) 179, 181, 220-24
arbitrage 72, 169, 256-62
art collecting (as investment) 181-83, 195-204, 211-13, 218-19, 225
  Times-Sotheby index 196-97, 201, 202, 203-04
Atlantic Richfield, 63-64
Auction 209, 214, 277
Audubon, James 189
autograph collecting (as investment) 179, 181, 192-95, 212
automobile collecting (as investment) 208-09
Ayres, Col. Leonard P. 35

Bagehot, Walter 74
Baltimore: stock exchange 16
Balzac, Honoré de 189
Bank of New York 76
bankers' acceptances 155
banking: bankers' acceptances 155
  Eurodollar deposits 155
  interest on accounts 96
  investment by banks 39, 42, 85
    See also institutional investors
  loans against bonds 148, 173
  loans against stock 42, 148
  and short-term money market 155
barbed wire collecting (as investment) 209
Barron's 24, 35-36, 63, 110, 135
  on Dutch tulip craze 73-74
  on mutual funds 275
Baruch, Bernard 56, 165, 274-75
bear market 13, 14, 39, 105, 264
Beardsley, Aubrey 216
bearer bonds 156
Beckett, Samuel 190
Big Board *see* New York Stock Exchange
Blake, William 189
bonds 60, 61, 62, 143-76
  bank loans against 148, 173
  commissions 156, 161, 162-63, 169
  convertible 61-62, 139-40, 162, 166-72
  corporate 75, 143, 145, 147, 162-72, 173
  conversion value 170, 171-72
  interest 162, 163, 164-65, 166, 168, 170, 171, 174, 176
  government 145, 147, 149-59, 173
  bearer 156
  "flower" 158
  interest 96, 149, 150, 156, 159
  maturity date 152, 154, 157-58
  registered 149, 156-57
  savings 96, 149-52, 153
  treasury bills (certificates) 152-56
  treasury bonds 152, 156
  treasury notes 152, 153, 155
  government agency 158-59, 173

bonds *(continued)*
  interest 61, 96, 143-48, *passim*, 154
    corporate 162, 163, 164, 166-67, 168, 169-70, 171, 174, 176
    government 96, 149, 150, 156, 159
  market price 60, 61, 144-45, 146
  municipal 75, 143, 147, 159-61
  rating of 162, 164, 170-72
  speculation in 148, 173-76
  and stocks, comparison 146-47, 168-69
  straight 162, 169, 170, 171-72, 173
  and taxation 96, 148, 149, 150, 155, 159
book collecting (as investment) 179, 181, 187-91, 212
borrowing. *See* loans
Boston: stock exchange 16
Boswell, James 188
Boutet, Nicolas-Noel 209
brokerage 38-48
  arbitrage 72, 169
  bankruptcy of firms 234
  bonds, reluctance to handle 151
  commissions and fees 18, 38, 39, 48, 49-55, 77, 85, 89, 129, 138, 156, 161, 162-63, 169, 233-34
  commodities market 249-55
  insurance for individual accounts 42
  loans to investor 41
  loans to other firms 44
  new issues 73
  research departments 39, 48, 51
  securities should be held by investor 41, 42, 157
Budge, Hamer H. 100
Buffet, Bernard 183
bull market 14, 39, 250
Business Week 24, 274
buying: arbitrage 71-72, 169, 256-62
  calls 64-67, 70-72
  fill or kill (FOK) order 255
  limited order 46-48, 254-55
  market if touched (MIT) order 47-48, 255
  market order 46, 47
  odd lots 34, 50, 175
  round lots 34, 49
  stop order 46-47, 80, 81, 254
  See also margin

calls 64-67, 70-72
Canada: bank loans against stock 42
capital gains: long-term, and taxation 55, 56-57, 64, 96-97, 103-04, 259, 262
  mutual funds 96-97, 103, 104, 105, 110, 111, 112
  short-term, and taxation 55, 56-57, 259, 261, 262
  See also gains
Carr, Fred 28-29, 80, 109
Carroll, Lewis 190
Cave, Edward 200
Channing Growth Fund 104
Channing Income Fund 104
Chicago: Board of Trade 235, 241-42
  Mercantile Exchange 235
  stock exchange 16
children, investing for 58
closed-end investment companies 93-94, 129-40
  commissions 129
  dividends 131
  dual-purpose funds 134-39
  letter funds 132, 133
  letter stock 131-32
Cohen, Manuel F. 100
coin collecting (as investment) 179, 204-06, 212
collecting (as investment) 179-226
  approaches to:
    conservative 211-13
    expert 217-19
    speculative 213-17
    synergistic 219-20
    utilitarian 220-23
  auction houses 182, 223, 224
  dealers 223-24
  forgeries 194, 218
  literature on 277-78

Index

psychological factors 184-86, 210-11
Collectors News 180
comic-book collecting (as investment) 191-92
commercial paper 155
commissions: auction houses 182
  bonds 156, 161, 162-63, 169
  closed-end investment companies 129
  commodities market 233, 258-59, 260
  mutual funds 94-95, 97, 113-15, 117, 120-28
  odd-lot trading 50
  round-lot trading 49
  See also brokerage, commissions and fees
commodities market 229-67
  animal products 235
  arbitrage (spread or straddle) 256-62
  carrying charges 256-57
  commissions 233-34
    spread or straddle 258-60
  fundamental analysis 240-42, 244, 245
  grains 235
  hedging 266-67
  literature on 278
  losses 231, 244-45, 253, 264-66
  margin 233-34, 251-52, 258
  mechanical trading rules 245-48
  metals 235
  psychological factors 263-67
  short selling 252-54
  technical analysis 240, 242-45
  "whipsawing" 247
Commodity Exchange Authority 231, 234, 251, 256
Commodity Research Bureau: price index 253
common stock 16, 17, 19-20, 60, 62
  convertible bonds exchanged for 61-62, 139, 162, 166-72
  dividends. *See* dividends
  Fisher and Lorie study 18, 19, 122, 147
  letter stock 101, 131-32
  rights 64
  warrants 62-64, 71-72, 75
  See also stock
Competitive Associates 128
Connoisseur 189
convertible bonds 61-62, 139, 162, 166-72. *See also* bonds
Copernicus, Nicolaus 189
Copley, John Singleton 197
Corn, Ira 194
corporate bonds 75, 143, 145, 147, 162-72, 173
  conversion value 170, 171-72
  interest 162, 163, 164-65, 166, 168, 170, 171, 174, 176
  margin 170, 171
  See also bonds
Curb, The. *See* American Stock Exchange

Dacey, Norman: *Dacey on Mutual Funds* 276
Dante, Alighieri 212
Darwin, Charles 189
Defoe, Daniel 188
Department of Agriculture: statistics 240
Department of Labor: statistics 18
Detroit: stock exchange 16
De Vegh Mutual Fund Inc. 124-25
Diebold Technology Venture Fund 132
District Banks for Cooperatives 159
Diverco, Inc. 97-98
diversification 79, 88, 89, 133
dividends 18, 21, 60, 61
  closed-end investment companies 131
  mutual funds 96-97, 102-03
  reinvestment of 18, 96-97
  and short selling 45
  in stock 21, 96-97
  taxation 58-59, 96, 131
Dodge, Mrs. Horace E. 161
Donchian, Richard D. 246-47
Dow, Charles 33
Dow-Jones industrial average 33-34
Dow theory 33

Drexel Equity Fund, Inc. 125
Drexel Hedge Fund 128
dual-purpose funds 133-40
Dunn and Haigitt's Financial Services 247
du Pont, Francis I. 42
Dutch tulip craze 73-74

Eakins, Thomas 198, 199
Ecological Sciences Corporation 28
Educational Computer Corporation 73
Edwards, Robert: *Technical Analysis of Stock Trends* 274
Eisenhower, Dwight D. 194
Electronic Data Systems Corporation 12-13, 73
Eliot, T. S. 190
Energy Fund 125
Engel, Louis: *How to Buy Stocks* 274
Enterprise Fund 28
Eurodollar deposits 155
Export-Import Bank 159

Fabricand, Burton: *Beating the Street* 275
Farmers Home Administration 159
Farouk, King 214
Faulkner, William 190
Federal Home Loan Banks 159
Federal Land Banks 159
fees. *See* brokerage, commissions and fees; commissions
fill or kill (FOK) order 255
Financial Analysts Journal 45
financial pages 23-24
  corporate bonds 164-65, 166
  stocks 21-22
  See also *The Wall Street Journal*
Fisher, Lawrence 18, 19, 122, 147
Fleischman, Lawrence 199
Fletcher Capital Fund 113
"flower bonds" 158
Forbes 24, 137
  on mutual funds 275
  on stamp collecting 179

Fortune 24, 187, 267
Founders Mutual Fund 123-24
Frankenstein, Alfred 219
fundamentalists. *See* investment techniques, fundamental
Fund of Letters 132
Fundscope 103, 105, 275
  study of load and no-load funds 120-21, 125
Funt, Allen 214-15
furniture collecting (as investment) 200-02, 212, 221-22, 223-24

gains: let profits run 79-81, 83, 264
  long-term 55, 56, 64, 96, 103-04, 259, 262
  never lament hindsight profits 82-84
  short-term 55, 56-57, 259, 261, 262
  should outweigh risks 84, 263-64
  take some out of market 85, 264, 272
  See also capital gains; dividends; interest
Galbraith, John Kenneth 23
Galsworthy, John 187-88
Gemini Fund 134, 137, 138, 139
General Electric 33
Getty, J. Paul 12, 218
Gimelson, Bruce 193, 194
Gogh, Vincent van 213
Gold, Gerald: *Modern Commodities Futures Trading* 247-48, 278
Goodman, George J. W. ("Adam Smith") 276
government-agency bonds 158-59, 173
government-agency notes 155
government bonds 145, 147, 149-59, 173
  bearer 156
  "flower" 158
  interest 96, 149, 150, 156, 159
  maturity date 152, 154, 157-58
  registered 149, 156-57
  savings 96, 149-52, 153

Index

Government National Mortgage Association 159
Graham, Benjamin: *Security Analysis* 35, 274
Gwinnett, Button 192, 195

Haack, Robert 50-51
Hamilton, Charles 192
Hammer, Armand 198
Harnett, William 219
Harrington, Michael 23
Harrison, William Henry 194
Hart, Pop 199
Hasbrouck, Lotus and Muriel 25
Hawaii: municipal bonds 160
Haydn, Franz Joseph 193
Hedge Fund of America 127-28
hedge funds 126-28, 132, 133
hedging: commodities market 266-67
  investment as hedge against inflation 14
  Mongolian hedge 65
  mutual funds 126-28, 132, 133
  puts and calls 65
Hemingway, Ernest 190
Hemisphere Fund 134, 136-37, 138, 139
Heritage Fund 127, 128
Hirsch, Yale: *Manual of Mutual Funds* 276
Hoffman, Heinrich 190
Hogan, Frank 185-86
Homer, Sidney 176
  A History of Interest Rates 276-77
Hubshman Fund 127

income 147-48
  investment for maximization of 103
  investment for retirement 14
  See also dividends; gains; interest
Income and Capital Shares 134, 137, 138, 139
income funds 103, 104, 105
inflation: bond market 168
  and collecting 179
  investment as hedge against 14
  savings bonds 149, 150
The Institutional Investor 100, 276
institutional investors 15, 16, 51, 85
  bonds 166, 176
insurance companies, investment by 39, 85, 166
  See also institutional investors
Integrated Resources, Inc. 73
Inter-American Development Bank 159
interest 60-61
  bank accounts 96
  bonds 61, 96, 143-48 *passim*, 154
    corporate 162, 163, 164-65, 166, 168, 170, 171, 174, 176
    government 96, 149, 150, 156, 159
    municipal 159, 160
  compound 98-99
  government-agency securities 159
Internal Revenue Service: dividends 61
  municipal bonds 160
  short selling 45, 57-58
  See also taxation
International Bank for Reconstruction and Development 159
International Business Machines 33-34
investing: advisory services 24-26, 239-40
  for children 58
  by collecting. *See* collecting (as investment)
  counselors 78
  knowledge needed for 18-20
  principles of: average up, not down 82
    diversification 79
    gains outweigh risks 84, 263-64
    let p ofits run; take losses quickly 79-81, 83, 264

investing *(continued)*
    move with trend 81-82, 175, 265
    never lament hindsight profits 82-84
    never risk money you can't afford to lose 84, 264
    take some profit out of market 85, 264, 272
    technique, consistency in 84, 263
    tips, refusal to act on 79
  psychological factors. *See* psychological factors in investing
  reasons for: avoid taxes 14
    conserve capital 14
    hedge against inflation 14
    keep what already have 102-03
    maximization of income 103
    retirement income 14
  See also buying; selling; institutional investors; small investor; speculation
investing techniques 34-37, 45-46
  consistency, importance of 84, 263-64
  fundamental 17, 26-28, 29, 31, 32-33, 48, 81, 240-42, 244-45, 255
  mechanical trading rules in commodities market 245-48
  Monthly Investment Program 138
  odd-lot theory 34, 175-76
  technical 27, 29-34, 47, 81, 240, 242-45, 254
investment companies. *See* closed-end investment companies; mutual funds
Investment Company Act 119
Investors Mutual Fund 121

Janeway, Eliot 150
Jarves, James Jackson 217
Johns, Jasper 213
Johnson, Dr. Samuel 270
Jones, Alfred Winslow 127
The Journal of Commerce 239, 278

Keltner, Chester 244
  How to Make Money in Commodities 246, 278
Kennedy, John F. 194, 216-17
Kentucky Fried Chicken 29, 235
Keystone B-4 103

Landseer, Sir Edwin 183
Lasker, Bernard 54
Lawrence, T. E. 190
Lazarus, Paul 250
Leasco Corporation 62-63
Lefebvre, Jules 183
Lehman Corporation 130
letter funds 132, 133
letter stock 101, 131-32
Leverage Fund of Boston 134, 138, 139
Lichtenstein, Roy 215
Lilly, Josiah K. 210
limited order 46-48, 80, 81, 254-55
Lincoln, Abraham 193, 212, 217
Lipper Corporation 102
"liquid" market 15
literary material, collecting of (as investment) 179, 181, 187-95
loans: by banks, against bonds 148, 173
  by banks, against stock 42, 148
  by brokerage 41, 44
  free carry 174
Loeb, Gerald 79
  The Battle for Investment Survival 274
London *Times* 190, 196, 277
  Times-Sotheby art index 196-97, 201, 202, 203-04
long-term gains 55, 56, 64, 96, 103-04, 259, 262
long-term losses 55
long-term trends 27, 253
Lorie, James 18, 19, 122, 147
losses: commodities market 231, 244-45, 253, 264-66

Index

fundamental vs. technical analysis 31-33, 244-45
as investment principle 79-81, 83, 264-65
mutual funds 18
option transactions 66-67
and taxation 55-56
Lublin, Abraham 199-200
Lynch, Thomas 195

McCallum, Henry D. 209
magazine collecting (as investment) 191-92
magazines, financial 24
Magee, John: *Technical Analysis of Stock Trends* 274
Manhattan Fund 104-05
Mardis Industries International 206, 207
margin 41, 42-43, 44, 251
bonds, corporate 170, 171
commodities market 233-34, 251-52, 258
over-the-counter stock 75, 76
puts and calls 69, 70
Marin, John 199
market if touched (MIT) order 47-48, 255
market order 46, 47
market price: bonds 60, 61, 144-45, 146
stock 17, 60, 61
"marking to market" 44
Massachusetts Investors Trust 112
Mates Investor Fund 91, 100-01, 102, 111, 132
Merrill Lynch, Pierce, Fenner & Smith 18, 44, 52
Minnie Pearl's Fried Chicken System 28
Mongolian hedge 65
Moody's Bond Survey 164, 171
Moody's Industrial Manual 30
Moody's Stock Survey 26
movie-magazine collecting (as investment) 191
Monthly Investment Program (MIP) 138
municipal bonds 75, 143, 147, 159-61
municipal notes 155

mutual funds (open-end investment companies) 15, 19, 31, 34, 39, 42, 51, 73, 85, 88-140, 166
buying a tax bill or credit 111-12
capital gains 96, 97, 103, 111, 112
capital-gains funds or growth funds 104, 105-06, 110
capital losses 111
commissions (load) 94-95, 97, 113-15, 117, 120
load versus no-load funds 120-28
comparison with other forms of investment 122
compound interest 98-99
dividends 96, 103
hedge funds 126-28, 132, 133
income funds 103, 104
initiation fees 92
letter stock owned by 131-32
literature on 275-76
ownership of stock in single company 107
redemptions and forced sales 102, 115, 116, 117
redemptions in kind 117
reinvestment of capital gains and dividends 96-97, 98
size of 107-09, 112
special funds 91-93, 103, 125-26
See also institutional investors

Napoleon 212
National Shareowners Association 54
National Stock Exchange 16, 45
See also stock exchanges
Nebenzahl, Kenneth 189
newsletters, financial 24-26
newspapers. *See* financial pages; *The Journal of Commerce; The New York Times; The Wall Street Journal*
Newton, Sir Isaac 189
New York Stock Exchange 16, 19, 33, 45, 47, 54, 90
and commissions 50, 52, 53, 54

New York Stock Exchange *(continued)*
  Dow-Jones industrial average 33-34
  Fisher and Lorie study of common stock 18, 19, 122, 147
  institutional trading 85
  "Monthly Investment Program" 138
  preferred stock 61
  suit against 54
  warrants 62
  See also stock exchanges
The New York Times 23, 275
Niagara Share Corporation 130
Nixon, Richard M.: on regulation of securities business 53
  on stock market (1970) 14, 17
Norris, Frank 249
Northwestern Steel & Wire Corporation 30-31, 46, 47
notes: government agency 155
  municipal 155
  treasury 152, 153, 155, 156

odd-lot trading 34, 50, 175
Odlum, Floyd 129
O'Hara, John 190
Omega Equities 101
open-end investment companies. *See* mutual funds
options. *See* calls; puts; rights; warrants
oriental-rug collection (as investment) 208
over-the-counter market 16, 19, 47, 75-77
  new issues 75
  warrants 62

Palmer, Mrs. Potter 215
paperweight collecting (as investment) 185, 214
Parke-Bernet 196-202 *passim,* 204, 208, 209, 216, 218, 219
Payne, John Howard 193
Peale, Charles Willson 197-98
Penn Square Mutual Fund 125
pension funds, investment by 39, 73, 85. *See also* institutional investors
Performance Systems, Inc. 28
Perot, H. Ross 12-13, 14, 42, 73
Picasso, Pablo 189, 220, 222
Pitcairn, Theodore 222
Pittsburgh: stock exchange 16
Plohn, Mrs. Charles 203
Poe, Edgar Allan 193
Polaroid 20
Pollock, Jackson 219
porcelain collecting (as investment) 181, 203-04
preferred stock 60-61, 62. *See also* stock
print collecting (as investment) 181, 199-200, 213
psychological factors in investing 20, 26-27, 28, 29, 34, 40, 78, 85, 269-72
  collectors 184-86, 210-11
  commodities market 263-67
Putnam Duofund 134, 136, 138, 140
puts 64-70, 71
Puvis de Chavannes, Pierre 183

Raphael 218
ready market 15
Redfield, Edward 199
Redouté, Pierre 189
Regan, Donald 52
Reitlinger, Gerald: *The Economics of Taste* 277
Rembrandt 181, 200, 218
Republic Corporation 76
Revere, Paul 203
rights 64
round-lot trading 34, 49
T. Rowe Price Growth Fund 121, 125
Rubloff, Arthur 214
rule of seventy-two 98

Saarinen, Aline: *The Proud Possessors* 278
Salomon Brothers & Hutzler 276
San Francisco: stock exchange 16
Saul, Ralph 52
savings bonds 96, 149-52, 153

Scudder Duo-West 134, 138, 140
Scudder Special Fund 125
Seaboard Airline Railroad 28
Securities and Exchange Commission 53, 234
   mutual funds 93, 100, 117, 132
   short selling 252
security analysis. *See* investing techniques
selling 15, 17, 18
   arbitrage 72, 169, 256-62
   forced sales 102, 115, 116
   market if touched (MIT) order 47-48, 255
   odd lots 34, 50, 175
   over-the-counter market 75
   puts 64-70, 71
   rights 64
   round lots 34, 49
   stop order 46-47, 80, 81, 254
   See also short selling
Shahn, Ben 199
Shakespeare, William 193, 212
share. *See* stock
Shaw, George Bernard 193
short selling 43-45, 48, 252
   "against the box" 57
   arbitrage 72
   commodities market 253
   uptick rule 45, 48, 72, 252
short-term gains 55, 56-57, 259, 261, 262
short-term losses 56, 261
short-term market: Eurodollar deposits 155
   government agency notes 155
   municipal notes 155
   treasury bills 152-53, 154-55
silver collecting (as investment) 181, 202-03, 212, 213, 222
small investor 15, 34, 52, 175
   bonds 143, 153, 175, 176
   brokerage commissions and research 39, 50-51, 52-53
   buying on margin 41
   commodities market 253
   mutual funds 34
   short selling 45
SMC Investment Corporation 132

Sotheby's 196, 198, 202, 203, 204, 208
   Times-Sotheby art index 196-97, 201, 202, 203-04
Southern Gulf Utilities 28
South Sea Bubble 74
Soutine, Chaim 213
Space-Time Forecasting 25
specialists 47, 233
speculation 133, 229
   bonds 148, 173-76
   in collecting 213-17
   commodities. *See* commodities market
   hedge funds 126-28, 132, 133
   letter funds 132, 133
   new issues 72-74, 75
   psychological factors 269-72
   puts and calls 64-67
   rights 64
   warrants 62-64, 71-72, 75-76
"spot" price 256
spread: bonds 156
   commodities market, arbitrage 256-62
stamp collecting (as investment) 179, 205-08, 209, 212, 213-14
Standard & Poor's Corporation: bond ratings 162, 164
   Stock Guide 275
Standard Shares 131
stock 14, 75-76, 146-47
   bank loans against 42, 148
   and bonds, comparison 146-47, 168-69
   common 16, 17, 19-20, 60, 61-64, 71-72, 75-76, 100, 122, 131-32, 140, 147-48, 162, 166-72
   dividends. *See* dividends
   hedging 65
   letter stock 101, 131-32
   listings 21-22. *See also* financial pages
   literature on 21, 273-76
   margin. *See* margin
   market price 17, 60, 61
   new issues 72-74, 75
   odd lots 35, 50, 175
   preferred 60-61, 62
   puts and calls 64-71

Index

stock *(continued)*
  registered in name of investor 41, 42
  rights 64
  round lots 34, 49
  warrants 62-64, 71-72, 75
stockbroker. *See* brokerage
Stockbroker 83
stock exchanges 16
  commissions 50, 51, 52-53
  specialists 47, 233
  See also American Stock Exchange; National Stock Exchange; New York Stock Exchange; over-the-counter market
stock indexes 33-34
stock market: bear market 13, 14, 39, 72, 105, 179
  bull market 14, 39, 250
  movement in trends 80, 81-82, 115, 265
  new highs 23
  number of investors 14
  ready or "liquid" market 15
stop order 46-47, 80, 81, 254
"straddle": commodities market, arbitrage 256-62
  puts and calls 65
"strap" (puts and calls) 65
"strip" (puts and calls) 65
Stuart, Gilbert 197, 198
Surveyor Fund 130

taxation 55-59
  bills and credits in mutual funds 111-12
  capital gains 148
    long-term 55, 56, 64, 96, 103-04, 259, 262
    short-term 55, 56-57, 259, 261, 262
  commodities straddle 259-62
  dividends 58-59, 96, 131
  dual-fund capital shares 136-37
  interest on bonds 96, 148, 149, 150, 155, 159
    exemption from 155, 159
  investing for children 58
  losses, short-term 56, 261
  preference tax 55
  puts and calls 71
  short selling 45, 57-58
  See also Internal Revenue Service
technicians. *See* investment techniques, technical
Technicon Corporation 12
Telex 147
Temple, Shirley 180, 191
Tennessee Valley Authority 159
Thomas, Dylan 190
Tiffany, L. C. 216
treasury bills, bonds, notes. *See* government bonds
Tri-Continental Corporation 71-72, 130-31
trusts, investment by 39
Tsai, Gerry, Jr. 104, 105
Turov, Daniel 63
Twain, Mark 13

uptick rule 45, 48, 72, 252

Vagnozzi, Egidio Cardinal 100
Value Line Development Capital Corporation 132
Vega, Joseph de la 82-83, 272
Vlaminck, Maurice de 213

The Wall Street Journal 18, 19, 20, 23-24, 115, 130, 157, 163, 176, 239, 273-74, 275
Warhol, Andy 215
warrants 62-64, 71-72, 75
Washington, George 193, 194, 212
weapons collecting (as investment) 209
The Weekly Bond Buyer 157, 276
Weight Watchers International 71
West, Benjamin 197-98
"whipsawing" 247
Whistler, James McNeill 200
Whitehead, Edwin C. 12, 13
Wiesenberger and Company 101-02, 120
Wilson, Ed 241-42
Working, Holbrook 267

Yeats, William Butler 190